Pray for Rain:

A College Baseball Story

by Jason Wuerfel

<u>Warning:</u>

This is a novel about college life and collegiate baseball. The characters walk, talk, and act like college kids. Therefore, be warned that this book contains profanity and sexual content.

All characters and events are a product of the author's imagination and in no way represent anyone or anything that happened in real life. All such relations to real people or events are strictly coincidental.

For Sarah - my editor, my best friend, and the love of my life.

Acknowledgements

I would like to sincerely thank everyone who helped in the creation of this story. You are all very special people and your help meant more to me than you know. I put my heart and soul into writing this story because it is a subject I deeply care about, and I appreciate how you respected me and my writing even while I was forcing it down your throat. An extra thank you goes out to my wife, Sarah, my parents, and my former teammates at the University of Michigan, Alex and Eric, for their support and helpful analysis, suggestions, and revision.

I would also like to humbly thank everyone in the Michigan baseball family whose interest in my project inspired me to continue to write even when I was unsure of myself. Michigan baseball is my second family and I love and respect everyone associated with it. Thanks to all the coaches at Michigan who took a chance on an undersized small school catcher. Thank you for teaching me how to play the game right, how to take pride in the way I play, how to compete, and how to be a man. Thanks to all my teammates who believed in me and became some of the best friends I will ever have. Thank you for showing me what hard work and dedication really was, when we were forced to grow up fast under the pressure of college baseball. Lastly, thanks to all the parents and alumni for your unconditional support. I could not have made it through without you.

Foreword by the Author

I had the best time of my life playing baseball and majoring in English at the University of Michigan from 1999-2003 and I had a difficult time dealing with graduation and the end of my athletic eligibility. I had four years of fall, spring, and summer baseball stuck in my head; memories of people who were good friends for a day, a summer, a year, or four years. Then, suddenly, I could no longer add to those memories – baseball was a chapter that was over in my life and there was nothing I could do about it – so I started writing. I found that as I created characters and made up this baseball story I could lose myself and transport back to Michigan for one last day under the sun. So I relived that day over and over again, coming back as much as I could, and a couple years later I had a novel.

I hope everyone who reads this story will enjoy it as much as I enjoyed writing it, but first, a few caveats: I did not create any characters as mirror images of people I knew in college or through baseball. The plot is another creation of my imagination and the behavior of the players, fans, coaches, and administration in no way mimics how things are run at the University of Michigan. I created the circumstances only because I thought it made a good story. I wrote it as a story, so please read it as a story, and know that I have nothing but love and pride for my alma mater – Go Blue!

Prologue
Until Next Year

For all sad words of tongue and pen
The saddest are these: "It might have been."
       -John Greenleaf Whittier

They called me Squat. No, not just because of my physical appearance, but because I never played. Yeah, I can admit it now, I didn't see the field very often, but I was a Wolverine just the same - a Michigan man - and that's something no one could take away from me with a stupid nickname. Besides, the statistics aren't what we talk about now when we get together again at alumni golf outings or reunions, those things turn to dust and fall away like the hair that used to be on my head. No, what we remember are our times together, the friends we had, and the friends we've lost along the way. That's the true value of being a part of something like Michigan baseball; it's how you feel when you're with your teammates, like you're something bigger and better than yourself.

I think it's only now, many years later, that I can reflect and realize how lucky I was to be part of such a great tradition, and how great of a time I had, even though I was a whiny bitch while going through it. Those are things you don't get a grip on until you're done. Then, on the day I woke up and realized that my baseball career was over, all I wanted to do was run out and tell every high school kid I could find, "Be an athlete. It's the best decision I ever made, and it will be the best decision you will ever make, too." You'll find everything you need in athletics, and the experience can't be replaced. You might be too busy gasping for air, bleeding or throwing up to notice at the time, but those things build character.

I've made the best friends of my life through baseball, and the most valuable things I know, I know because of my experiences in baseball. High school baseball and summer travel teams helped me get into shape, meet people, and find a girlfriend. College baseball taught me the value of teammates and hustle, but also how to be humble, and how to handle failure and adversity. Heck, during one of my summers playing baseball I even found religion. It was in my senior year that I finally learned how to deal with pressure situations, so now any work deadline is a breeze. There isn't a place on earth where I have ever felt as much passion as I did when I was on the baseball diamond; it's where I could love and hate others with more intensity than I've found possible anywhere else. Man, do I miss it.

It's tough for me to explain, but trust me, if you haven't experienced that level of competition, it's hard to find anything that compares. No matter how intense your intramural flag football team was, or how competitive you are at video games, you still aren't close. After you feel the intensity of the college game, it's tough to go back to normal life, where, compared to collegiate athletics, it seems like no one has the same passion. Many ex-collegiate athletes deal with depression after their careers are over, I know I did. There is nothing we can do better in life than the sport we played, and it becomes frustrating not to be able to integrate that skill into everyday life. It becomes a hole where nothing else fits just right. This is why as great as the experience of college athletics is, and as much as it does for a person, nothing can prepare you for how to deal with the day it's over.

After my last game, I woke up with those words revolving around my head for weeks, "It's over." I guess it hit me so hard because I had such problems looking past my playing days. I just couldn't do it. It was impossible for me to look ahead and say, "You know what? Someday I'm not going to be able to play this sport again." I know now that if I would have said that to myself, I never would've been able to put all of my effort into baseball. If I really believed one day in the near future the day would come when I could no longer wake up and strap on my cleats for the rest of my life, I wouldn't have been able to push myself as hard as it took just to make the team.

The rulebook states that after four years of competition you're no longer eligible to play. You don't get cut. You don't get fired. In fact, you don't get anything except for a handshake and a "good luck" from the coaching staff. You promise to stay in touch and then you walk away. It isn't that you're suddenly not good enough to play, it's just the rules. Four years, and then you're history. Out with the has-beens and in with the soon to be has-beens. The most tragic part about the end of an athletic career is that everyone's career, barring a championship, ends in a loss.

I first saw the end coming the moment my junior year was over. When I saw the look on the faces of the seniors, it started to click in my mind that their pain wasn't very far from being my own. It was the first time I realized the real heartache after the final game wasn't that one last tally in the loss column. The real heartache was the dispersing of friends, the ending of an era, and the knowledge that the one day you'd have to wake up and tell yourself, "It's over," had finally arrived.

*****

Don Archie leaned forward in his chair and spit out a cheekful of sunflower seeds before continuing with the broadcast. "That makes two outs and the excitement continues to grow here in St. Paul where the Wolverines are up by two runs and are one out away from their tenth conference tournament championship. Carl Beckman, the Gopher second basemen will walk to the plate with men on first and second. He will either be the winning run or the final out in this elimination contest. Harold, your thoughts?"

The overweight man sitting next to Archie cleared his throat before speaking into the microphone. "Beckman is two for three on the day with two singles and, according to his teammates, he likes to put sugar on his Lucky Charms cereal in the morning. I mean, it already has marshmallows in it, I just don't get why anyone would need that much sugar." Harold's hands swirled around his head while he talked, motioning like he was sprinkling something and then spooning cereal into his mouth.

Don shook his head before asking, "What would the Wolverine Broadcasting Network do without you and your useless information?"

"I'm not sure, Arch," Harold said with a laugh. "Don't look at me like that. Most people don't use sugar on Lucky Charms. I'm surprised you didn't know that."

"It was a rhetorical question." Harold shrugged and Archie swallowed hard before turning his attention back to the game. "While we bicker up here in the booth, John Cooper has pitched a gem of a game today. It looks like Cooper will stay on the mound for the Wolverines to face Beckman even though he has hit him hard twice today and closer Michael Merlin is ready in the bullpen."

"You can say that again," Harold said with a grunt. "Coop has always had trouble with two outs. I'm surprised Coach Witherton isn't going to go with Merlin to finish this one off; the guy has been absolutely lights out this year." There was a radio silence as Don put a hand over his microphone and muttered, "asshole," toward his partner.

"Thanks for the jinx, Harold, really swell." Archie sighed before continuing. "John Cooper is now staring down Beckman and looking in for the sign. Cooper wheels and deals a get-me-over-curve for strike one. That's a big strike, folks. Two more and the Wolverines can call themselves champions. Harold, your thoughts?"

"It reminds me of a funny story about Cooper, Don. As Michigan baseball lore has it, Coop got diarrhea so bad on the spring trip his freshman year that he crapped his pants on the mound during his first collegiate start." Harold pointed to his backside while talking, and then refolded his arms.

"My God, Harold, only you could make people change the station when the conference championship is on the line." Don's icy stare didn't have an effect on Harold's lackadaisical demeanor, especially after twenty-six years of broadcasting together.

Don steadied himself and said, "Beckman digging in again as Cooper winds and throws a fastball is called ball one off the outside corner. Man, that was close and the Michigan fans wanted that one. The look on Cooper's face says he didn't like the call either. Wow, it would have been nice to get that call."

"You can say that again," Harold said.

Archie ignored him. "Cooper looks in for the sign with a one and one count. He checks the runners, and here he comes to the plate. It's a curveball and it catches the corner for strike two! Yes sir! Michigan is now one strike away and this stadium is rockin'. The next pitch will mean the season for the Wolverines! Harold, what do you say now?"

"Coop really snapped that one off," Harold said. "One strike away."

Don leaned forward for the next pitch. "And here it is, this could be the last pitch of the Big Ten tournament. Coop wheels and deals a high hard one. BECKMAN SWINGS AND CONNECTS! BECKMAN LIFTS THE BALL TO STRAIGHT AWAY CENTER. THE CENTER FIELDER BEN MARKER TURNS HIS BACK TO GIVE CHASE. THE RUNNERS ARE ROUNDING THE BASES, IF THIS FALLS TWO WILL SCORE. BECKMAN DIGS FOR SECOND, HE THINKS IT'S DOWN. MARKER IS LOOKING UP AND THIS BALL IS…"

Harold groaned and Archie muttered a few cuss words under his breath before returning to the microphone. "And in desperation the Michigan center fielder Ben Marker climbs the wall for one final stretch, but the wind will give this ball a gentle shove over the fence and Beckman has his first home run of the season. I say again, a walk-off three run homer by unlikely hero, Carl Beckman, will bring a bittersweet end to the Wolverines' season and launch the Minnesota Golden Gophers into the NCAA Regionals next weekend."

Harold scratched his head and said, "Sugar on the marshmallows, who knew?"

"What a heartbreaker for the Wolverines," Don said with his palm planted on his forehead. "The Wolverines, whose trying season this year gleamed brightly with hope after upsets against Ohio State, Penn State, and Illinois in their first three games here at the Big Ten Tournament. But two straight losses to Minnesota will have Michigan looking back for answers and forward for promises as they hope to return a veteran squad next year.

"And while Minnesota begins their celebration at home plate, the Wolverine players and prideful fans can only sit and think of what might have been."

Harold closed his eyes in response, the impact of the moment finally hitting him. The program cut to commercial and they both looked down on the field, trying to get a visual reaction from the players who had just begun to experience the most heartbreaking time of their lives.

*****

With my view from the bullpen, I saw Coop hang his head motionless as he stood on the mound. Our starting catcher stared blankly at his back, suddenly unsure if the bonds of friendship gave him the status necessary to approach. There were tears in the eyes of even the toughest guys on the field. Ben Marker in center field took off his hat and glove and quietly fell to his knees, trying to turn back time with his mind.

On the plane home the seniors reminisced about their time spent initially as followers and eventually as leaders of the team. They talked openly about the combination of four or five years of early morning lifting sessions, grueling running over rough terrain and under stopwatches, late nights of studying crammed after intense practices, sacrificing free time for extra practice and summers away from home to play the game they loved. It had all been done with the fear that at any moment the head coach would take it all away with the words, "You're cut." It was tough to watch them come to grips with the fact that their time as a Michigan athlete had come to an abrupt close.

Before I knew it, the men I had matured with over the most difficult years of my life were shaking my hand at the year end banquet and trying to convince me how good our team was going to be the next season. Then they each took their turn at the podium, some laughing, some crying, as they shared stories that made us all proud to be Wolverines. As hard as it was to listen to their stories and realize I wasn't going to share the playing field with any of them again, I knew my senior year was going to be a much tougher experience. *A year away*, I remember thinking, *my time at that podium is only a year away.*

Part I:

The Roster

University of Michigan Baseball
Top Returnees

Name	Pos.	B/T	Ht	Wt.	Yr./Elig.	Hometown
Michael Merlin	P	R/R	6'2"	200	5th/Sr.	San Diego, Cali.
John Cooper	P	R/R	6'3"	210	Sr./Sr.	Detroit, Michigan
Ben Marker	OF	S/L	5'9"	185	Sr./Sr.	Chicago, Illinois
Tom Kindleman	1B	L/L	6'4"	225	Sr./Sr.	Dallas, Texas
Wes Roth	IF	R/R	6'2"	180	Sr./Sr.	Kalamazoo, Mi.
Lou Whitley	3B	R/R	5'11"	210	Sr./Jr.	Cincinnati, Ohio
Paul Varner	OF	R/R	6'1"	190	Jr./Jr.	Marquette, Mi.
Chase Warner	P	L/L	6'1"	195	Jr./Jr	Appleton, Wis.
Wilson Jack	P	L/L	6'4"	180	Jr./Jr.	Boston, Mass.
Bill Hum	P	R/R	6'0"	190	Jr./So.	Kalamazoo, Mi.
Glen Schmalz	IF	R/R	5'7"	160	So./So.	Royal Oak, Mi.
Don Franklin	P	R/R	6'4"	215	So./So.	Dayton, Ohio

Top Incoming Freshman

Name	Pos.	B/T	Ht.	Wt.	Hometown
Paul Walker	C	R/R	6'0"	210	Fort Wayne, Indiana
Albert McKinley	1B	L/L	6'6"	235	Chicago, Illinois
Pete Alger	OF	R/R	6'0"	160	Saline, Michigan
Tucker Howard	P	L/R	6'2"	190	Los Angeles, California

Chapter One
Coop and the Squatster

"Only two things are infinite, the universe and human stupidity, and I'm not sure about the former."
-Albert Einstein

I'd move back into my apartment each fall feeling the same false hope that I could actually score some playing time during the upcoming year. This year would be different though. I was a senior and I stepped foot on campus like I was important for the first time. The only snag was the surprising resignation of our entire coaching staff, which had been replaced by some alumni guy who was coaching a Division II team in Grand Rapids, Michigan. But I didn't let it affect me, at least not initially, because first I had to deal with my dumbass roommate, All-American starting pitcher, John Cooper.

*****

Click.
"Hello, Wolverine fans and welcome to another edition of Wolverine Sports Magazine. I am your host, Joe Macino, and boy, do we have a loaded show for you today. First, we will review last year's football season and then give you a preview of this year's squad; a superior recruiting class promises to help bring another national title to Ann Arbor. A little later on, Coach Harnick will offer his opinion regarding Michigan's championship chances. Then, we will run down last year's sports highlights and lowlights, as the Wolverines made another strong push for the Director's Cup, awarded yearly to the best athletic program in the nation. Also included in this edition, we will check in on baseball, where some off-season coaching changes promise to bring the Wolverines back to prominence on the diamond this coming spring. All of this and more, when we come back on Wolverine Sports Magazine."
John Cooper blinked away from a television induced coma, rubbed the laziness out of his face, and staggered over to the kitchen. He stood up too fast and his knees buckled so he reached out to steady himself on the nightstand by the couch. He paused for a second to let his dizziness subside, tugged on the waistline of his stained sweatpants, and plotted his course for refreshment. His sticky hands reached for the refrigerator door, hoping that there would be something edible inside. The door creaked open and he squinted against the

light of the fridge. He was the first of his roommates to return for the school year and the fridge was empty except for a few miscellaneous pieces of fruit, fruit cups, canned fruit, and eggs, all unused and clearly ruined by a summer of neglect.

Coop stood up straight, scratched his bare, unwashed chest, and slammed the fridge door shut. He looked around the kitchen, and then around the rest of the apartment, surveying the situation. He wiped the counter by the sink with his pointer finger, and brought what he found close to his face. An unhealthy film of dust had settled over the entire apartment during its summer vacancy. Coop and his roommates threw an end of year party the night before they went home for the summer. Coop planned on his roommates cleaning up the mess, but it looked like they had thought the same thing about him.

Coop walked back over to the TV to see if the baseball portion of the show had started yet, but all he saw was the oversized head of Coach Harnick. Coop brushed some stale potato chip crumbs off the couch and sat down. The air conditioning had been broken since they left the year before and John's sweat made the couch stick to his skin. He peeled his back away from the couch and leaned over to turn on the standing fan positioned in the corner. He pushed each button a few times before he saw it wasn't plugged in and realized he was going to have to get up to turn it on.

He shook his head and said, "It's not that hot, I guess," and laid back down.

"We have some tough teams on the schedule this year" Coach Harnick said on the television, "and we have a lot of potential, but potential is just a French word for someone who hasn't done anything yet." Roy Harnick liked to play it safe on camera, but the way he carried himself, and the stupid smirk on his face, said he was anything but modest. "Do we have a good recruiting class? Yes. Do we have a better team than last year? Maybe. But right now it doesn't matter what kind of players we have, what really matters is what kind of team we are by the time we take the field when it really counts."

"Bullshit, Harnick," Coop yelled at the television. "I haven't even heard of two of the teams on our schedule. I've heard this same crap out of you since I was twelve, just be a man and tell them how bad you're going to kick the crap out of them!"

Coop glanced at the clock. The football review and preview had taken two-thirds of the show. Not surprising since Michigan football generated an ungodly amount of money for the athletic department.

The interview with Coach Harnick ended and Joe Macino looked into the camera before it broke away to a commercial. "Up next on Wolverine Sports Magazine, the Wolverine baseball team has a new sheriff in town, and he has the track record and the determination to take this program to the next level. After the commercial we will have interviews from returning All-American John Cooper as he talks about his new coach Tom Nichols. Next on Wolverine Sports Magazine." Joe Macino disappeared from the screen and a poorly made local commercial appeared in its place. Coop sighed, thought about getting up to go to the bathroom, but decided against it after realizing how far away it was.

Then Coop heard a key slide into the lock of the apartment door. He listened as the person holding the key accidentally locked the door instead of unlocking it and slammed into it face-first when he tried to turn the doorknob. Coop got up from the couch, walked over to the door, crossed his arms, and prepared a smirk.

*****

Coop was standing there waiting for me when I opened the door and I knew from the look on his face that he had been listening to me in the hallway. "Wipe that stupid look off your face," I said.

Coop laughed. "How'd that feel?"

"Shut up and help me with my crap." I turned around, propped the door open with my butt, and grabbed two of the black trash bags I was using to move my stuff. Then I turned back to the door, sucked in my stomach, and tried to squeeze through.

I looked at Coop and grunted for help when I couldn't fit. "Don't just stand there, dumbass." Coop's smirk turned into a full-fledged grin when he saw me struggling with my stuff. He had a reputation for being a lazy bastard, but he didn't mind what people said about him as long as he didn't have to work. He crossed his arms and watched me struggle with my bags.

"Lose any weight this summer?" he asked with a chuckle. He grabbed one of the bags away from me and tossed it into the center of the room.

"Yeah," I said between breaths. I rested for a second to answer his question, "Never go south for summer ball, man. Holy shit, it's so hot down there, much too hot for a northern boy like me." Then I turned back to the hallway to grab some more of my stuff. John was holding the door for me when I turned away, but when he heard Wolverine Sports Magazine come back on the television he let the door go in order to get a better view. So while I was putting a trash bag under each arm the door was swinging shut behind me. I turned around just in time for it to slam into my forehead. With no free arms to help me balance, I tipped over and fell hard on my butt.

"Damnit, Coop, you son of a bitch!" I yelled when I got on my feet and into the apartment. "Now my left eye is all blurry and I'm going to have a goddamn bruise on my forehead the size of your ego."

"Shut up!" Coop yelled. "Holy shit Squat, can't you see I'm on TV?" He snapped his neck back to the TV. I gave him the finger in response, but I walked around behind the couch so I could see the TV, too.

"I had a great year last year," Coop said on the screen. "The talent is here on our team, we just need someone to help us realize our potential. There is no doubt I will have another great year next year, and I would love to help win a championship for Michigan before I go pro." I groaned and Coop shot me a dirty look.

On the television Joe Macino paused to make sure Coop was finished talking before asking his next question, "Are you already saying that you don't plan to spend your senior year in the Maize and Blue?" Coop watched himself puzzle the question for a few seconds.

"What professional club wouldn't want me? I'm 18-4 since entering college and it's not like I've had a ton of run support." He tried to hold in a laugh, but failed. "Look, school is always going be here, my arm isn't. There are some big bucks waiting for me out there and I mean to squeeze those teams for every cent I can while I can still throw over 90." Coop smiled into the camera. Lying on the couch on the other side of the TV, Coop smiled back at himself.

Coop was a cocky bastard, but he was right. The money he would see after his senior year would be way less than the money he would get after his junior year. College players don't have any leverage on the negotiations if they can't use the threat of returning to school the next year.

"Well John, I would like to shift gears here," Joe Macino said. "Let's talk about the new coaching staff."

"Okay."

"What are your first impressions?"

"To tell you the truth, Joe, I haven't had time to sit down with all of them yet."

"How about Coach Nichols?"

"I talked with him briefly on the phone after the press conference, but that's it."

"What was that phone call like?"

"It was a little awkward. After being in college for two years, and having the same coaching staff during that time period, it was different to hear a new voice talk Michigan baseball. I am a little nervous about the changes that might be taking place in the next few months here, but I'm sure they're all for the better of the program. It's a difficult situation when it's my last year to play college ball. There needs to be trust, understanding, and communication in a player-coach relationship, and that type of relationship is tough to establish in one year. I just felt like I was getting a handle on the type of people my former coaches were before they parted ways with the university."

"You mean resigned?"

"Yeah, I don't know much about it, but I think we'll be all right this year. I just know I'll do my part. And I'll try to help the new coaches get adjusted any way that I can."

"Alright John, best of luck to you and the Michigan baseball team on the diamond this coming spring. Thanks for stopping by."

"Hey, dick-face!"

Coop looked at me with a sigh. "What?"

"Nothing. Don't worry about it, I got it."

"Good, because I wasn't going to help, anyway." Coop closed his eyes and I chucked a trash bag at his face, scoring a direct hit.

Coop groaned and grabbed the bag. "Oh, I thought you were serious."

"Shut it, egghead, and take the bag to my room."

Coop nodded and grabbed the bag at his feet. He walked toward my room and opened the door, but as soon as the door opened, he dropped the bag and covered his nose.

"Oh my God, Squat. Are you kidding me? If there was a loving God in heaven he would not let such a scent exist." I frowned, picked up a bag and threw it at Coop's back. "Ouch, you fat bastard. Don't be so sensitive."

"Kiss my ass, Coop," I said. "Just pick up my shit and throw it into my room if you can't stand it."

Most of the guys on the team didn't understand why we roomed together; Coop was tall, skinny, flamboyant, insensitive, and one of the top players in the nation. I, on the other hand, was short, overweight, thin-skinned, and spent most of the baseball season picking splinters out of my ass on the bench.

"R.J., listen man, you know me. I didn't mean any harm. It's just that your room smells."

"You suck ass at apologies."

"Yeah, I know," Coop said, adding, "have you heard from Kindleman?"

"No, you?" We walked back to the living room and sat down on the couch.

"I haven't heard anything, do you know where he went to play this summer?" Coop asked.

"He played for the Torrington Twisters in the New England League. We send a couple of guys out there every year because old man Witherton has a good relationship with the owner; I think they played in college together." I paused after mentioning the name of our old coach.

Coop grunted. "So much for that."

"Yeah." I didn't really want to talk about it. "Anyway, I heard it's pretty good baseball, but there is pretty good baseball everywhere. I played down in the M.I.N.K. league this summer. It stands for Missouri, Iowa, Nebraska, and Kansas. There's a team or two in each state. It was great competition."

Coop nodded. "How did you play?"

"Alright, I guess. I mean, I played as well as I could since I almost melted during each game. The first two weeks I was down there it did nothing but rain, so when the rain finally stopped, it was over a hundred degrees and we had a schedule full of double headers. I swear sometimes my head was baking in my catcher's mask."

"That's rough man."

"You're telling me. One day, when it was over a hundred degrees, I was standing on first base after getting a single when the guy batting behind me hits one in the gap. So here I am, barreling from first, rounding second and picking up the third base coach. He is waving his arm for me to go home and I think 'Oh my God, my entire body is going to explode,' but at the very least I score with no play at the plate."

Coop tried to look interested. "That's great."

"Well, there were already two outs, and the next batter hits the first friggin' pitch on the ground straight to the first baseman and the inning is over. So here I am, throwing on my equipment and running on the field just in time to feel like I was getting heat stroke."

"Wow."

"I felt like I was going to die. Did I mention it was over 100 degrees?"

Coop looked down at his chest and then back at me when he realized I was done talking. "I'm glad you liked it." I knew I had a tendency to ramble, so I decided to change the subject.

"So how about the team this year?" I asked.

"Which one?"

"I meant the football team, I think I know how we'll do."

Coop grunted. "I'm so sick of the damn football team. They get all the coverage. I don't know when the university is going to figure out that there are good players on the other teams, too."

I punched him in the arm. "Don't be bitter, hot shot. Just because Wolverine Sports Magazine put you at the end of the show doesn't give you a reason to act like a jackass on TV."

Coop shrugged. "Whatdaya mean?"

"Whatdaya mean, what do I mean? I mean nice friggin' interview."

"What about it?"

"Wow, you really are a dick, aren't you? First of all, you aren't exactly rushing to make a good impression on our new coaches."

"Who cares?"

"Second of all, the guys are going to rip you a new one. Or how about the fact every scout in the nation who saw it just wrote 'complete asshole' on your scouting report? That can't help your draft status."

Coop reached down his pants to scratch himself. "The only thing I'm worried about is what agent to sign with. This Michigan alumni guy said he could get me over three hundred thousand if I go in the top five rounds."

"Is that it? A monkey could get you more money than that if you go that high. Shit, you should hire me as your agent, I could get you millions."

"Too bad I don't know a monkey."

I grabbed a napkin off of the counter and scribbled some notes before saying, "Screw you. Just sign this if you don't believe me." Coop grabbed the pen and scribbled his name. "Ha," I said, "now that you've signed this contract I'm officially your agent."

Coop snatched the napkin out of my hand and thrust it in my face. "Put this in the bathroom on your way out," Coop said. "We don't have any toilet paper."

"I forgot how much of waste of space you are," I said. When Coop didn't respond I said, "Listen, I'm beat, I'm going to take a nap." I grabbed the napkin, got up, and walked to my room. Coop sighed and called after me louder and louder until I slammed my door shut.

"Aw, Squatster, man, don't worry about it. Aw, come on man, don't walk away. I'm sorry! I said I'm sorry! DON'T WORRY ABOUT IT MAN, WE'RE UNTOUCHABLE THIS YEAR, ANYWAY! YOU HEAR ME SQUATSTER? INVINCIBLE! BIG TEN'S, REGIONALS, SUPER REGIONALS, COLLEGE WORLD SERIES, BABY! YOU HEAR THAT, SQUASTER? ALL THE WAY MY FAT LITTLE FRIEND!"

Chapter Two
Benji and Shakes

"A slick way to outfigure a person is to get him figuring you figure he's figuring you're figuring he'll figure you aren't really figuring what you want him to figure you figure."
        -Whitey Herzog

        I was roommates with Coop and Tom Kindleman, but the teammate I connected with the best was Benjamin Marker, our fearless center fielder. I guess I liked him so much because he was a lot like me; he didn't have a scrap of talent in his whole body. However, he managed to out hustle and out work every guy on our team year in and year out. The guy was just flat out fun to watch play the game. It was incredible how Benny could overcome his talent handicap on the baseball field, and yet he could never get rid of his social anxiety. I guess that's why I thought it was hilarious when I heard he had to sit through a five hour car ride with a guy more socially inept than he was.

*****

        Benjamin Marker yawned, tightened his grip on the wheel, and squinted down the dark, deserted road in front of him. He looked at the clock, trying to focus through tired eyes. It read 2:30 in a neon yellow tint. He had been driving for five straight hours now, not including the two hours he got lost trying to pick up Albert. All together, Benny had been up for close to thirty hours straight, preparing his things to move into his new apartment, and his body wasn't used to going very long without proper rest.
        Benny felt his eyelids start to close and he slapped himself in the face, making the freshman sitting next to him jump a bit in his seat. Albert, sitting on the passenger's side of the '85 Ford Ranger's bench seat, watched Ben out of the corner of his eye.
        Albert's voice cracked a little as he asked, "Want me to drive?"
        Benny shook his head and said, "Sorry about that, sometimes I get into a trance while driving, almost like I'm sleeping."
        Albert shifted in his seat and Benny rushed to rephrase. "Well, I guess it isn't quite like sleeping, per se. I just zone out once and awhile. It's easy when you're just driving down the freeway and no one else is on the road."

Albert nodded slowly and Benny gave up trying to explain. Benny rubbed his cheek where he had slapped himself and then he ran his hand up to the side of his head and massaged the temple in slow circles before returning both hands to the wheel.

"Is your head alright?" Albert asked when he saw Benny wincing.

"Yeah," Benny said, "it's just a headache. It's what you get after spending most of your life running head first into outfield fences." Benny did a double take after finishing his sentence. Across the dark interior of the car he could see Albert's face twitching like it was being electrocuted.

"So," Albert said. His lip twitched nervously again.

"Uh," Benny said, searching for words. "Are you glad to be starting college?"

Albert cleared his throat and stuttered a bit while saying, "I'm really excited."

"What classes did you register for?"

Albert shook his head. "I'm not sure. I'm gonna hafta check my schedule when I get my computer set up."

"You have a computer, huh? Are you into video games?"

"Not really, I just use it for school."

Ben gripped the wheel a little harder and the leather made a squeaking noise under his white knuckles. "What position do you play, again?"

"I play first base," Albert said.

Benny nodded. "Our first baseman is going to be a senior this year. You should have a few solid years of playing time after he graduates."

Albert made some noises like he wanted to talk, but nothing came out.

After a few seconds Benny said, "What?"

Albert's voice shook in rhythm with the twitching of his face as he said, "I thought the first baseman graduated."

"No," Benny said. "We graduated a guy named Max. He played a little first base, but mostly he DH'ed. Tom Kindleman is our starting first baseman. He can swing it pretty well. He struggles a little bit defensively, but he's a good stick in our line-up. He's a great guy. He's a bit slow upstairs, but hey, he's from Texas." Ben trailed off when he noticed the expression on Albert's face. Ben watched as he twisted his lips and eyebrows, trying to register the information.

"Didn't you ever check out the website?"

"No."

"Shit, Al," Benny said as he reached over to slap him on the knee. "There aren't many people that can just step in on a Division I level and contribute right away, I don't care what sport they're playing. It's just a year, and you'll probably get red-shirted anyway, which means that you will have four full years to be a starter."

Albert looked at his feet and grimaced.

Benny sighed. "Albert, I don't want to sound harsh, but you need to suck it up. We have a few guys on our team that will eat you alive if they see you feel sorry for yourself like this. Besides, Kindleman will be gone next year and you will be the only first basemen on the roster. Besides that, who is to say that Tom won't go out and break an ankle right before the season? But you have to realize that the coaches are going to keep recruiting good players behind you. In order to keep the program moving forward they are going to try and replace you with someone that's even better. You can't rest on your accomplishments at this level."

"Yeah," Albert said, his gaze drifting from his feet back to the open road. "Maybe I should have gone to junior college."

Benny shook his head. "Over Michigan? No way."

"Well, I got drafted in the 36th round this year by the Montreal Expos and they told me I should go to junior college."

"Of course they did," Benny said with a sigh. "If you go to junior college and become a superstar between now and next year's draft, they can still sign you. As soon as you step foot in the classroom of a four year university, major league teams lose their rights to you until you turn 21 or until after your junior year."

Albert's legs were now trembling as he replied. "At least I would have known that I was going to start this year."

Benny didn't hear Albert's last comment because he was busy staring at his trembling legs. "Are you feeling okay?"

"Yeah, it's just this thing I got."

"Thing?"

"People have always teased me about it, but it's no big deal. It doesn't affect me anywhere except socially. I think it helps me concentrate a little better at the plate. Kids in school used to call me 'Shakes.'"

"Shakes?"

"Yeah, Shakes. Shakes McKinley."

"That's not bad," Benny said. "Hell, it even has a little ring to it."

"You think?"

"Yeah, I think. I think you'll be all right with that, Shakes. Jesus, when I was a freshman they called me 'shit for brains'."

"Really?"

"Yeah, really. It's a good thing that Hansen came along and acted dumber than I did. I would've been stuck with that nickname for life."

"They still call this Hansen guy 'shit for brains'?"

"Yeah, but most people just call him Squat."

"Squat? Is there a story behind that?"

"Yeah," Ben chuckled, "he's a catcher, he's short and stubby, and he never plays. He gets ripped on a lot."

"That's kind of harsh, don't you think?"

"It's a harsh world, Shakes, it's a harsh world." The orange night sky of street lamps in Ann Arbor glowed in the distance and a familiar sensation rushed back to Benny's bones. Turning on his blinker, Ben slapped Albert on the back and said, "Home sweet home."

Chapter Three
The University Towers

"I'm going to play with harder nonchalance this year."
        -Jackie Brandt

If Coop was the most talented guy on the team, and Benny was the toughest, Michael Merlin was definitely the coolest. I can't think of anything bad I can say about the guy. However, he had some serious issues he never dealt with until his senior year. Even then, instead of looking at his lifestyle and making a decision to change, he thought all he would have to do was change his company, but it didn't quite work out that way.

*****

"What a fucking cluster-fuck," Don Franklin said as he maneuvered through move-in day traffic. People were scattered all over the roads and sidewalks as far as Don could see. Driving around Ann Arbor during an average day was hard enough, but driving through Ann Arbor on move-in day was a death sentence. The liberal minded urban developers who planned the area thought it would be better to discourage driving by cramming in a bunch of high density housing and no parking spaces. If that wasn't enough to worry about, the students at Michigan were notorious for walking in front of traffic. An average of two students were killed by the campus buses each year.

Don honked the horn at a pair of students carrying a couch across the street in front of his car. "Fuck, can you believe this shit, Smalls?"

"Well, what did you expect DFF, it's move in day," said Glen Schmalz, called Smalls by most, from the back of Don's 1992 Chevy Blazer. Smalls coughed and a cloud of dust flew up around his head. "It smells awful back here."

"Well, that stuff has been sitting back there for a month, what the fuck do you expect? You're the one that didn't want to take all your stuff out of here when we were done playing summer ball. And don't call me DFF, I'm a sophomore now. No more stupid freshman nicknames." Don slammed on the gas and swerved at the couch-toting pair in front of him, adding a loud honk to the screeching wheels as they drove by. Smalls looked out the back window as they flew past the two mouthing the word "sorry."

Smalls coughed again. "Are we there yet? I'm going to choke to death back here."

"Quit your whining, the apartments are right here. Look, there's Merlin's car. He must have already moved his stuff in." Don flipped on his left turn signal and waited until the oncoming traffic dispersed before turning into the parking lot.

*****

Michael Merlin smiled from the balcony of his apartment as he watched his two new roommates drive in. He closed his eyes and took a deep breath. When he opened them back up he took a pull off of his beer and looked out over downtown Ann Arbor. This was Merlin's first year staying in the University Towers, but it was his fifth year on campus. It was a little more expensive than a typical college apartment, but nothing in Ann Arbor was cheap. The life of a commuter at U of M was a hard one, and Merlin took a drink for all of those that tried to find a place to park around campus on a daily basis. That is what made below average apartments close to campus so expensive.

"Supply and demand," Merlin said out loud. "Thanks, Economics class."

Merlin could see freshmen herding in and out of a bookstore below, and he got a sudden feeling like he didn't belong. Merlin red-shirted his freshman year, making a fifth year possible, but he always planned on getting drafted and leaving school early Unfortunately, his bad habits didn't make that possible. It was only at the point when his friends graduated and moved away that Merlin saw that he was going to have a change in his life whether he liked it or not.

Merlin hated change. He was a creature of routine and addiction. Once he got used to something, he could never understand why someone would want him to do something different. That was one of the reasons the coaches decided to red-shirt him his freshman year; he wouldn't listen to what they had to tell him. They wanted him to make some major adjustments in his pitching motion, they said he threw across his body too much and didn't use his lower body enough. They said that if he continued to pitch with the arm action that he had, it might cause a serious injury.

He sighed at the memory and took another drink, pondering what a fifth year meant. One more chance to prove to the pro scouts that he could make it at the next level. Talent had never been an issue for Michael. His problems stemmed more from unreliability, or as his teammates called it, a serious drinking problem. He had a dynamite season on the field the year before, but self-destructed in the draft when the major league teams all received a police report with his name on it. After that, he knew he needed to straighten out in order to realize his dream, and the two sophomores pulling into the University Towers' parking lot were a big part of his plan.

Merlin's roommates from the year before were a big part of his problem, and even though the thought of two new people sleeping in his apartment made him feel uncomfortable, he knew it was necessary. His roommates from the year before didn't play much, and with the end of their baseball careers imminent, they knew that it wouldn't hurt the team if they went out and partied nights before morning lifting, before practice, even before the games. Merlin, whose drinking problems started during high school, couldn't help but tag along.

Merlin heard the elevator make a loud noise as it hit his floor and he threw the beer over the railing in a panic.

He turned around as Don was walking through the open apartment door. "Merlin, what the fuck is going on man?"

Merlin shook his head. "Don 'Fucking' Franklin, how was the drive?"

"Not bad, our junk is a little rank from sitting in the back of my fucking car for the last month, but we didn't have to drive very far."

"I can see that your language has cleared up over the summer there, DFF," Merlin said with a smirk.

"Dude, quit that DFF stuff, I'm a sophomore now."

"You'll always be Don 'Fucking' Franklin to me." Merlin laughed. "Where's Smalls?" Merlin walked out the apartment door to see all five foot seven inches and a hundred and sixty pounds of Glen Schmalz struggling with a thirty-eight inch television by the elevator.

Merlin walked over to help him. "DFF, how about helping your roomy carry in some of your stuff?"

"Well, it's his TV," Don said under his breath, still inside the apartment.

"Here Smalls, let me help you with that."

"Thanks Mike, good to see you." Merlin bent down to pick up the TV, carrying half of it backward into the apartment. "Where's Don?" Smalls asked after setting down the TV.

"I'm in here," Don said from inside one of the rooms. Merlin shrugged and suggested they get the TV hooked up. A few seconds later, Don walked out into the living room with a terrified look on his face. "Merlin, dude, there are only two fucking bedrooms in this place."

Merlin sighed and finished connecting the cable to the back of the TV before answering. "I told you about that last year Don, I just don't think you were listening. Besides, it's not like you've never been over here before."

"I don't think we have ever been over here before, Mike," Smalls said while straightening out the TV.

Merlin laughed. "Well, why did you sign the lease without checking the place out first?"

"You told us it was a great location," Franklin whined.

"I think you were drunk at the time," Smalls said.

Merlin shrugged and said, "Oh well, I'm the fifth year senior here. You two are shackin' up in the smaller room, I've already moved in my stuff."

Franklin shot a look at Smalls, but Smalls just shrugged and told them he was going back to the car and unload more stuff. Franklin tossed him the keys to the Blazer and plopped himself down on the couch in front of the TV.

"C'mon DFF," Smalls said. "Get the lead out of your ass, man. We got a lot of stuff to move in."

Franklin got up out of his seat and Merlin plopped down in the same spot. "I'll save your spot, DFF."

"Blow me," Don said as he walked out the door.

Merlin laughed and turned his attention to the television where Coach Harnick was blabbing on and on about football. Then Joe Macino turned his eyes into the camera and said, "Up next on Wolverine Sports Magazine, the Wolverine baseball team has a new sheriff in town, and he has the track record and the determination to take this program to the next level. After the commercial we will have interviews from returning All-American John Cooper as he talks about his new coach Tom Nichols. Next on Wolverine Sports Magazine." Merlin put down the remote, walked to the fridge, and grabbed a beer with each hand.

Chapter Four
Hunt House

"Courage is the art of being the only one that knows you're scared to death."
  -Harold Wilson

We had an interesting freshman class that year, to say the least. Hanging around the freshman was a surreal experience because we could see so much of ourselves in them. It was almost like for every one of us leaving, there was someone coming into the program just like us. I looked into their eyes and saw the same emotion I remember feeling when I was in their position. At the beginning of a college career, it's almost like there is an entire life left to live that has just begun.

*****

Pete turned off his alarm and rubbed his eyes softly and slowly before sitting up in bed. He squinted through the sunlight that was coming through the window in his room, then looked around and sighed. Trophies were piled high on his shelves and desks. Certificates of achievements littered any open spot on the wall. They read things like, "First-Team All-State Outfielder," "Academic All-Region Basketball," "First-Team All-Conference Quarterback." Pete got out of bed and walked over to a Michigan flag he had hanging on the wall and traced the outline of the M with his finger. While looking at the flag he caught a look at himself in the mirror and turned to flex. He flexed his muscles in several different poses, but none of them made him look big. Pete was six feet tall and scrawny, something that made colleges unsure about signing him, but no one could argue his talent.

Pete heard a loud crashing noise from the floor below and he clenched his fists. His parents had been up since dawn, making sure that everything was securely packed away in the van and ready to haul. Pete already found it hard to sleep the night before moving into college, but his parents had kept him up all night as they made their own preparations.

"This is going to be great," Pete mimicked his Dad's voice into the mirror. "My boy going to college. I bet you are beside yourself with excitement."

Pete's thought process was interrupted by the sound of someone coming up the stairs and he braced himself for frustration.

"Peeeeeete," his mother yelled, trying to be charming. "Pete, wake up, big day ahead of you, stud."

"I'm up, Mom," Pete said, getting a towel out of his closet. Pete's mother burst into his room just as he was dropping his shorts to get ready to take a shower.

"Are you excited?" she asked with a large smile on her face.

"Mom," Pete said, trying to remain calm, "I'm getting ready to take a shower, can you give me a minute?"

Pete's mother looked down to see that he had nothing but a towel covering his body and laughed. "Oh, Pete, I'm your mother for crying out loud."

"Don't be weird, Mom, just give me some privacy please." Pete's mom rolled her eyes and shut the door on her way out. Pete secured the towel around his waist, waited a few seconds for his composure to come back, and headed out into the hallway. He only got a few steps toward the bathroom before his younger brother Roger came barreling out of his room and ran straight into his legs.

Roger hugged Pete hard before pulling away and mumbling something under his breath. Pete knelt down to Roger's level in order to look his kid brother in the eye. "Why are you up so early, Rodge?" Pete ruffled Roger's hair before he noticed a tear streak down the side of Roger's face; he had been crying.

"What's wrong, big man?" Pete said. "Did you have a bad dream?"

"Pete?" Roger's tiny voice said.

"What is it?"

"You goin' away today?" Roger sniffled loudly before Pete could think of a reply.

Pete held up his right hand and pointed to the palm. "Look, here we are here in Saline. Here is where I am going, Ann Arbor, the University of Michigan." Pete moved his pointer finger a couple of millimeters. "See how close we are? It's just a short drive; I'm not going very far at all. Okay?"

"Okay, Pete," Roger said while reaching in for another hug.

"All right, Rodge, I gotta take a shower. Maybe you should go back to bed?" Pete gripped his towel tightly as he stood up.

"I love you, Pete," Roger said, retreating back into his room.

"I'll see you soon, Roger." Pete watched Roger disappear before he walked into the bathroom.

"Get it in gear, son! Adventure awaits us in Ann Arbor!" Pete's father yelled from downstairs. Pete closed the door to the bathroom, locking it with a quick twist.

*****

Twenty miles away at the South Quadrangle dormitory, or the "Squad," as students called it, there were hundreds of freshman trying to move

28

refrigerators, computers, and boxes of clothes up the stairs and overcrowded elevators. Albert McKinley, on the other hand, had been alone in his dorm room for nearly a week. Albert didn't know anyone but Ben Marker, so he sat alone in his dorm, and only left to eat and buy his books. He spent most of his time playing computer games and hoping that Benny would call. Albert wanted to go down to the field and get some work in before official practice started but he couldn't bring himself to do it because he was too nervous.

"You can never hit enough," Ben had told him during that long awkward car ride from Chicago. "I try to hit before and after practice if I can." Albert was sure that Benny had spent the last few days hitting, throwing, and working out down at the field, and it made him sad to think that Benny hadn't called to ask if he wanted to tag along. He had Ben's cell phone number too, but he was afraid to call. He had the courage to pick up the phone, but he always called his parents instead.

"Hi, Mom," he would say as soon as he heard someone answer the phone. Albert's father was always away on business.

"Hey honey, how are things going?"

"Great," he would lie, "got some good hitting in today. My arm feels really good; I can't wait for practice to begin."

"That's nice. Are you making any new friends down there yet?"

"You bet, Mom. The guys on the team are really cool."

Albert spent so much time entertaining himself during that first week he hardly knew what to do once he heard people starting to move in. A loud crashing noise woke him up one morning while he was asleep in bed, and he wasn't sure what he should do. The only personal contact he had for the entire week leading up to move-in day was short conversations with the employees at the bookstore and the man that worked at Wendy's.

An hour after dozing off to sleep, he heard a knock on the door. Rolling over in bed, he started to rub the laziness out of his eyes when he heard a key go into the lock. Albert looked down at his baseball boxers and he felt his throat start to clench and the muscles on his face start to twitch. When the door started to open he put his head back in his bed and shut his eyes.

"Hello?"

"I don't think he's here yet."

"Dad, get the fridge."

"Oh wait, there's stuff in here."

"Jesus, he's asleep, be quiet."

"We're terribly sorry."

Albert rolled over in bed and grunted like he was dreaming.

"He's asleep."

"Tucker, don't wake him."

"Quiet, Mom. Go help Dad, I'll get him up."

Albert cringed. He heard footsteps approach his bed and a hand coming down to wake him up.

"Hey, are you Albert?"

Albert groaned. "Hmmm?"

"What's up, I'm Tucker. Look, I'm sorry about the quick introductions, but if you don't want my mother and the rest of my family to see you in your baseball boxers, I suggest you get out of bed and throw some clothes on."

Albert jumped out of bed and walked over to his dresser where all of his clothes lay neatly in piles and in the drawers. Grabbing a t-shirt and pair of sweats, he was fully clothed just as Tucker's father pushed the door aside with a small refrigerator riding on top of a dolly.

"Thanks for helping, Tucker. Damnit, I think I broke my back," said the thin balding man pushing the dolly. After setting the fridge on the ground, Tucker's father grabbed his back with his left hand and stuck his right hand in Albert's face.

"Hi, I'm Tucker's father, Mr. Howard."

"Albert McKinley. It's nice to meet you, sir." Albert shook his hand.

"Ha!" Mr. Howard yelled, making Albert jump a half step back, "Sir! Did you hear that Tucker you ungrateful and arrogant little snot? He called me sir! What a match you two will be."

"Can it, Dad," Tucker said from the back of the room before addressing Albert, "You sure jumped out of bed quick there, guy."

"I'm a light sleeper," Albert said.

Just then Tucker's mother and two sisters burst into the room from behind Albert, knocking the door into his back and sending him stumbling toward the middle of the room.

"Oh, we're so sorry," they chimed together, adding, "Won't you look at this dreadful little room." Before Albert could open his mouth, all three of them were sticking to him like glue.

"Hi, I'm Mrs. Howard."

"I'm Becky."

"I'm Lisa."

"You two will get along just fine."

"My, you're a big one aren't you?"

"I see that you are very neat."

"Tucker isn't so neat."

"You'll have to put him in line."

"You'll have to give him some lifting tips."

"He just loves baseball."

"It's all he talks about."

"College is an exciting time."

"Ann Arbor is so precious."

Albert felt nauseated. He was relieved when the women all huddled and decided to go back to the car and start hauling up the rest of Tucker's stuff.

Mr. Howard sat on the lower bunk bed with a groan. "It's nice to have women that don't mind hauling some clothes, but I guess there's more heavy stuff for us fellas to get out there. Let's go Tucker, we aren't going to carry everything for you, and I don't care about your damn arm either, it will be fine."

"Hey, this arm is going to support you someday," Tucker said, following his dad out the door. Albert offered his help and followed closely behind.

"I can carry something if you want," he said, "I'm dying to get out of this dorm room. I've been here by myself for a week."

"What did you do with yourself?" Mr. Howard asked as they walked down the stairs of South Quad. As Albert told Tucker and his father about his early arrival, Pete and his father were carrying the family's extra microwave up the same stairwell.

"Hey there!" Pete's father said, starting to drop his end of the microwave.

"Hi," Mr. Howard said, not paying much attention as he walked past.

"This is Pete," Pete's father said to Tucker and Albert.

"Hey, Pete," Tucker said, trying to appease the man, "where are you from?"

"Saline," Pete said, feeling his cheeks starting to burn. "C'mon, Dad, let's let these people get back to moving."

Mr. Howard nodded said, "Nice to meet you, Pete."

"Wait," Tucker said, "what's your last name Pete?"

"Alger."

"Oh, great," Mr. Howard said. "Pete Alger, outfielder from Saline, Michigan. This is my son Tucker Howard. It looks like you three will be teammates this year."

"Small world," Pete said. "Where's your room?"

"Albert and I are in 3116 Hunt."

"I'm right next door," Pete said. "I wonder if the entire freshman class is in the same hallway."

"Are there many freshmen?" Albert asked from the background.

"No, not too many," Mr. Howard said. "Not a lot of players graduated last year, I think there are only about eight freshmen or so."

"Well that would be great if you guys were all in the same hallway," Pete's father said.

"I think Coach Nichols told me that he wanted all the freshmen in the same hallway. He is really big on developing team chemistry. It is the biggest reason I decided to sign here," Tucker said. "Anyway, we better get to the car before my mom and sisters break all my valuables, I'll see you around."

"See ya," Pete said.

"Good you meet ya," Pete's father said.

Pete waited for Tucker, Tucker's father, and Albert to pass by before shooting a dirty look at his dad. "Just pick up the microwave and let's get it to the room," Pete said, "Mom will have a heart attack if we leave her alone by the car. I swear I don't know why she worries so much."

"Ann Arbor is not like Saline," Pete's father said, picking up the other end of the microwave, "much more crime. Many more people."

"Give me a break, Dad. Thirty-eight thousand students all paying between fifteen and thirty thousand dollars a year to come here, I don't think they are looking to steal a box of underwear from the car. Mom should be helping us."

"Oh, Pete, what are you going to do when you can't complain about your stupid parents?"

Chapter Five
Half the Staff

"The secret of managing a club is to keep the five guys who hate you from the five who are undecided."
 -Casey Stengel

Ray Fisher stadium, home of Wolverine Baseball, was named after one of the greatest baseball minds ever to come from the University of Michigan. Ray Fisher coached the Wolverines for thirty-eight seasons, had an overall record of 636-295-8, a conference record of 283-135, won fourteen conferences championships, and one national title. After playing college ball at Michigan, Fisher pitched ten years in big leagues where he had an overall record of 100-97. The stadium, named after him in 1967, has been the location of Wolverine Baseball since 1912. If I was Tom Nichols, I would have been nervous, too.

*****

"Coach?"
Tom flinched.
"Coach?"
Coach Tom Nichols looked at Gene Calloway, his assistant coach, who was sitting on the other side of his desk. "I'm listening," he said while rubbing his eyes.
"With all due respect, Tom, you've been flaking out ever since we took this job," Gene paused for a second. "Is everything okay? I'm starting to wonder why we left Grand Valley State; we had a pretty good thing going there, you know."
"I've had a lot on my mind," Tom said. "What about you? You and Susan all squared away on living arrangements?"
Gene chuckled. "Look who you're talking to, of course I have."
Tom nodded. "Sarah and I have had a difficult time finding someplace affordable. Any ideas?"
"Just one," Gene said. "Let's talk baseball. I didn't come to the ballpark today to find you a cheap two bedroom apartment within driving distance of Ann Arbor. I came to talk baseball, so let's do it." Gene flipped through a large three-ringed binder that was sitting on his lap. "Let me throw these names at you: Bob Steiner and Mitchell Lewis."

Tom wore a confused look. "Remind me."

Gene looked up from his notebook. "They're our two new collogues."

"Come again?" Tom asked.

"You need to learn how to check e-mail.," Gene's lips quivered as he talked. "It looks like our almighty athletic director, Morgan Polanski, took the initiative to fill the assistant coaching positions without asking us."

"For crying out loud." Tom rubbed his eyes. "Tell me you at least know something about these guys."

"Just what Morgan sent me in the e-mail." Gene paused to read. "Bob Stein. He graduated from Traverse City High School, 1974. Then he graduated from Central Michigan University, 1979. Head coach of Ann Arbor Pioneer High School, 1982-2002."

"What kind of coaching record does he have?"

Gene fired through a few more papers. "His career record at Ann Arbor Pioneer is 486-132, five state championship teams, and nominee for the Michigan High School Baseball Coaches Association Hall of Fame. It looks like we have one of his former players on the roster right now, an R.J. Hansen." They both looked at each other and shrugged.

"Speaking of players," Tom said

Gene grunted. "I'm way ahead of you, what do you want to know?"

"Start with pitching."

"Let me just say that the word on the street isn't exactly really positive about the attitude of the team we're inheriting. You'll have to work some of that team bonding bullshit or something. You might have to be kind of a hard-ass for a while, think you can handle it?"

"Look who you're talking to," Tom laughed.

"I'll believe that when I see it."

"Just get on with it, Gene."

"Okay, okay," Gene cleared his throat. "Our bright spot is that we have two returning All-Big Ten selections in John Cooper and Michael Merlin."

Tom stopped Gene by raising his hand. "Cooper, is that the loudmouth from Wolverine Sports Magazine?"

"That'd be the one. Last year's bio in the media guide says he went to high school in Michigan, at Birmingham Brother Rice. All-American in high school, drafted in the 17th round after his senior year."

"Brother Rice?" Tom said.

"Yep."

"Catholic league boy, eh?"

"Looks like it."

"Just what I need, another Catholic League kid."

Gene sighed. "Tom, I hate to tell you this, but not every kid that comes out of the Detroit Catholic League is going to turn out like Shane McMillon."

Tom ignored him. "What about this Merlin?"

"I've heard his stuff is electric, but he has a rap sheet as long as your boring speeches."

Tom chuckled. "How bad can it be?"

"He's a closer. He finished last year with a 2.12 ERA and 10 saves. He's a California kid, looks like he ran into a little trouble with the law last year." He paused. "I guess there might be some eligibility issues we may want to research. Anyway, he didn't get drafted as a red-shirt junior. So there it is, the leadership on our pitching staff is going to come from an asshole and a fifth-year felon."

Tom frowned. "Super. What else?"

Gene smirked. "Off the top of my head?"

Tom nodded.

"The rest of the staff is pretty inexperienced. Top returnees include sophomores Don Franklin and Bill Hum, and juniors Wilson Jack and Chase Warner. All of them pitched somewhere around twenty to thirty-five innings last year. Other than that, we just have a few guys with a couple of appearances."

"Well, we should be okay. I think this recruit I got with the remaining money could be an immediate impact player."

"I'll believe that when I see it."

"Why do you say that?"

Gene cleared his throat. "Tucker Howard, he's the pitcher you are talking about, right? Cincinnati native, father played here in the 70s? Scouting report says the kid needs a year or two for his coordination to grow into his body."

"Do you have his underwear size in there, too?"

Gene smiled and looked down, pretending to read. "Size medium, 32-34 inch waist."

"Boxers or briefs?"

Gene looked down again. "Boxer-briefs."

Tom laughed. "What about my hitters?"

"Most of last year's starters are returning. Not that they did spectacular or anything, but at least they're experienced. The only starters we lost are at catcher, third base, and left field. At first base there is two-year starter, senior Tom Kindleman from Dallas, Texas. At second, we have Wes Roth, he is from the Kalamazoo area. Our shortstop is Glen Schmalz, from Royal Oak. The center fielder is Ben Marker from down around Chicago, and the right fielder is Paul Varner. He's from Marquette." Gene raised his eyebrows and waited to see Tom's reaction.

"A Yooper, eh?"

"Yooper or not, his stats are good enough to start for us."

Tom's face changed expressions. "Let's not let him know that, or anyone for that matter. I want every spot on the field to be open. In order to be successful we need to create a new look, a new start, a new tradition."

"The motivation stuff is your department," Gene said. "But I think you're looking at this all wrong. It's not like they're complete failures. There are a couple players left from a Big Ten Tournament Championship team five years ago, and they went 28-28 two years ago. Take it easy on them Tom, they've had some major changes in this program over the last few years, and it's not like we're working with nothing." Gene glanced at his watch. "Sorry, Tom, but I need to get going. There are a couple loose ends I need to deal with at home." Gene waddled over to the door and left without another word.

Tom took the few minutes peace to reflect. He had over forty players on his roster, and he would have to cut to thirty-two. Telling more than ten of these players that they would not be able to play baseball for Michigan would be the worst and most stressful part of his life over the next month and a half. Getting the cuts over early in the year would help him transition into the task of building team unity, but he knew there would be second guessing. He was always scared to make the wrong decision, and since he had never seen any of the returning players play, he knew he was going to have to spend an extra amount of time analyzing every detail.

Tom couldn't help judging people on the first impression; he had been doing it all his life. His assistant coach and best friend, Gene, was the perfect example. They played together at Michigan and Tom was almost solely responsible for Gene's role as the team outcast. He often looked down on him, and rallied the team to make fun of Gene because of his mechanical habits and oversized body frame. It wasn't until Tom got to know Gene a little better, during the long road trips, that he started to realize how much they had in common. But when Tom thought of regret, he could only see one name, Shane McMillon.

Tom inherited Shane as a player during his first year coaching at Grand Valley State University in Grand Rapids, Michigan. Shane was promised the world by the previous coaches and he wasn't shy in expressing his frustration with his new head coach. It was Tom's opinion that Shane just didn't have the proper attitude needed to endure a college baseball season. Plus, that kind of bad attitude was contagious, and the last thing Tom needed was a locker room full of players talking about how bad of a coach he was before his first season even started.

Tom didn't underestimate the power of Shane's negative attitude and the effect it would have had in the locker room, but he did underestimate his ability. After sending the athletic department enough threatening letters for Tom to pile up to his knee, Shane transferred to Saginaw Valley State at the semester. SVSU was a highly competitive Division II program that Grand Valley would have to go through in order to win a conference championship. Sure enough, the two teams were neck in neck going into the last weekend, and GVSU had to travel to Saginaw for a series that would decide the championship.

Tom never felt so much torment as he did during that series. He could feel the eyes of Shane's parents on his back during each game. Shane was starting and starring for Saginaw Valley, and Tom started to regret that he cut him. When the conference championship came down to the last game, and the last at-bat, it was only fitting that it was Shane at the plate.

Tom knew it was gone before Shane even swung. Hell, he knew it before Shane even stepped in the batter's box and they sent in the sign from the dugout. Tom knew that it didn't even matter if they had tried to intentionally walk Shane in that moment; something was going to happen, Tom could smell it in the air. As the pitcher looked in for the sign, tiny electric shocks went up and down Tom's arms, making his hair stand on end from his head to his toe. Then it came. A curveball, a hanger, the ball was hit so hard and left the park so fast that no one even had time to cheer. Everyone's mouth hung open at the sight of one of the longest balls they'd ever seen hit.

Tom could still remember the look in Shane's eyes as he rounded the bases. His eyes continued to breathe fire, even after he had his revenge. Then, as Shane rounded third and his third base coach jumped and cheered, waiting to give Shane a high five for his spectacular act, Shane slowed down and stared right into the dugout, pointing his finger straight at Tom. His face wore more pain than Tom knew what to call it, but he knew it wasn't satisfaction. As Shane crossed home plate, and the game ended, Tom knew that everyone on the other team felt like a winner save one. And it was his fault.

Chapter Six
Straggling In

"Success depends on the support of other people, the only hurdle between you and what you want to be is the support of others."
-David Joseph Schwartz

There's something exciting about coming back to the field for the first time each year. I always wanted to see my friends, tell stories, and show off my bulging muscles from a summer worth of lifting. There was always a feeling of starting fresh, even if the year before was terrible, and for me they usually were. So the fall was my time to shine and catch up with old friends.

*****

Benny parked his truck behind Ray Fisher Stadium, or "The Fish," as we called it, and turned off the ignition. He picked up his equipment lying next to him on the truck's bench seat, unbuckled his seat belt, and reached for the door handle before stopping himself. He raised his head again, taking one more look at the words "Ray Fisher Stadium" built in a semi-circle around the likeness of Ray Fisher throwing a baseball and closed his eyes. Ben thought back on three years worth of memories and mouthed the word, "senior." He shook his head, the word felt funny on his lips.

Don Franklin, standing outside Benny's truck, had to knock four times before Benny's body responded at all. When Benny came to he opened the door of his truck and greeted the grinning faces of Don Franklin, Michael Merlin, and Glen "Smalls" Schmalz.

"How long have you guys been sanding there?" Benny asked.

"Long enough to see you drooling over the sight of the ballpark," Smalls said.

Benny shrugged and said, "What can I say, I love this place. How were your summers?"

"Jail was nice," Merlin said. "I met some good people, did a little networking."

Benny skipped over the subject and looked at Smalls and Franklin. "How was it playing in the Great Lakes League, guys?"

"Two words," Franklin blurted. "Lima, fucking, Ohio."

Merlin chuckled. "That's three words, DFF."

Benny and Smalls laughed, but Don didn't retaliate until they were inside the locker room. "I'm not spending another year being the butt of every joke, so you guys can just knock that shit off right now."

"Save the drama, Franklin," Smalls said while grabbing a stool off of his locker. "I will always get made fun of because of my last name, and you don't hear me bitching about it."

"He has you there, DFF," Benny said. "Besides, I think Squat has it twice as bad as either of you."

"You're killing me, Smalls!" A gruff voice yelled from the entrance of the locker room, making the four of them jump a bit. They turned to see the bearded face of Paul Varner, a junior outfielder, and the self imposed dictator of verbal punishment. Smalls took a look around the room, zeroing in on Franklin as if to say, "See what I mean?"

Varner laughed and threw his gym bag at Franklin. "What's up ladies?" Franklin grabbed his bag out of the air, stood up, and chucked it in the bathroom.

Varner laughed and walked into the bathroom to retrieve it. "Nice velocity, DFF." Everyone except Franklin suppressed a laugh, sending the locker room into an awkward silence.

*****

There are few people that I care for less in this world than William McGee. He was a red-shirt sophomore during my senior year, and not only did he think he was a lot better than he really was, but whatever supplements he was taking to grow his freakishly large muscles, it seriously affected his attitude. Everyone joked about his 'roid rage, but sometimes I had to wonder if he really was on the juice.

So when I caught a glimpse of his gigantic back trying to open the outside door to the locker room at The Fish, I groaned loud enough to get a reaction out of Coop.

"Are you giving birth over there?" he asked as we walked toward the stadium.

"You see McGee?"

Coop looked toward the stadium and said, "What? Are you still afraid of that big dumb animal?"

I shook my head and kept my silence as we approached the ballpark. Coop and I greeted McGee once we reached the stadium and opened the door for him. I guess he didn't have enough brain cells left to remember the combination to the lock over the summer.

Merlin, Franklin, Smalls, Benny, and Paul Varner were all inside the locker room by the time we got there. It wasn't uncommon for the guys on the team to get to school early so they could work out before Fall Ball started. But today a group of freshman came wandering into the locker room while we were there, and torturing the freshman was a much better past time than working out.

"You hear about the team so far?" McGee asked the group of freshman, who were talking amongst themselves in the corner of the room. "I heard we have over forty players coming in."

"Forty people?"

"How many starters are returning?"

"How many are pitchers?"

"How many catchers do we have?"

"Is that a lot?"

"What does that mean?"

"It means," said McGee, who was now staring at his shaved chest in the bathroom mirror, "that eight or more of us are going to be done with baseball in five weeks."

"Five weeks?"

"Forty people on the roster?"

"Seriously?"

"How many outfielders do we have?"

"I know one thing for sure, I ain't gettin' cut." Everyone looked toward the door when they heard a slow southern accent. There, with a Dallas Cowboys duffel bag in his hand, was Tom Kindleman, my other roommate, decked out in cowboy boots and hat. His smile was just wide enough to keep the chew in his mouth. His other hand held a Mountain Dew bottle with an inch of brown spit inside.

"Hi, Tex," McGee said from inside the bathroom, still checking out his muscles.

Varner walked over as if to shake Tex's hand, but gave him a sucker punch in the stomach instead. "Cute outfit, Tina."

"Hi, Tex," Coop said, coming up from behind Varner. "How was your summer?"

"Okay," Tex said.

"Still a man of few words," I said while trying to push my way to the front of the group.

Tex looked me up and down before shaking my hand. "You clean the apartment?"

"Nope. She's waiting for you, big man. She told Coop and I that there's only one man that's allowed to take a vacuum to her carpet." Everyone laughed except Varner, who was on his way back to his locker.

"Look who turned into a fucking comedian over the summer," Varner said.

"Kiss my ass, Varner," I snapped.

"Anyway," Tex said, "I hate to break it up, but I'm running on a tight schedule. I need to get to my locker so I can get ready to go hit, what are y'all doing right now?"

"I came down to see if I could meet the new coaches," I said. "I might take a few swings out in the cages if they aren't in."

Tex nodded and turned toward the rest of the guys in the locker room "What about you guys?"

"Smalls and I are going to go get a lift in," Don said. Smalls nodded.

"I'm up for anything," Benny said. "I'll go hit with you if you want Squat."

"Sure."

"Aight," Tex said, picking out a new locker, "I'll meet you guys out there."

I walked toward the door that led to the coaches' offices, opened it, and peeked down the hallway. The light was off in the head coach's office, and it didn't look like anyone was around. I felt like a freshman for a second looking down the hallway, still nervous about meeting his coaches for the first time. I shook the nervous tension out of my body as soon as it came. *I'm a senior now*, I thought, *I need to act like it*.

"No one's here." I shut the door and walked back toward my locker to get a bat. "Are you ready to go, Benny?"

"Always."

"See you out there, Tex."

Coop brushed past us as we left the locker room. "You guys do that. I'll go take a shit," he said, making a beeline for the bathroom.

*****

Merlin watched Benny and Squat leave the room going toward the field, and then turned to the freshman still hiding out in the corner. "Can any of you speak?"

The first freshman to step up had a difficult time talking because of a strange spasm in his neck. "I'm Albert McKinney," he said, "Ben Marker gave me a ride here."

"Well, isn't that fantastic," Varner said from his locker.

"Shut up, Varner," Merlin said, "you have to make the freshmen feel more welcome than that."

"I'll make them feel welcome," McGee said, pulling on his penis. Merlin laughed in his head and Varner laughed out loud. Don and Smalls, who weren't really paying attention to the conversation just gave the group a couple head nods and walked out of the locker room, heading toward the weight room.

"I'm sorry, guys," Merlin said. "You can continue. Who are you?" Merlin pointed toward the scrawny kid in the bunch. He pointed his finger at his face as if to ask, "Who, me?" Merlin answered the visual queue, "Yeah, you."

"I'm Pete Alger."

"Good, Pete. Who else?"

"Tucker."

"Tucker?"

"Yeah, Tucker."

"What kind of name is that?"

"I just came to stake my claim for a locker, so I'm out of here fellas," Varner said, heading toward the door, "don't be too nice to those fuckers, eh?" Varner laughed as he exited the room. Two more players entered as Varner left, stopping for a second to give Varner a handshake. The first one had an ear to ear grin on his face, revealing a row of bleached teeth. The man behind him was a bit shorter, but almost as wide as he was tall. His short sleeved t-shirt was cut up the seam on the sleeves to make room for his huge biceps. Physically, he was about the same size as McGee, except a bit shorter. The only way to tell the two apart was that McGee had a lighter complexion.

"Froshies," the tall skinny one yelled before anyone else could get another word out. "Who wants a little tour of Ann Arbor, and a chance to get to know two of your teammates a little better?"

"Well if it isn't my man Wes and his evil step-sister Lou," Merlin said. "Is it 'wear your little brother's t-shirt day' Lou?"

"Fuck off," Lou said in a deep voice.

Merlin walked over to Lou and pinched his t-shirt between two fingers, trying to get a look at what it said. "What is it today, Lou? Oh, Abercrombie had a pretty good volleyball squad in '84, huh? State Champs? Congratulations!"

Lou's face started to turn red, but the tall kid he came through the door with started talking before he could think of a comeback, "Hey Magic Man. We just want to help make some of these freshmen feel a little more welcome."

"Knock yourself out."

"How about that one right there?" Lou said, pointing toward Albert.

"Which one?" Wes asked.

"That one."

"Me?"

"Yeah, you."

"C'mon son, time's a wasting. Say goodbye to your classmates."

"Bye, guys."

"Bye, Tex," Lou said as he walked out of the locker room. Tex, who had been taking his time changing into his shorts and cleats, just gave his teammates a salute before they exited the room. Then, McGee got up off of his stool and walked over to the full length mirror and started to swing.

"Why don't you put some underwear on if you are going to swing in front of the mirror," Merlin paused, "for the freshmen's sake."

"Fuck them," McGee said. "They'll get used to it." Merlin took another look at the three freshmen, still sitting in a bunch in the corner of the room.

"You guys have a voice?" Merlin asked.

"Yeah," said one of the three.

"Tucker, right?"

"That's right."

"And Pete?" Merlin pointed toward the smallest of the three, who was trying his best to cower behind Tucker.

"That's right," Pete said in a squeaky voice

"What about you?" Merlin pointed his finger at the last unknown freshman.

"Paul Walker."

"Like 'Walker, Texas Ranger?'"

"Yeah." Paul hung his head a bit, it wasn't the first time he had heard the comparison.

"I'm Mike Merlin. Some guys call me Mr. Wizard, or the Magic Man."

"Or alcoholic," McGee said.

Merlin was unfazed by the cheap shot. "Or that." Merlin shrugged and looked over the freshmen again. "Hey, you guys want me to give you a tip?" They nodded their heads in unison. "Take your gloves and cleats back to your dorm rooms at night. Don't let them out of your sight during Fall Ball."

"Merlin," McGee said with a shocked look, "are you serious?" McGee usually didn't have anything really intelligent to say, and unless it was about baseball, beer, or girls, it was usually just, "Are you serious?"

"Why?"

McGee shot Merlin a threatening glare in response. Merlin laughed, tossed the newspaper on the center table, and laid down on the couch. "Someone wake me up when DFF and Smalls get back."

*****

Meanwhile, Benny and I decided to sit in the stands and catch up a little while waiting for Tex.

"So how has life been treating you?" I asked after we sat down.

"I can't complain, who would listen? I'm still playing baseball, and it doesn't get much better than that. I guess you should ask me in a couple years." Benny's eyes glazed over as he looked at the field. "Field looks outstanding."

"Sure does."

We sat in silence for a few seconds before Ben starting talking again. "Seniors," he paused. "Wow, it just seems like yesterday that we first put on the Michigan uniform."

I sighed loudly. "I know what you mean, it hasn't quite hit me yet that I'm going to be in the working world next year. I have no idea what I'm going to do, what about you?"

"I don't even want to think about it. I guess I'll just tour the country for awhile, going to every open tryout that I can. There are five independent baseball leagues, and a couple more starting up, so I'm planning on chasing the dream and going from tryout to tryout until I run out of money."

"Independent ball? I'm sure you'll make it. That's exactly what Dubbs did."

43

"Who, Walt?"

I nodded, forgetting for a second that Benny and Walt, or "Dubbs," as we called him, had never been on good terms. "He told me that he just wasn't ready to give it up. He felt like he had to work the baseball out of his system. He played a little last summer in the Frontier League. He might know some people, do you have his number?"

"No."

"Remind me to give it to you, it's on my cell phone." I stood up and looked back down the tunnel in towards the locker room. There was still no sign of Tex.

"Man, if Dubbs can catch on with an independent team, I know that I can."

"Shit, Ben, you should be playing for an affiliated team."

"Get real. No one wants an undersized center fielder with a below average arm and no speed."

"Yeah, but you're a baller, man. The scouts are too stupid to see who's a baseball player and who isn't. The only reason they draft anybody these days is based on raw talent, which is bullshit anyway. I would take real talent over raw talent any day; there is a big difference between an athlete and a baseball player."

Benny raised his eyebrows. "Are you trying to say I'm not an athlete?"

"Yeah, I guess I am," I said with a laugh. "No, seriously, I meant that you have instincts and heart, and they can't measure that on a scouting report. That's why it can't get you down if you don't get picked up right away. Who cares? If you catch on with an independent team, or if the right scout sees you they'll be able to tell that you live to play this game. Hell, since I don't ever play, I think the best part of the games are watching you play. It's inspiring."

"Yeah well it's too bad that you aren't the one scouting me in the stands. I swear if that bastard Cliff from the Brewers gives me some shit this year about my size I'm going to punch him in his fat head."

"Violence is never the answer, Benjamin." We exchanged a laugh and I continued by saying, "Look at it from my point of view; at least the scouts are giving you crap. Scouts don't make fun of nobodies, only players they are looking at who they don't think are very good. Me, I don't even sniff the playing field, and even if I did I'm not good enough for a scout to make fun of me. I just want to make the team and be around baseball and the guys for one more year."

"C'mon Squat, quit talking like that, you'll get some playing time this year. The catching spot is wide open and you're a senior. As for myself," Ben knocked himself twice in the head with the knuckles of his left hand, "major league organizations tend to frown upon the type of recent medical history that I've had."

"What are you talking about?"

"Well, it seems that my tendency of going head first into the outfield wall after fly balls has started to catch up with me."

I smiled. "I remember when you hit the wall at Ohio State last year. You almost knocked the goddamn thing down, saved two runs. Man, that was a hell of a play."

"Thanks, I couldn't see out of my left eye for two innings after that."

"No shit?"

"No shit." Ben looked back toward the locker room tunnel, still no Tex.

"Grab the ball bucket, I'm sick of waiting for that slow-ass Texan," I said.

Benny grabbed his batting gloves and tossed them into the bucket of balls we brought with us from the locker room. He grabbed his bat with his other hand and walked down the steps, onto the field, and toward the batting cages.

"As I was saying," Benny said as they were about half way to the cages, "something serious happened this summer. The new coaches don't know about it, and I'm not sure if I am going to tell them. Can you keep a secret?"

"I don't know Ben, that's a lot of responsibility."

Benny laughed. "Okay, forget it."

"I'm joking, dick, you can't do that. You have to tell me now."

"It wasn't much, just a concussion from hitting the wall again," Benny said.

I wasn't surprised; Benny had two concussions in his first three years at Michigan. No one played the outfield like he did - he was fearless. He would run over his own grandmother to catch a fly ball without even stopping to check who he stepped on.

"But then," Benny said just as they reached the cages, "I started getting these headaches. Some of them got so bad that I would throw up. The doctor said I was starting to do some heavy damage to my body and that I should consider hanging them up."

"No shit?"

"No shit." Benny frowned. "You know me, I could never do that."

"Yeah, Ben, I know you all right." We lifted up the netting to the cage and stepped inside just as Tex appeared from the locker room. I changed the subject. "Hey, there's Tex."

"It's about time," Benny said.

I grabbed the bucket of balls and walked to the far end of the cage and turned up the L-screen that been knocked down by the wind. "Benny," I said, trying to pick my words as carefully as possible, "just how bad was this concussion?"

Benny turned his head and looked behind him. Tex was still crossing the field, far out of earshot. "Pretty bad. I'm not going to stop playing, but I think my 'running into the fence for a fly ball' days are over for good. I might do some permanent damage if it happens again. But don't worry; you don't throw hard enough to hurt me anyway."

I laughed. "We'll see about that, fucker." I got back behind the screen and threw one over Ben's head, sending him straight to the ground.

"Jesus, asshole, I was just kidding. Try not to kill me."

"Any time I want, Benji."

"Yeah, right, anytime you want." Ben grunted and got back up to his feet. He knocked the dust off himself before settling back into the left-handed side of the batter's box. Ben threw right-handed but hit from both sides of the plate. His left handed swing was much different than his right handed swing; he didn't have much power so he tried to go to the opposite field a lot. But hitting in the cage against me, with my easy-to-see straight-over-the-top catcher's delivery, he decided to try and show me up.

I spoon fed the next pitch down the heart of the plate and Benny used every piece of his body to drive the pitch up into the top of the batting cage just as Tex was walking up on us.

"Yahtzee!" Tex yelled with a laugh, starting to take a few warm up swings.

"Yeah, keep talking Tex," I said, "your first pitch is going right between your shoulder blades." I turned my attention back to Benny, who had dropped his bat and was holding his left hand over his eyes as if he was straining to see how far the ball went.

"Show off," I said while grabbing another ball out of the bucket.

"Just bring it in here, meat," Benny said, picking up his bat.

Tex took the chew out of his lip and threw it on the ground so he could laugh without the threat of choking on his chewing tobacco. "I missed you guys."

Chapter Seven
Baseball and Girls Don't Mix

"It was too bad I wasn't a second baseman; then I'd probably have seen a lot more of my husband."
    -Karolyn Rose, ex-wife to Pete Rose

Wes and Lou were, as lightly as I can put it, the worst role models you would ever want for your kid. I'm sure if Mr. and Mrs. McKinley knew what kind of company Albert was keeping on that day, they would have rushed to Ann Arbor and made him transfer. I know this because I, like Albert, was easily influenced by Wes, or "The Weasel," when I was a freshman, and I regretted it for my entire college career. I was so ruined by the decision that he persuaded me to make, that I didn't even try to make it right until my senior year. Then things got even more complicated.

*****

"Hey, baby! Party at South Fifth tonight!" Wes yelled out the window of his pickup truck. The man in the passenger side, Lou, laughed deep and loud, making the inside of the truck shake. In between them was freshman Albert McKinley, who blushed hard and slumped down in his seat, trying not to be seen.

"This is the best time of the year," Wes said. "The girls are just getting back from their long lonely summer vacations. Freshmen girls are breaking free of mommy and daddy's protective hold and lookin' for a good time." He bared his teeth at Albert and snickered. "That back there are the two best places to pick up chicks in Ann Arbor, Al," Weasel continued, "South Quad and West Quad."

Lou closed in on Albert's face and said, "You get any numbers yet or what?" Lou elbowed Albert in the ribs. "Any hot new freshman athletes ripe for the pluckin'?"

Albert cleared his throat before saying, "I just moved in yesterday."

Wes thumped the steering wheel. "No excuses, froshy. I was baggin' girls the first night. Let's make another round and find you a woman."

"I already have a girlfriend."

Weasel's eyes widened. "Holy shit, a girlfriend? That's a four letter word around here." Weasel stepped on the gas and turned into the driveway at the South Fifth baseball house.

"Where are we?" Albert asked.

"Where are we?" Weasel repeated. "It's the baseball house, bro." Weasel and Lou both got out of the car and Albert followed.

"Which," Lou said as they approached the house, "is going to be your home for every Thursday, Friday, and Saturday night for the next year."

They ascended the front porch steps together, but Lou stopped Albert once they hit the door. "What the fuck is wrong with your leg, dude?"

*****

The speech that Albert "Shakes" McKinley received when he got in the house was a speech that many freshmen heard during their first year in college. Some people call it the "don't have a girlfriend when you go to college" speech, others call it the "long distance relationships never work" speech, but the baseball players at the University of Michigan called it the "baseball and girls don't mix" speech. The premise was simple; Wes and Lou wanted Albert to dump his girlfriend.

"How can you really enjoy your time here," Wes said, "when all you can think about is what she is doing there? Besides, if you want to contribute to the team, you have to get rid of all distractions. A girlfriend is distracting enough, but a long distance relationship? It's not going to work, trust me. Women are very important to a man's morale. That's why we party and pick up chicks. Not to abuse them, just to ensure that we are positive people once we get out onto the field. We are obligated to keep ourselves happy off the field so we can be the best we can be on it. If you take a relationship like the one you have with your girlfriend, where you're used to constant emotional satisfaction, and you take it away from a man, the results are never good. That is why proximity is the most important factor in choosing a girlfriend. It's really simple, Al. You need to have your mind, body, and heart here in Ann Arbor in order to help this team and stay eligible. Trust me; you won't be able to handle it if your mind or heart is always with her."

Albert just sat there, not sure what to make of the arguments that had been laid before him. While he thought back on what his new teammates had told him, his eyes wandered around the house. The house on South Fifth was the designated baseball party house, or so Wes said. The evidence of his claim was confirmed by the strippers' pole located just a few feet from the front door. "You'd think that would make girls turn up their nose," Wes had told him earlier. "It was really just a joke at first, but you would be amazed how the chicks get down on that thing." The pole made Albert wonder what his girlfriend was doing at that exact instant.

"It boils down to a trust issue," Lou said.

"That's right," said Wes, "It all comes down to trust. Do you want to worry about what your girlfriend is doing during every second of the day while she's two hundred miles away?"

Albert shook his head.

"I didn't think so."

*****

After Benny, Tex, and I got done hitting, I went off to one of the bookstores on campus to get my books. I was waiting in line to check out when I first saw Cassie Roth.

"Hi," she said with a confident voice.

"Hi." I wish I could have come up with something a little more charming, but it wasn't everyday some random girl just walks up to me and starts talking.

"I was standing in line next to you and I saw that you have a Michigan Baseball t-shirt on," she said.

"Yeah," I said, "I am." I looked down to make sure. "I mean, I do."

"My name is Cassie Roth."

I winced on the inside. "Roth?"

"That's right," she said. "I'm Wes Roth's sister. What is your name?"

"R.J." I looked her up and down, trying to decide if she was worth the hassle of having to deal with "The Weasel." "I didn't realize Wes had a sister."

"I'm a freshman, so that's probably why you haven't seen me around before. Are you going to the party this Saturday night? Wes said that he wants to start this year off with a bang, so they are going to get some kegs together for after the football game."

"Yeah," I said, "if it's baseball related, I'm sure I'll get dragged along whether I like it or not."

"Great, I'll see you there." She reached over and touched me on the arm before she walked away. I tried to retain my composure and act natural. I hadn't had any female contact since I broke up with Beth my freshman year. I glanced over to where Cassie had returned to line and her girlfriends broke their whispering circle just long enough to give me a smile and a quick wave. I tried not to blush, and since I had a bunch of school books in my hands, I just nodded back.

"Hey," someone behind him said, "keep the line moving."

I looked ahead to see about three empty feet of space between me and the person in front of me. I smirked and shuffled my feet forward, but my thoughts drifted back to Cassie, Wes, and my freshman year. Wes was the reason I broke up with Beth and I hadn't had a date since. Two minutes later the same guy yelled at me to move ahead and I pushed Beth out of my head.

Chapter Eight
Fight for your Right

"I can resist everything except temptation."
-Oscar Wilde

The weekend before school started was the best weekend to be a college student at U of M. There's usually a home football game and campus turned into one huge party because no one had to worry about going to class on Monday. This specific Saturday night, after the football team defeated Western Illinois 42-10, all the guys were having a great time at South Fifth. Coop decided to bring his temporary girlfriend, Laura, one of the many whom he stayed with "until he got a better option." I know, a total scumbag, but he was my friend.

I, on the other hand, was dressed to kill, and looking for Cassie. I barely remembered what it was like for a girl to pay attention to me, and I felt like a new man. However, the attention I paid to the way I looked would go all for naught on this night, where two interesting interactions would overshadow my efforts.

*****

Coop burrowed his way through the crowded line by the keg. "House cup, watch out people, got a house cup here." Coop grabbed the tap from some kid he didn't recognize and started to fill his cup in front of a dozen or so pissed off party goers. "Sorry, guys. House cup gets to cut, it's my party."

Coop squeezed his way away from the angry mob after he filled his cup and saw the familiar face he couldn't match to a name. "Hey, Coop, what's up?" the man asked.

"Hey, what's up?"

"Working, you know," said the man, "paying the bills."

"Super," Coop said. "Check ya later." Coop turned away from his unknown companion just as Pete walked out of the house.

"Hey, Coop," Pete said, "who's this?"

Coop shrugged. "Who is he? Who are you? Who cares? Take it easy fellas." Coop tried to wiggle away from the conversation, but the crowd held him up.

"I'm Pete," he said. "Pete Alger. I'm a freshmen outfielder. We met the other day in the locker room."

"I'm Matt," the guy standing behind Coop said.

"Matt," Coop said with a flourish. "That's right, now I remember. You were a senior here when I was a senior in high school. I met you on a recruiting trip." Coop sipped his beer and tried to escape again, but now Pete was blocking the way.

"Really?" Pete said to Matt, "how did you like your time here at Michigan?"

"I don't think you want to get me started," Matt said.

Coop raised an eyebrow. "What brings you to the neighborhood?"

"Just relivin' old memories."

They sipped their beers and smacked their lips, searching for what to say next.

"You're kind of pathetic coming back to college parties, dontcha think, Matt?" Coop asked before adding, "Jesus, did I say that out loud?"

Matt sighed. "You're right, I agree. It's over for me, finito, finished, done, history, it's in the books, you can look me up, I'm a historical figure. One day the seniors are putting handfuls of Vaseline in your spikes and the next you're just relivin' old memories. One day you're wearing your letter jacket around a Division I campus and the next no one on the team knows your name."

Matt started to go on, but Coop shushed him. "Dude, quiet with the initiation stuff."

"Vaseline?" Pete asked.

"Don't worry about it," Coop said to Pete before turning back to Matt. "And, as for you, lay off the suicide trip, guy. Everyone knows baseball doesn't last forever."

Matt started to backpedal on the porch. "I probably shouldn't have even come over here tonight. I was just in the neighborhood and I saw the house and... forget it. I just have one more thing to say, and then I have to get home," he paused. "Think about it this way: You know who your father is, and maybe your grandfather. But what about your great grandfather? Your great great grandfather? I mean, unless you're Jesus Christ or Santa Claus, you can bet that your great great grandchildren aren't going to know much about you either. And you think baseball means something? Look at me, I played here five years ago and who am I? Just the old man who shows up at the college parties." Matt tossed his empty cup into the bushes and walked back around the house and disappeared down the sidewalk of South Fifth Avenue.

*****

"Who was that guy you were talking to?" I asked. At the time I couldn't remember Matt's name, but Benny and I were sitting on the couches on the porch of South Fifth watching Coop talk with Pete and Matt.

Coop shrugged. "Matt something. I can't remember his last name. He played baseball for Michigan a while ago and now he specializes in going to parties and giving suicide speeches."

"He played here?" Benny asked. "On the baseball team?"

"Yeah," Coop said, "I think I remember meeting him on my recruiting trip."

"It's not like me to not remember someone who played at Michigan," Benny said. "Oh well, let's go tell some stories. I got this hilarious one about a host mom and a pineapple."

*****

Around one in the morning, after Coop had gotten his fill of baseball stories from Benny and I, he made his way back onto the dance floor, and found his girlfriend dancing with a few of her friends. Coop wasn't a bad dancer, but his fun was cut short when someone ran into the back of him, spilling his beer all over everyone around him. Lou was standing a few feet from Coop and he saw what happened. There were two large drunk guys on the dance floor, later identified as freshman football players who were being red-shirted.

"Hey, what the hell man, you spilled beer all over everyone!" one of the partiers yelled in Coop's direction.

"Someone ran into me!" Coop yelled back. When Coop turned around to get a look for himself, he could see that Lou was standing next to Wes, and they had the two football players in the crosshairs. Coop quickly suggested to his girlfriend that they call it a night.

"Aw, come on Johnny, I'm having fun," she whined in a half-drunk tone.

"No, for real, we need to go." Coop nodded toward the door.

On the other side of the room Lou was yelling into Wes' ear. "If those assholes bump into me one more time, I'm going knock the mother fuckers out." Weasel grinned, and waited for the two guys to come close again. When the time was right he nudged Lou himself, right into the back of one of the two football players.

"Watch it, fuck-face!" Lou screamed.

Weasel stepped up to Lou's side. "What the hell is happening here, Lou?"

"These assholes are spilling beer all over everyone," Lou screamed back.

"You assholes!" Weasel yelled and took two steps forward to get into the other football players face. A couple other baseball players in the room saw the trouble start and jumped up to help.

Coop decided there was no more arguing with his girlfriend so he grabbed her around the waist and carried her out of the room. He set her down near the front door as it broke out and the next thing he knew, Lou was slamming one of the players up against the wall behind him.

"GET THE FUCK OUT OF MY HOUSE," he yelled as he opened the door with one hand, he tossed him onto the front porch with the other. Coop covered Laura's head with his arms, trying to shield her in case there was an errant blow.

Then Coop heard Lou yell again from behind him, "WHERE IS THAT OTHER ASSHOLE!"

"WE GOT HIM OVER HERE!" Weasel yelled, pointing toward the large mass that was getting kicked and beaten by half a dozen players on the floor. Lou walked over and grabbed him by his collar and dragged him toward the door.

"AND YOU GET THE FUCK OUT OF HERE, TOO!" he yelled, kicking him in the ass as he tried to get up. The two players limped off the porch, yelled some profanities, and then walked away.

*****

It's too bad I missed it, but it made me forget about getting stood up for a while.

Chapter Nine
The Other Half of the Staff

"With my team I am an absolute czar. My men know it. I order plays and they obey. If the don't, I fine them."
        -John McGraw

Coach Nichols didn't like the idea that someone in administration went behind his back to hire his assistant coaches without passing it by him, but he rolled with the punches because he was living his dream job. However, he was having trouble delegating any kind of responsibility to his two new co-workers because he didn't know anything about them. Of course, this was all stuff that us guys on the team didn't find out until much later, because for some reason as a player you always figure that the coaches know exactly what they're doing, and never have any disagreements. I didn't find out until I was much older that authority figures can be just as lazy and as irresponsible as the people working underneath them.

*****

Tom looked at his watch and then at the three men sitting in front of him. It was six p.m., and Tom felt like he had spent the entire summer in his office. "Mitch, any news on an equipment manager?"

"Yes," a short blonde haired man answered. "We just got that filled today. We only had one application, but after interviewing him I'm confident that he can do the job."

Gene shuffled his feet. "Mitch, I'm not sure how much experience you have with college baseball, but we're going to need two equipment managers. One just isn't going to cut it."

"I think he can handle it. He's a medical student, near the top of his class. He says that he needs something to keep him occupied." A single drop of sweat dripped down Mitch's forehead.

"Occupied?" Tom said. "Last time I checked, Mitch, med students don't exactly have a light load. How does this guy realistically think he can handle this sort of commitment?"

Mitch pointed toward the office door with his thumb. "I could go get him. I'm sure he could speak for himself better than I can."

Tom made a motion with his hand that gave Mitch his cue to leave the room. Bob Stein, a thick man with hairy arms, waited for Mitch to leave and said, "This guy is a real friggin' fruitcake, huh?" Bob ran his tongue along the inside part of his bottom lip where he usually had a chew during this part of the day.

Tom sighed. "Coach Stein, I realize that we have only been working together for a little less than a week, but respect is something that is very important within the teams that I coach, and it will be very important within this coaching staff. If you have some kind of beef or quarrel with Mitch, you need to take care of it before we get this thing rolling, because if the coaches can't trust and respect each other, we can't expect our players to. Is that understood?"

Gene snorted. "The jury is still out on you anyway."

"What the hell is that supposed to mean?" Bob asked in a voice bordering on a yell.

Tom was saved from the awkward moment when Mitch led a tall, strong-looking kid through the office door. "Have a seat," Tom said. "Mitch was just telling us about you, and we have a couple of concerns." Tom stopped himself. "I'm sorry, I don't think I caught your name."

"Carl Burtinski, but most people call me Q-Bert."

"Q-Bert?"

"That's right," he said matter-of-factly.

"And the Q?" Gene asked.

Carl looked across the room and fired back his answer without missing a stride, "Q-Bert was a popular arcade game in the eighties. Before the big high quality graphics boom that the world experienced in the nineties, many people enjoyed how simple the games operated, and some still prefer their gaming style to today's realistic alternatives, but I digress. Q-Bert was a game that featured a strange Pac-Man style rip-off that jumped up and down a pyramid, trying his best to stay away from monsters. Each tile that he landed on lit up, when you lit up all the tiles on the pyramid, and you passed on to the next board.

"I guess people call me Q-Bert for the combination of my last name and my strange behavior. About as strange as a purple Pac-Man rip off jumping up and down a pyramid while being chased by monsters." There was a moment of stunned silence. "It was one of the first video games in three dimensions."

Coach Stein hit himself in the forehead with his palm, "Great job, Mitch. This guy's weirder than you are."

"Coach Stein," Tom said while shaking his head. "I'd appreciate it if you would watch your mouth."

Q-Bert was unaffected by Stein and immediately stood up for himself. "Actually, I know that I am the only one that applied for this job, it's not like anyone really went out of their way to post it or anything. Secondly, I can do this job with my eyes closed, it's not like it really involves that much besides a little time, which I certainly have plenty of."

Tom waved his hands in the air after Q-Bert was done talking. "But you're a med student."

"I have a lot of time on my hands because I only sleep for twenty minutes every two hours. Last year I wrote a research paper from a physics perspective that looked into the benefits of so-called 'performance enhancing drugs' for athletes. I have always been a sports fan, and this year I wanted to do something a little more recreational with my spare time. I don't like sleeping for long periods of time; it makes me feel like I am wasting time that I could be doing something productive. So I take a twenty minute nap every two hours, just enough to keep me going. It's all programmed into my watch." Q-Bert lifted his arm up to eye level so everyone else in the room could see that he was wearing an expensive looking digital watch. "As soon as I am awake for two hours straight, a little alarm goes off and I fall asleep right on the spot. From what I am told, you could kick me in the head and I wouldn't wake up. It didn't start out like that, but I have sort of conditioned myself to respond that way. That way I don't have to waste any time trying to fall asleep. Then, after I sleep for twenty minutes, another alarm goes off and I am fully awake and so on and so forth."

"Well," Tom said, "are you sure that you can handle it yourself? Usually there are two equipment managers."

Q-Bert grimaced. "I like things a certain way, and I don't want to have to deal with anyone who doesn't do things the way I do. I've never really been that great at teamwork."

Everyone stared at each other for a second before Tom realized since he was the head coach, it was his responsibility to break the silence. "Okay," he said, "I don't have any complaints then, but I expect you to let us know if you start to get overwhelmed."

"No problem."

"Bob," Tom said, "are you satisfied?"

Bob crossed his arms and ran his tongue along the inside of his lip before nodding his acceptance.

"Good," Tom said, leaning back in his chair. "Okay, Q-Bert, from now I want you to start working on organizing the equipment room and the shed outside by the batting cages. Just start picking things up and make an inventory for me whenever you get a chance."

"I've already started," Q-Bert said, "just let me know when you want the results." Q-Bert got up out of his seat and headed toward the office door, but Gene decided he needed to ask a question just before he disappeared back toward the locker room.

"Carl?" Gene said. "I mean, Q-Bert. What did you find out from your research last year? About the performance enhancing drugs?"

Q-Bert smiled before answering, "I'm sorry but I can't divulge any of the information yet. I ran a probe into some major league baseball organizations and because of confidentiality agreements the Major League Baseball Players Association made me sign, I am legally unable to answer."

Then he shut the door on the group of coaches and walked back down the hallway.

"What a douche bag," Bob said. "And besides that, how are a bunch of ball players going to react when they have to share the locker room with that guy. He talks like a goddamn robot for Christ's sake." Bob finished talking and there a loud crashing noise in the hallway. The four coaches got to their feet and looked out the office window to check out it out. They stood on the inside of the office door and looked down at Q-Bert, who was lying on the ground and snoring loudly.

"Point noted, Bob," Tom said, "but we don't have time to nitpick right now. Q-Bert will have plenty of time to show whether or now he can handle the responsibility of being equipment manager all by himself, but let's shift gears for right now and talk about practice." Tom let everyone get back to their seats and before he grabbed a piece of paper off of his desk that detailed the daily practice plan. "Since this is the first time that this coaching staff has worked together as a group, we need to get right into some game situations. Plus it will help us get a better look at some of the players, whom we haven't seen play yet. Therefore, after a few days of conditioning on the first week, I want to get into scrimmages as quickly as possible."

"Tom," Gene interrupted, "I'm not quite sure how much the pitchers will be able to go after one week of practice, so let's be smart about their arms, okay?"

"Of course, but with eighteen pitchers on the Fall Ball roster, we can get some pretty good work in if each of them can go thirty to forty five pitches or so. Any complaints?"

"Nope."

"Okay, good. Now, before we leave, I want to stress that I anticipate our players might be a little defensive over the sudden change in the coaching staff. So, let's lay off the mechanical stuff for the first week and half or so and just let these kids play. The last thing I want is for them to view any of us as the type of coach that comes in with preconceived notions about their work ethic or their passion. We didn't recruit them out of high school, so let's use this time as our 'recruiting process,' so to speak. We need to get them on our side before we can really teach them anything. Any questions?"

"Yeah," Bob said, "how exactly do you want us to do that? Hold their dicks for them while they go to the bathroom."

Gene and Mitch both rolled their eyes and groaned, but Tom forced himself to answer in a reasonably low tone, "Not exactly, Bob. I just want them to feel comfortable around us. You have to understand that we are all new to them, and we can't act like we are better than them, or give them the impression that we wouldn't have recruited them if we would have had the chance. The last thing you want your players to feel like when you come in as a new coach is that they aren't good enough or that they don't deserve to be where they are. And I think that if we come in throwing a bunch of mechanical stuff at them that is the exact feeling that we are going to generate.

"Now, that being said," Tom paused for a moment to collect his thoughts, trying to shift his terms to Bob's liking. "I don't want these kids to think this place is a country club. Michigan, like I have said before, is very dear to my heart, so I will not allow anyone to slack off. Remember, we are looking for reasons to cut kids on this team, and I don't really care if they are the most talented kid on the field; if they have a bad attitude, don't hustle, or don't buy into the team concept, then I will give them some more time to focus on their academics, if you know what I mean."

"I read that," Bob said with a satisfied grin.

"Good," Tom said. "Today is Monday and our first team meeting is Wednesday at four o'clock here in the locker room. Mitch, I want you to take the folder I gave you with the team rules and get enough copies so everyone can get one. Gene and Bob, make sure you guys make yourselves friendly around this place and introduce yourselves to players as they come in to work out. As far as the lockers are concerned, I am guessing that the players will take care of it themselves. Mitch, just make sure that Q-Bert gets the name plates done before we get this thing rolling. I want everything to look as professional as possible.

"Thursday we are running the two-mile. If anyone doesn't make it in less than fourteen minutes, they will show up every weekday morning at six in the morning until they do. If I remember right, the players will probably have their first initiation this Saturday night, so those that miss it will have a new motivation by Monday if they still run it the same way they did when Gene and I went here. Friday's conditioning will be my call after we find out what kind of shape our team's in. I don't want to emphasize conditioning too much when we still have six months until our season starts, but we need to make sure we get the message across that when you come down to this field, you need to come to work.

"Next week's practices will be fairly uniform, and we will be working together to come up with lineups for the intrasquad games after we get some information from the pitchers to see how their arms are feeling. Basically, we will have stretching, throwing, team defense, position split defense, hitting drills, and finish it off with a scrimmage. That may be modified for the first few days until we learn a little more about the players. Everyone still with me?"

*****

I swallowed hard, knocked on the door, and shoved my head inside without waiting for one of the new coaches to get up and answer. Bob Stein was my high school coach at Ann Arbor Pioneer, so it gave me a little boost of confidence to butt in on their meeting. "Hey coach," I said in a deep, masculine voice, "got a second?" I looked at Coach Stein, trying to hide the desperation in my eyes.

"I'm Coach Nichols."

"R.J. Hansen. It's great to finally meet you."

"Hey, Squat, how have you been?" Bob asked. He got out of his chair and shook my hand. Relief washed over me in a warm wave.

"Hey, Coach Stein," I said. "I heard that you applied for the job, but I wasn't sure that you got it. It's really great to see you."

"You two know each other?" Tom asked.

"Sure," I said, "Coach Stein was my coach in high school."

"Squat is a local boy," Bob said. "He went to school and played for me right down the road at Ann Arbor Pioneer High School."

"Great," Tom said. "Anyway, Coach Stein will be working with the catchers, and Coach Lewis here will be working with the outfielders."

"Hi, R.J.," Mitchell said. I remember thinking that he looked young enough to be my little brother.

"And this is Gene Calloway," Tom said. "He will serve as the pitching coach."

"It's good to meet you R.J.," Calloway said, "but we were in the middle of a meeting and I'm afraid I don't have much time to chit-chat today."

"Oh, I'm sorry," I said, feeling a touch of regret, "I didn't realize I was interrupting." .

"It's okay," Tom said, "but the wife has dinner cooking at home, and she is a woman that doesn't like to be kept waiting."

I let out a forced laugh as I retreated toward the door.

*****

"Squat?" Gene said as soon as the door shut.

"Just a nickname they gave him here at Michigan. He's a catcher."

"Any good?" Tom asked.

Gene took a second before answering. "He has a big heart. He's a cornerstone kid, you know? He might not be worth two shits in the batter's box and behind the dish, but he is the kind of kid whose presence on the team and in the locker room could win you a championship."

"Oh please," Gene said, "you are going to fit right in with Coach Feelings over here." Gene pointed at Tom and laughed.

Tom winked at Gene before he answered, "You know what Bob? I think I know exactly what you mean."

Part Two:

Fall Ball

University of Michigan Baseball
Fall Depth Chart

Catcher
1. Evan Lancaster
2. Steve Tawas
3. Paul Walker
4. R.J. Hansen

1ˢᵗ Base
1. Tom Kindleman
2. Brad Kelly
3. Albert McKinley

2ⁿᵈ Base
1. Wes Roth
2. Eli Kleinfeldt
3. Tyler Bowers

3ʳᵈ Base
1. Lou Whitley
2. Nelson Cruz
3. Dean Shively

Short Stop
1. Glen Schmalz
2. Simon Bowers

Left Field
1. Jordan Burton
2. Pete Alger

Center Field
1. Ben Marker
2. Brett Vernon

Right Field
1. Paul Varner
2. Timmy Benson
3. William McGee

Starting Pitcher
1. John Cooper
2. Chase Warner
3. Wilson Jack
4. Bill Hum
5. Don Franklin
6. Kelly Summers
7. Zach Anderson
8. Sam Weir

Relief Pitcher
1. Nick Elston
2. Oliver Press
3. Clive Hunter
4. Sander Utley
5. Quinn Marchowski
6. Tucker Howard
7. T.J. Regan
8. William Kingston
9. Mike Stevens

Closer
1. Michael Merlin

Chapter Ten
Team Meeting

"I'm not the manager because I'm always right, but I'm always right because I'm the manager."
    -Gene Mauch

Everyone showed up early for the first official team meeting under our new coach. Even my lesser liked colleagues were Division I athletes for a reason, and two of those reasons were punctuality and commitment. For me there was no greater motivator than fear, and I was still trying to dream up a way I could make the team. I tried my best to hide my uneasiness, but most of those guys knew I was nervous about the new coaches before I even got to campus, and even though most of them were really bad at it, some of my better friends tried to calm me down when they sensed me start to freeze up.

"Yo, Squat," Coop said while the team was sitting around waiting on the coaches to emerge from their offices, "tell me again about this girl you met."

Some of the guys sitting nearby turned their heads to hear me answer, including Wes. "I asked her to come to the party last weekend," I mumbled under my breath, "but she never showed up."

Wes looked disgusted. "Please tell me you at least get her number?" When I shook my head he said, "Jesus, Squat, you're a setting a bad example for the freshmen. You're pretty fucking pathetic, you know? There is no way you are going to see her again on a campus this size. Maybe I'll take pity on your stupid ass and put some extra work in to get you a girl this weekend. I don't remember hearing the words 'Squat' and 'girl' in the same sentence since we were freshmen. Not since I saved your life by talking you into dumping that broad you dated in high school. What was her name?"

"Beth," I said.

Tex was sitting on a stool next to me and his head snapped around when Beth came up. "Lay off, Wes," Tex said.

"I don't think I asked you anything, Cowboy."

"I mean it. Lay off."

"Whatever."

Coop leaned in to whisper in my ear so no one else could hear, "Don't worry about that asshole."

"I'm not," I spat.

Coop cleared his throat and leaned back in, "What's the story with Beth, anyway? Have you heard from her lately?"

I gritted my teeth. "Fuck off, Coop. I haven't talked to her for over two years."

"Maybe now is the time, huh?" Coop winked at me, which made me even more pissed. "I mean, c'mon Squat, you know that the reason you haven't found anyone else at Michigan is because you still love her."

"Hey," I said while grabbing his sleeve, "I said fuck off. Who do you think you are? Dr. Phil? Enough about Beth already."

"Whispering hurts feelings," Varner said from a few stools down. "No secrets in this locker room, eh?"

Coop shook his arm loose and looked at Varner. "We were just talking about how hot your mom is Varner, what do you think?"

"I'll kick your ass, that's what I think."

"Hey Coop," Merlin yelled with a nod of his head, "I heard a rumor." The room stopped and turned its attention toward Merlin, who just sat there, saying nothing.

"Spit it out, Merlin."

"What?"

"Goddamnit Merlin," Varner said.

"Okay, okay, the rumor is that we are running a timed two miles tomorrow."

Albert McKinley's eyelids shot open and a squeaky voice escaped his throat, "What? Do you usually run on the first day like that?"

"Hey pussy," Varner said, "who said you could talk?" McGee chuckled and slapped Varner on the back.

"I was just asking a question," Albert said in a defensive tone.

"That's not the point, froshy," Varner said. "You're new here, so learn your place. It starts with keeping your mouth shut, which includes not shoving your stupid quivering lips into the conversations of the seniors, eh?"

Merlin sighed. "Don't be such a tight wad, Varner. There is a time and a place designed for you to be a dick, and it is coming up soon enough. So just let these kids breathe for a while, will you?"

Varner shifted in his seat, preparing to talk, but Bill Hum, a pitcher who only thought of things in the context of the movies he saw, beat him to the punch, "It's okay, Merlin, Varner is still coming to grips with the fact that we aren't in *Dazed and Confused*."

McGee stared down Hum, "Are you serious?"

"Yeah," Varner said, "stay out of it, movie boy."

Hum smiled. "Relax, Varner. I know *Dazed and Confused* was a great movie, but you don't have to try to live out the whole initiation thing every year."

Coop moved quickly to speak. "No, Merlin. I had not heard that."

"Why thank you, Coop. I was just wondering if you had." Merlin stared at McGee and gave him the middle finger just before the door to the coaches' offices opened.

There was dead silence in the locker room as soon as Coach Nichols walked through the door. Even though he had not earned the respect from most of the players, we knew how to fake it. Division I athletes thought of their playing time before just about anything else. And in this moment, the hush over the room told the coaches that, at the very least, we knew what it took to kiss the coach's ass.

"Well, men," Coach Nichols said. "Here we are. My name, for those of you whom I have not yet met, is Tom Nichols. On my right is Gene Calloway, he will be working with our pitchers. On my left are Mitchell Lewis and Bob Stein. Coach Lewis will be working with the hitters and outfielders, while Coach Stein will be working out the catchers. The infielders will be mine." He paused, taking a long look around the room. "I will also be providing input into our hitting and trying my best to stay out of Gene's way on the pitching front.

"I'm sure you're all anticipating our first practice. It may or may not have leaked out that we will be running the two-mile tomorrow. You must make it in less than fourteen minutes or I will see you every morning at six thirty in the morning until you do make it. Now," he paused again, letting the shock seep out of our faces, "a few words about this place of which you have the privilege to step foot."

Coach Nichols took a moment to collect himself, rubbing the bridge of his nose with his thumb and forefinger. We would come to learn that Nichols always liked to express himself emotionally in front of us. He believed in being vulnerable in front of his players. He thought that we could relate to and play for a coach that showed his true colors, and so that's what he always tried to do.

"We, gentlemen, are Michigan. We are Wolverines. You are now part of one of the most storied programs in the nation. We are the oldest sport on campus, and one of the oldest in the country. We have two national championships, thirty-two Big Ten championships, and nine Big Ten tournament championships. Michigan baseball has had more players represented in the Major Leagues than almost any other university in the nation.

"When you have Michigan written across your chest, you are carrying those men and this tradition with you. You represent this tradition everywhere you go, and it is my responsibility to weed out those of you who will not represent those men and this tradition at the standard I was taught when I sat in your position. In case you didn't know, Gene and I both took our turn playing for the Maize and Blue."

"Currently," Coach Nichols continued, "we have forty players on the Fall Ball roster, and as I am sure most of you already know that Title IX has affected this school's policy so that we must limit our roster size to thirty-two. Now, I want you to know up front that this is a fact that I do not like, but it is something that we all have to deal with. No one will be exempt, and all spots are open. All I have to go by are your stats from last year. However, while you will find out that Coach Calloway here lives and dies by the numbers, I do not. The roster lists your height and weight, but it does not take into account the size of your heart; and that is precisely what I will be measuring this fall.

"It takes no talent, men, to hustle. The slowest man on the planet still has the ability to run as fast as he can. This game demands that you give it your all at all times. The first time an outfielder dogs it, it will be the difference between a diving catch and a ball that gets past him and rolls to the wall. The first time that a catcher slacks off, a ball in the dirt will surprise him and the base runners will advance or even score. The first time a pitcher thinks that he is rolling on the mound, he will leave one up and we will be waving to it as it sails out of sight.

"Therefore, if this is a game that is built around explosion and hustle, why would we take practice any easier? We wouldn't. We won't. The difference between the people who make it on the roster and those who get cut, and the difference between the people in the field and those on the bench, will be their ability to lay everything on the line, not their raw talent. You are all talented, and if you think you can be lazy and still shine above the rest of this group, you are dead wrong. And if you don't know what it means or what it feels like to give everything that you've got, I suggest you find out before tomorrow, because once we start this thing, once we strap that Michigan across our chests, it will be time to put up or shut up.

"I know this university is steep in its tradition, and its ways. I assume that most of the upperclassmen know how to work, because I am confident that the work ethic has been passed down from class to class, just like I received it, just like I passed it on when I graduated. Upperclassmen, it is your job to help these freshmen, and those below you that still might not have figured it out, to know what it means to be a Michigan man.

"These are your teammates. This is your fraternity. On the field is where we learn our brotherhood and where you earn your right of passage to play for this university. You will play with passion, enthusiasm, and determination. The underclassmen need to be ready to follow and the upperclassmen need to be ready to lead. You froshies have the ego, that's okay; you'll need it to survive at this level. But the returnees have experience, and a chemistry that you have to work yourself into or you will be replaced by someone who has.

"The human body is an amazing thing. It has about four hundred muscles, and the doctors that study this shit say that if it was possible to move every single muscle in your body in the same direction at the same time, you could literally move a mountain. The Big Ten, men, is a mountain. Now if we plan to move it, we all have to be pushing in the same direction. If you hold us back, you will be left back; I hope I have made that clear. I don't care what you batted last year, who your parents are, or which cheerleader you were humping in high school," Tom paused, waiting for the laughs to die down.

"If you think, 'man, there is no way Coach Nichols can cut me,' think again. Just because you hit fifteen home runs or had a ton of strikeouts last year does not mean that you weren't the reason this team has been losing. Sometimes the all-star is really the asshole that drags down the entire ship.

"Now for the team rules," Coach Nichols motioned for the person on the end of each aisle to pass down little blue binders that sat in piles next to them. "While the rules are being passed out let me briefly hit upon a couple other subjects.

"First of all, when you see our new equipment manager walking around, I want you to introduce yourself and make sure that you thank him for the hard work that he has already put into his low paying job. The cleanliness of this locker room and the organization of the equipment room, mud room, and equipment shed outside are all thanks to him. His name is Carl Burtinski, but he has requested to be called Q-Bert."

Merlin raised his hand, not waiting for Coach Nichols to call on him before he started talking, "Is that like the video game?"

Nichols ignored him. "Q-Bert is a medical student who is on fire for the opportunity to be a part of this team, and that is what he is, and that is how I want you to think of him. He is as much of a part of this team's success as any one of you. He couldn't make it to the meeting today, but I am assured that you will see him around the office more than some of the coaching staff.

"Okay, so now that you have the folders in front of you, I want you to open to the first page. For the seniors and freshmen, there should be two names printed on the inside cover. One of those names should be yours, and the other is the name of your mentor. A mentoring program can be extremely beneficial to a sports team, so I want you to take it seriously. Every senior has been paired with a freshman, and it is that senior's responsibility to do anything in their power to make the freshmen feel comfortable in what, I am sure, is a new and terrifying world. A new coaching staff, on one level or another, is something that none of you, or none of us, really expected, so let's make the most of it.

"After I get done going through these basic set of team rules, you are free to go for the day. Are there any questions before we get into the rules?" Coach Nichols smiled when no one raised their hand. The goofy bastard always had a way of controlling the room. "Alright, men. Let's get down to business."

Chapter Eleven
A Fat Man and a Long Run

"I tried real hard not to get any muscles so I wouldn't hurt them."
    -Dan Quisenberry

        The next day during the two-mile run, I knew I was in trouble by the time I finished my fifth lap. Coach Stein looked at his watch while I ran past and yelled, "Goddamnit, Squat, you better unhitch the trailer!"
        I reached down and touched my side as I rounded the corner on the track, trying to locate the spot where it felt like my insides were bursting out. From behind me I heard, "Looking good, Benny," from Coach Lewis just before Benny lapped me.
        "You gotta dig deep, Squat," Benny said with all the breath that he could muster up, "don't let this shit beat you!"
        "I can't," I coughed. "I can't breathe."
        "Hang in there," Benny said. "I'll be right back."
        Benny pulled away from me like I was standing still. Merlin was jogging not too far ahead of me and Benny slowed down to yell at him for a second. "You better kick it in gear if you don't want an early morning tomorrow."
        "It's okay," Merlin said to Benny's back, "I'm a morning person anyway!" I could tell Benny didn't think it was funny as he sprinted away from Merlin. Hustling was pretty much all Benny had, and he couldn't stand anyone who didn't push it as much as he did.
        I watched as Benny went by different groups of players running together, giving encouragement as he passed.
        "Let's go fellas," he said as he passed a couple red-faced freshmen, "you can do it, just use your arms." Two hundred meters later the coaches were telling Benny that he had one lap to go. Ten seconds later he started to lap me again.
        "Dig deep, Squatster," Benny said as he ran past, "get on my heels man, c'mon, you can do it!" Benny took the outside lane around me and then cut across into my lane. When he started to feel like I was dropping back, he slowed down to run with me.
        "Let's go Squat, this is all you. Don't give up." I looked at Benny with defeat in my eyes. "C'mon Squat, take it up a notch. You have to stay at least a

hundred meters behind me." After Benny said that he took off with everything he had left.

Down the home stretch Benny felt like someone was sprinting up on his heels and he looked over his shoulder to see Merlin, hands and knees flying high. "Don't worry Benny!" he said with a gasp, "I'm not going to beat you. I still have one lap left, but I just realized that I lied - I'm not really a morning person." Then Merlin flew past Benny just as Benny hit the finish line.

"One lap to go, Merlin," Coach Lewis yelled, "and you're finished Benny, great job. Twelve minutes and nine seconds."

Benny put his hands on his knees in order to support himself as he watched most of the team kick it into gear for their final lap, suddenly aware of the possibility of a few early morning runs. Benny stood up to take a deep breath right as I was crossing the line and he glanced at Coach Lewis' watch.

"One minute, twenty-five seconds!" Benny yelled. "Move it!" It sounded more like a threat than encouragement, but we both knew anyone who couldn't make the two-mile was going to be rushed to the top of the list for people likely to get cut. Fortunately, when the thought of not being able to play baseball at Michigan anymore popped into my head I took off like I was possessed. My arms were locked in ninety degree angles and pumping up and down faster than I thought possible.

"Is that little fatso gonna make it?" Coop said to Benny after crossing the finish line. Franklin and Smalls crept up on the other side of Benny. Smalls bent over with his hands on his knees, trying to catch a breath while Franklin put his hands on top of his head.

"God, I hope so," Benny said.

"Those guys sure the fuck aren't," Franklin said with a nod. They stood in silence as a group of guys headed by Wes and Lou loafed past.

"Are you fucking serious, Franklin?" McGee said with a laugh as he passed by the players who had already completed the run.

"Shut your mouth and run," Coach Nichols yelled from behind Franklin, "and you better make this last lap in forty-five seconds or I'm going to see you tomorrow morning."

"I'll bring some doughnuts," McGee said as he kept trotting around the track, refusing to pick up his pace.

"Wow," Smalls said, coming up for air. "McGee has some nerve talking to the new coaches like that, huh?"

"Forget that, look at Merlin," Coop said just as Coach Lewis yelled that there were thirty seconds remaining. Benny looked down the home stretch to see Merlin churning toward the finish line. "Man that was a fast last lap for Merlin, but it doesn't look like the Squatster is going to make it."

"Shit," Benny said, instinctively starting to walk down the last leg of the track to yell at me. "C'mon Squat let's go!"

More and more players continued to finish their eight laps and the coaches congratulated them and showed them their times, but a cheering group for me was starting to form around Benny, including Coach Stein.

"Move it, Squat! Run! You're faster than that, let's go!"

"Fucking move it, Squat!" Franklin yelled.

My cheeks were burning red like a fire as I got within a hundred meters of the finish line. Coach Lewis yelled out, "twenty seconds!"

"Ah, shit," Coop said under his breathe, "Move it fat ass, move it!"

Benny kept yelling, but as I neared the finish line I couldn't hear a single voice. The group around Benny, filled mostly with upperclassmen who knew how much baseball meant to me, and how desperately I needed to finish under fourteen minutes, cheered with everything they had left.

"Five," Coach Lewis yelled. "Four, three, two…"

I lunged ahead like an Olympic sprinter for the finish line and then immediately fell down to my knees and rolled over onto my back. My friends rushed to congratulate me as Coach Lewis finished the countdown.

"One, zero."

The coaches turned their attention from the mass around what seemed to be one of their most popular players, to some of their stupidest.

"Looks like we are going to have five or six for tomorrow morning," Gene said with a sigh. "This appears to be a deliberate slap in the face, Tom."

"It looks that way doesn't it Gene?" Coach Nichols asked, still staring down the group that still had half a lap.

"Should I keep the watch going so they at least know where they are?" Lewis asked.

"They know where the hell they are," Coach Stein said, approaching the other three coaches after shaking my hand. "We are going to have to crack the whip on these assholes or else we won't get any respect from them."

"Oh, I think if they keep up this kind of behavior two words will do the trick," Coach Nichols said, pulling down the bill of his Michigan baseball cap.

Stein made a snorting noise. "What words would those be?"

Nichols turned and started to walk back toward the Fish with the rest of the team, pausing for a second to give Coach Stein his answer, "You're cut."

Chapter Twelve
The Announcement

"In a world filled with hate, prejudice, and protest, I find that I too am filled
with hate, prejudice, and protest."
    -Bob Gibson

    The next morning Nichols did everything short of threatening the lives
of the early morning work-out crew, and Wes and his groupies decided they
should get it over with and hustle through the two-mile. Some of them skipped
class after the run to sleep in the locker room. It was pretty clear they didn't
feel rushed to make a good impression on our new coaches.
    Later that day was our second practice. It was another short practice
and another day I puked so hard that it started coming out my nose. After the
puke fest the seniors called a team meeting on the field and told the freshman to
wait in the locker room. The meeting was to get organized for initiation
because Wes and company had a laundry list of stupid little tortures to put the
freshman through.
    When we got back into the locker room Varner, whom I decided did
things like this because he was neglected as a child, took it upon himself to try
and scare the freshman as much as possible. He did a pretty good job of it too,
jumping up naked on the table in the middle of the room and waving his hands
with threatening promises of pain and torture to come from the weekend
activities. When Varner was finished with his juvenile tirade, McGee walked
past him on the way to the shower and slapped him on the ass as hard as he
could, causing bedlam to break out.
    McGee and Varner started grappling, totally unconcerned with the fact
that both of them were still naked and not worried about who or what they ran
into. When they ran into and knocked down Coop, I was waiting for him to get
up crying about his arm, but instead he got to his feet and jumped right in on
the wresting match. That didn't last more than ten seconds before McGee
shook him off his back and head first into the coffee table just as Bob Stein
burst into the room to see what the commotion was.
    Coach Stein had not learned the names of most of the players on the
team yet, so he wasn't sure what names to yell out when he saw two of them
wrestling naked on the side of the locker room while the rest of the team
huddled around Coop, who was gripping an open gash on his forehead. Stein

was too shocked to speak at first, so he just stood there and stared at us until everyone was quiet.

"What the," he finally managed to say before having to pause, "what the fuck is going on here?" McGee and Varner kept wrestling in the background, oblivious to the coach's presence. "Hey assholes," Coach Stein yelled, waiting until they stopped to continue talking, "what the hell do you think you're doing"

"Coach, Coop hit his head on the table," said someone in the crowd.

"Is he breathing?" Coach Stein asked.

"Yeah."

"Well, don't let him bleed on the carpet. And you two," Coach Stein pointed at McGee and Varner, "no more horseplay in this locker room, or else I'll have to come in here and show you how shit gets done, and you don't want that." He scratched his head. "Is this the sort of homoerotic bullshit that goes on around here?"

"Just when Squat's around," Varner said from back of the room.

"Kiss my ass, Varner," I said.

Varner pointed at me and said, "See, Coach, I told you."

"Shut up, you bearded freak," Coach Stein said. A silence fell over the room before he spoke again. "The rest of the coaches are waiting on me," he said, "we're going to meet today until we can figure out how we can win with a team full of smart ass perverts." Bob turned and exited the room and everyone started to regain their composure after they realized that Coop would live.

When the door closed behind Stein, Varner said, "Don't worry about Coach Bob there. He's just a local high school dickweed sitting on a cloud-nine power trip after getting this job. But all that chewing tobacco has worn a whole through his brain."

Tex started feeling his head, "Can chew do that to you?"

"It's a figure of speech, eh," Varner said with his Canadian accent, "but you know it's not good for you, right?"

"Well, yeah."

"Tex," I broke into the conversation, "didn't they ever have any of those propaganda posters in your high school of the guys with half a face after getting their lip and throat removed because of cancer?"

"Nope." Tex shrugged off the idea and went back to cleaning up his locker area.

"Forget it," I said. I went back to the middle of the room where Coop was still on the ground, holding a wad of red paper towels up to his head. "You all right, Coop?"

"Why, what happened?"

Everyone that was still in the room laughed. I helped Coop to his feet and into the bathroom to get a look at the wound.

Meanwhile, Wilson Jack, a lanky left-handed pitcher who was a complete loose cannon, was making his way out of the locker room while saying, "You know what the best part of all this is? Tomorrow we get to wake up and do it all over again. And the next day, and the next day…" The locker room door shut behind the mob and the locker room fell silent again.

"Aw, look," I said, examining the top of Coop's head, "it's just a little scratch. Man, those head wounds sure can bleed."

"The fucker hurts," Coop said, trying to position himself in the mirror so he could look at it. He gave up and said, "Go get your coat, I'm ready when you are."

"Okay." I walked back into the locker room where Tex was slipping on his cowboy boots. "You almost ready?"

"Yep," Tex said.

A few minutes later, we were all getting into my car when Coop started to talk. "Just like that, huh?" he said.

"Huh?" Tex asked from the backseat.

"It doesn't take much does it?"

"Coop," I said, "I can't decipher these cryptic codes and drive the vehicle at the same time. Now if you want to play twenty questions, I'll pull the car over, just let us know what the hell you are talking about. Do you think you need to go to the hospital?"

"No," Coop said. "You know what I'm talking about. It's scary that one second I'm an All-American and the next I could be a paraplegic."

"Yeah I know," I said. "I guess that's why I never wrestle anyone; I don't want to jeopardize the millions of dollars I'm going to sign for this spring."

"Don't be an ass."

"Forget it, dude," I said. "Let's go get something to eat, huh?"

"I got stuff at home, guys," Tex said from the backseat.

"What?" I asked.

"I said that I have food at home, so if y'all are going to go get something to eat, you can just drop me off right here." Tex didn't wait for an answer, instead he just jumped out of the car as soon as I hit the next stop sign and walked by the car with a wave.

"Thirty-five thousand students on this campus," I said as I watched Tex out the window, "and I had to pick the two weirdest fuckers in the whole university."

"I love you too, Squat," Coop said with a laugh.

Chapter Thirteen
A Night to Remember

"(Tommy) Lasorda's standard reply when some new kid would ask directions to the whirlpool was to tell him to stick his foot in the toilet and flush it."
        -Steve Garvey

Almost every senior was resistant to the idea of being a mentor, including me. The freshman class was supposed to be clueless, ignorant, and shy. It was a feeling all of us had to deal with during our first year, and some of us took exception to the fact we were being forced to let the freshmen feel comfortable in their new surroundings.

Well, at least we still had initiation.

*****

"I don't even know half of these morons," Varner said while some of the upperclassmen waited on the porch of the South Fifth baseball house the night of initiation. "Plus half of these poor assholes are going to get cut anyway. It makes me feel bad for them that they have to go through this stuff if they aren't even going to be on the team."

"Someone take a picture," Merlin said. "Varner is showing a moment of compassion."

"Have another, Merlin," Varner replied, making a motion with his hand like he was drinking a beer.

"Hey," Merlin said, pointing his beer-filled right hand toward Varner, "I'm already three down, be-otch. You're way behind."

"Everybody is always behind you, Mr. Wizard," Varner said under his breath.

"Take it easy, Varner," Tex said, but Merlin just shrugged it off.

"Quiet, Tex," Varner said, "I'm just looking out for my teammate. Excuse me if I want to make sure Merlin doesn't screw up another payday like he could have had last year."

Merlin shrugged. "No biggy, I can't drink and drive again if I don't have a license."

"What do you say, boys?" Wes asked. "Maybe we should just bag this crap. Let's just get the freshman drunk and call it good. No one cares about this stupid initiation stuff anymore."

"I care," Benny said.

"You would," Lou said with a chuckle.

"You're damn right I would," Benny said. "Because, unlike you, I give a shit about the tradition of this university."

"Tradition?" Wes said. "The only thing this is good for is laughing at the freshman, that's it."

"Forget it, Wes," Benny said. "Just forget I said anything."

"Anyway," Merlin said while shooting a glare at Benny. But before Merlin could come up with a way to change the subject, a black car with tinted windows pulled up in front of the house. Its front right wheel ran up onto the curb a little bit as the driver pulled it to the side of the road. The group of seniors sat silently, trying to strain and see who was inside the vehicle.

"Hey, I recognize that car," I thought out loud.

"Who is it?" Tex asked.

Varner got up and walked down the steps on the porch, looking inside the car as the driver started to open the door. He turned around to address the rest of the group before the driver came into view, "It's just Nichols," then he turned to yell at the car when Coach Nichols came into view, "What's up coach? You come for the party?"

"Boys," Nichols said as he exited the vehicle, "I'm afraid I have some bad news."

*****

"What time is it?" Pete asked. The freshmen had been huddled outside South Quad by the flagpole since 8:30, even though they weren't told to be there until 9:30. None of them wanted to be late and intensify the pain they anticipated for the night's activities. A little bit of the process always leaked out to the freshmen before the night arrived, but never enough to give them a real feel for what was going to happen. Just enough to make them more terrified than they would be otherwise.

"I have quarter after," Tucker said, sliding his watch back under the sleeve of his shirt. Tucker scanned the street for any signs of one of their teammates. An unfortunate consequence of going to an academically prestigious university was the anti-social behavior of the student body. Student after student rushed past the group of freshmen without even a glance, their heads down, white-knuckled grip on their backpack straps, making a beeline for what Tucker presumed was the library in order to get an early start on their schoolwork.

Albert was concerned with how noticeably different campus seemed after move-in week where the only thing on the minds of the students was where to find the best parties for the night. Now no one would ever guess that the students at Michigan ever liked to party. Albert searched the groups of students walking in and out of South and West Quad for some hint of a smile, anything to distract him from the fearful vibes his friends were giving off.

"What do you think is going to happen to us?" Pete asked, trying to break the tension. No one answered right away, but Pete could tell it was what everyone was thinking about. Everyone, that is, except for Paul Walker, who had already started to annoy some of the other freshmen with his cool confidence. "I'm sure it won't be that bad," he said while rolling up the sleeves on his collared shirt to the elbow. Then he ran his fingers through his mid-length hair and pulled at a couple in the front, trying to make them stand on end.

"You're dressed pretty nice tonight, Paul," Tucker said.

"I always dress nice," Paul said. He grinned out of one side of his mouth and kept examining how he looked. His pants were freshly ironed, and his shoes glowed from being polished. "There's never any reason to look like a slob."

"Yeah, well, I think these initiations are tailor made for freshmen just like you," Tucker said, the statement making a couple of people in the group release a nervous laugh including Paul's roommate Sam.

"Are you laughing at me, Sam?" Paul said. Paul's grin had vanished, but Sam didn't seem too concerned.

"No, I was just telling jokes inside my head," Sam said. Paul took a couple steps toward Sam, who was sitting on the concrete ledge near the flagpole, and Sam stood up to get in Paul's face. Paul was easily thicker and stronger than Sam, but Sam had three or four inches on Paul and refused to be intimidated. "This isn't the time to act like Tommy Tough Guy, Paul."

Tucker turned his attention back to the street while his two teammates continued to bicker harmlessly behind him. There was no sign of anyone so Tucker walked over to sit down next to Pete and Albert, who were deep into a discussion of their own.

"What's up guys?" Tucker said as he sat down.

"Not much, just mulling over tonight," Pete said. Albert nodded.

"Try not to worry about it," Tucker said. "I don't think it is going to be anything too serious. There's no way that they could do anything to physically hurt us or anything like that, so I imagine there will just be a bunch of yelling and what not."

"Yeah, I know," Pete said. "It just bothers me that we are all going through initiation but there are some of us that aren't even going to make the team. Why wouldn't they at least wait until we made the cuts?"

"I don't know," Tucker said, "but I don't think we need to worry about that."

"What do you mean, we?" Albert said.

"Just look at some of those guys," Tucker said. Albert, Pete, and Tucker took a second to examine the other freshmen who had huddled around Paul and Sam, who were still spitting all over each other as they exchanged verbal blows.

"Well, there's another thing that makes me feel uncomfortable," Pete said. "I don't even know all of the freshmen, and I only know like five of the upperclassmen. The ones I do know, I'm scared to death of. All I do know for sure is that we have a shit-load of outfielders and we have a bunch of cuts to make."

"Calm down," Tucker said. "Those guys over there will be first on the chopping block. We will have to fuck up pretty bad to get booted off of this team."

"Calm down? I think you better take another look," Pete said. Pete's voice inflection caused Albert to flinch and put a few muscles in his face into a twitching frenzy. "Tucker, in case you haven't noticed, the only position that has more players to cut than in the outfield is on the pitching mound, you know? As in the position that you play? How can you just look at me and tell me to calm down? You should be freaking out too!"

Tucker tried to put his arm over Pete's shoulder but Pete shook it off his as soon as it made contact. Pete turned his head from Tucker, trying not to show that he was shaken. "Pete," Tucker said, "I'm telling you, you have nothing to worry about. We are on scholarship, man. Do you know what that means? It's like wearing the red jersey in football practice; it means that we can't be touched. Besides that, my dad and I have researched every player that's out for the team and I'm telling you, all three of us will be here when those final cuts are made."

"What does a scholarship have to do with it? Didn't you hear Coach Nichols during his big 'This is Michigan' speech? All he has ever done is emphasize that every spot on the team is open. There are no certainties here," Pete paused when he noticed Tucker was smiling at him. Pete turned his eyes back down to his feet, his cheeks turning red, "and it is really starting to piss me off that you aren't taking this seriously. We could be done with baseball in a matter of weeks. Finished. End of story."

"Pete," Tucker said, "I really don't think that I can hang out with you much longer if you keep acting so paranoid." Tucker sighed when Pete didn't laugh at his joke. "Look, no offense Albert, but Pete, you are I are the only two guys on this entire team that the coaches have even seen play. We're hand picked."

"Wait," Albert said, "You two were recruited by Nichols?"

"Yeah," Pete said. Albert started flexing his left hand in and out, trying to keep it from shaking.

"See?" Tucker said, "It looks like even Albert knows what I'm talking about." Albert nodded, but Tucker and Pete were busy looking over Albert's head to Sam, Paul, and the other freshmen who had finished fighting and now were sitting quietly trying to eavesdrop on their conversation.

"What are you guys talking about over there?" Walker asked.

"It doesn't concern you," Tucker said.

"No need to get excited," Walker said, and then went back into conversation with his group.

"Look," Tucker said, lowering his voice and getting a little closer to Pete so no one else could hear, "The higher ups in the administration will never let the coaches get away with cutting a scholarship player ahead of a non-scholarship player. Nichols and the rest of them want to save face in front of the university, especially in their first year. All they talk about is how much they love this job and how much they want to have it until they retire. That means they will do anything not to make waves, and I'm not lying when I tell you that cutting a guy like you or me, would make some serious fucking waves. Cutting a guy like Sam, or one of those other poor assholes over there will mean nothing. Maybe a phone call from an angry parent. Big deal, it's a lot better than the alternative."

"Yeah, right," Pete said. "Like who is going to give a shit about what names are on the University of Michigan baseball roster as long as the team is winning."

"Oh there are people that give a shit, Pete. Trust me."

"Quit saying, 'Trust me,' you make it sound like a bad soap opera."

"From what I hear, these things run like soap operas sometimes. Things have a tendency to get political in collegiate athletics; you just have to make sure you are on the side that can do the most fund-raising."

"Okay," Pete said, "this conversation is over. You are starting to talk in metaphors and I now, officially, have no fucking idea what the hell you are talking about."

"Hey, jack-offs," said a familiar voice from the area near the other freshmen group, "are you going to join us over here or what?" Pete, Albert, and Tucker stood up and starting walking before McGee had even finished the question. With all the talk about scholarships and who was going to make the cut, they had totally forgotten about initiation. It took them about two seconds to join the huddle of the other scared and helpless looking freshmen, but every step of those two seconds was filled with terrible thoughts of what might be in store for them in the midnight hours. None of them were even close to being right.

*****

They had been walking for about a half an hour now, and most of the people in the group had no idea where they were. There were lots of houses around, but no clear landmarks, and the freshmen hadn't had much time to orientate themselves to the area. Pete's mind drifted as the group walked in a single file line, quiet, unable to talk, and only able to look at the back of the person in front of them. The group was being led by McGee, who reeked of alcohol. *Boy, that's just a super sign for how things are going to go tonight*, Pete thought.

Pete was too scared too look anywhere but straight ahead, and after staring at Albert's back for a half hour his eyes began to blur a bit. When his eyes blurred he started to picture what was about to happen to him at initiation. He pictured verbal and physical abuse, getting beaten with sticks, stripped naked and humiliated, forced to drink, stuck naked in a basement unable to eat for days until they learned unity. He thought about it until he pictured everyone on the team hovering above him, yelling at him, telling him he could never make the squad and that he was terrible. A teardrop struggled to free itself from the corner of his eye as he sensed the group stopping.

"Hey," McGee said, stopping the group suddenly. Pete was looking at his feet at the time, and his mind didn't send his body the directive fast enough to stop him from running into the back of Albert. Albert grunted and rubbed his back with his right hand where Pete's chin had struck him, but he was too scared to look around and see what happened. "Did I hear someone thinking back there?" McGee asked, his eyes stretched open, and for a second Pete thought he saw them burning red. "Well, stop! No fucking talking, and no fucking thinking either!"

*****

"Here they come," I said with a sigh, "anyone volunteer to tell McGee?" On a normal initiation night, the South Fifth house would be pitch black and emitting strange noises to scare the approaching freshman, but this wasn't a normal initiation night.

"I think we'll make that your job, Squatster," Coop said while patting me on the back.

"Me?" I blurted. "Have Merlin go tell him, no one gets mad at Merlin."

"Merlin's passed out piss drunk," Wilson Jack said, now watching TV with his long legs propped up on the table in front of the living room couch.

I sighed and walked out onto the porch of the house, joining Lou and Wes, who were leaning on the porch railing and watching McGee approach with the group of freshman in tow. I walked up on them and said, "You guys want to tell McGee it's off?"

Wes gritted his teeth. "That goddamn Nichols, I can't believe this shit."

"What I don't get," Lou said, "is that Nichols gives us his bullshit talk about being a Michigan Man and then he tells us we can't have initiation. He went through it, he knows it's part of our tradition."

I looked down the street; McGee and the freshman were only about fifty yards away.

"I'll tell you what happened," Wes said, "some of the freshman had their mommies and daddies make a couple of phone calls, that's what happened."

I shook my head and said, "You really think so?"

Lou nodded. "I could see it happening."

"Nichols is no idiot, he saw what they did to Witherton," Wes said.

I continued to shake his head. "What does this have to do with Coach Witherton?" McGee was within ten yards now.

Wes looked at me out of the corner of his eye. "There were some complaints about the way he was running the program, so he was told he had to make some changes. He told the administration to shove it, so they forced him to resign."

"C'mon," I said, "I haven't heard anything like that, if that really happened..."

"It's true," Lou said. "Trust us."

"Stay right fucking there froshies," McGee said as he climbed the steps to the porch. Wes, Lou, and I looked back at him with expressionless faces.

"McGee," Wes said with a heavy sigh, "Squat has something to tell you."

Chapter Fourteen
The Boys of Fall Ball

"Baseball is simple. All you have to do is sit on your butt, spit tobacco, and nod at the stupid things your manager says."
     -Bill Lee

I had a tough time believing Wes and Lou's story about our former head coach, and I made sure not to tell anyone; the last thing we needed was a coaching scandal. Besides, the guys on the team were already upset about initiation being cancelled, and I didn't want to add to the fire. So I just went on about my business and pretended I never heard it.

The Monday after the foiled initiation Coop decided to show his dedication to Nichols' mentoring program by meeting Sam outside after class to walk him down to the field for the first official day of practice. He waited on a bench outside the Chemistry building with his arms spread out wide so everyone could see his Michigan baseball t-shirt when he noticed a girl walking straight toward him with a huge smile.

*****

"I'm a baseball player," Coop said as she approached.
She giggled. "I figured as much,"
Coop puffed up his chest said, "And you are?"
"Cassie Roth." She smiled as Coop processed the information, his thoughts slowed by her short jean skirt and halter top. He mumbled a few broken phrases before spitting out something that made sense.
"Roth," he repeated, "that sounds familiar."
"Well, if you really are on the baseball team, then you know my brother, Wes." She shifted her weight onto one leg and turned her head to the side, her lip gloss catching the sun's light and nearly blinding Coop.
"Holy shit," he said, "you're Weasel's sister?"
"Yeah, I know, there isn't much resemblance."
Coop took an extra second to stare her up and down while considering if she was worth taking heat from "The Weasel."
"Why are you looking at me like that?"
"I was just looking to see if you had a pen on you, so you could write down your number for me."

"Don't worry," she winked and dropped a piece of paper in his hand, "I already did." She turned and walked away, Coop's eyes following her until he heard Sam's voice from behind him.

"Hey, Coop, what are you doing here?"

"Just checkin' out the talent, froshy." He stood up and threw his arm around the freshman. "You're going to the field, right?"

"Yeah," said the wide-eyed freshmen.

"Good, let me talk at you on the way there."

Coop hadn't really prepared much of a speech, but as they were walking, he felt like he had a lot more information to share than he previously thought.

"As a freshman, you're always a target. Lesson number one is to stay out of the way of guys like Varner, because he sits around just waiting for you to do something stupid so he can nail you for it. It's unavoidable that you'll do something to get his attention, but you have to remember not to take it personally when he rips on you. You have to know going in that the upperclassmen are going to try and put you into your place. Freshman year was probably one of the most difficult periods in my life because I thought that everyone should welcome me with open arms, like I was going to be this team's saving grace. The problem is that the college game is all about the team. Things are different when you are in high school or summer ball, trying to attract a college or sign a pro contract. Here, especially at the highest level of Division I, everything is about the team, and anyone that steps outside that boundary and thinks they are above the team will be shot down quickly by the upper classmen.

"You also have to be careful around some of the sophomores, because they can be the worst of the bunch. Take Franklin for instance, we ragged the shit out of that guy during his freshmen year. For guys like Franklin, their freshmen year is still a fresh wound, and they will want to return the favor. The seniors won't always be around to mediate, but just make sure you don't step up to them like you are better than they are. They've been through way more than you, even in one year."

"You're kind of scaring me, Coop," Sam said.

"You should be scared. Aren't you a walk-on?"

"Yeah, why?"

"No reason. The coaches never tell us who's on scholarship and who isn't, but you can always tell by the way they treat their players. I wait and see who they favor and who they shit on. Then it's pretty obvious where the money is."

"Obvious?"

"You didn't really expect a level playing field as a walk-on did you?"

"I think those might have been their exact words. The old coach, what was his name?"

"Witherton," Coop said.

"Yeah, he sat down in my house and said…"

"I don't have any money for you," Coop interrupted. "But I promise that if you choose Michigan you'll get a fair shot."

"What are you saying? I'm not going to get a fair shot? That the coaches are going to shove me aside just because I don't have any money?"

"No," Coop said with a slight hesitation. "Well, yeah, I guess that's what I'm saying, sorry."

"Fuck Michigan," Sam said with a sudden burst of anger. "This is horseshit, how can you run a program like that?"

"You won't find anything different anywhere else. Coaches have to justify their decisions about who they give these scholarships to, and they can't do that and give a ton of playing time to walk-ons. The athletic department would be all up in their ass with questions like, 'why the hell did you give that kid a fifty percent scholarship to sit on the bench?'"

"Shit." Sam's frustrated look made Coop shift his focus.

"Don't get down. I'm not really good with tact. I just wanted you to know that it's going to be an uphill battle for you to make the squad. You'll have to be one and a half times better than a scholarship player or an upperclassman if you want to make the team."

"You think I can do it?"

"Well, you seem to fit the walk-on mold pretty well. My impression is that you are a hard worker, dedicated; you looked pretty strong in the two-mile, like you came in prepared and in shape. That's the kind of stuff you need to keep up if you want to make it."

"Thanks, Coop," Sam said.

By this point they had reached The Fish and Coop paused before opening the locker room door. "Don't thank me yet."

The locker room was packed with people and practice clothes, thrown everywhere after the mad dash to find the right size. Carl Burtinski stood at the far side of the locker room, barricading the equipment room with one arm and playing tug of war with Lou over a pair of pants with the other.

"I already gave you a pair, meathead," Q-Bert said. "You have to give the other pair back before you get these."

Benny decided to rush to the manager's aid. "Lou, what are you doing?" Lou turned his head to look at Benny and Q-Bert snatched the pants away while he wasn't looking.

"This guy is being such a tight wad with the stuff that we aren't even going to be ready for practice," Wes squealed in his high pitched voice.

Benny laughed. "Since when did you give a shit about practice?"

"Besides," Q-Bert interrupted, "if anyone here had the ability to act like a sensible and civilized human being we would have been done a long time ago." Wes smirked and Lou threw his hands in the air and retreated back to his locker. Q-Bert smoothed his ruffled t-shirt and cleared his throat before yelling so the entire locker room could hear his voice. "Attention. Your attention, please." Everyone looked up from what they were doing to listen to what Q-Bert had to say. "You all filled out a sheet on the first day where you wrote down your sizes," he waved a white piece of paper in the air. "I have issued you everything that you need for today's practice, and I will continue to hand out the equipment as we go. If something breaks I need to see it before I give you a replacement. If something you've been issued does not fit, I need to get it back before I give you another one," he glared at Lou. "Are there any questions?"

"Yeah," Paul Walker said, "I don't have any batting gloves…"

"Shut your mouth, freshman," Varner interrupted. "You speak when spoken to." He turned his head back to Q-Bert. "When the hell can I get some batting gloves, jackass?"

"The name's Q-Bert," he snapped, "and like I said, you have everything you need for today. You're only doing position splits, and by definition that means you won't be hitting. Thus, you don't need gloves."

Everyone returned to their business, satisfied by Q-Bert's explanation and what they found in their lockers. The freshman all exchanged excited glances as they got their first opportunity to don their Nike Michigan Baseball t-shirts, and they took turns pretending to go into the bathroom to use the urinal so they could get a glimpse of themselves in the mirror.

Pete was taking his turn walking past the mirror to get a glimpse of the "M" he proudly wore on his hat when he saw William McGee step in front of him, naked from the waist up, and start flexing. Pete completed the charade, trying to fake peeing as long as he could, waiting for McGee to finish looking at himself.

"What's up, Sally?" William McGee asked out of nowhere, not bothering to take his eyes off himself in the mirror.

"Not much, William," Pete said, zipping up and trying to rush past McGee, but McGee grabbed him by the shirtsleeve as he passed by.

"That's Mr. McGee to you," he said, releasing Pete after he finished talking.

On the other end of the locker room Varner and I were still getting out of our street clothes. I began to remove my shirt and the room got eerily quiet. As my shirt began to rise, a belly built through summer beer binges plopped out and over my belt line. As soon as Varner got sight of my stomach, he began to call out.

"Hoooooooly shit would you look at that, eh!"

I stood up straight like I just farted in church. I tried hard not to turn around and face the crowd that was now laughing in my direction, but I was doing a poor job pretending it didn't affect me.

"Hansen, you got to be kidding!" Varner yelled. "Look at that thing! You gotta lay off the cheese fries!" Everyone laughed whether they thought it was funny or not. Pete's awkward snicker caught Varner's attention from across the room.

"Oh froshy, you like that do you?" Varner said. Pete's face dropped as the room closed in around him.

"You think I'm pretty funny, Petey? Huh? What's that?" Varner held a cupped hand up to one ear. "I'm sorry, I can't hear you." Then he stood up as if wanting to fight. "Then you better shut your fucking face freshman and learn your place." He let out a fake sigh and sat back down. "Besides," he continued, "I am the only one that is allowed to make fun of shit for brains over here, isn't that right Hansen?" I didn't turn around when Varner gave me a slap on the back.

Chapter Fifteen
Position Splits

"I was never nervous when I had the ball, but when I let it go I was scared to death."
      -Lefty Gomez

The next day at practice I watched Nichols hit some fungos to the infielders while taking a water break before our position splits. I didn't have any concerns about our starting infield, but we didn't have much depth. The main question marks were Simon and Tyler Bowers, twin freshman unoriginally dubbed Pete and Repeat by the insensitive upperclassmen. They both said they could play third, short, or second, and they appeared to play all three equally as bad. Junior Eli Kleinfeldt and sophomore Dean Shively were two other infielders who had a good chance to make the team just because we didn't have many infielders, but they were both a year away from really contributing.

Albert "Shakes" McKinley, on the other hand, had great hands, a good arm, and solid instincts for a freshman. Unfortunately, he had his mentor, Tom "Tex" Kindleman, and sophomore Brad Kelly to compete with at first base, where Nichols was sure to only carry two players. Tex didn't have a whole lot of range or an outstanding arm, but he had experience and he was a leader. Brad had been sitting behind Tex for a couple years, but Shakes was turning out to be a pretty tough competitor himself.

On the other side of the infield Lou and junior Nelson Cruz were set to split time for the third consecutive year. Lou would get most of the starts because of his bat, but he had a difficult time fielding any ball that wasn't hit directly at him, so Nelson usually came into games in the late innings as a defensive replacement.

After a few minutes of hitting fungos to his infielders, Coach Nichols turned over his shoulder and sighed at Coach Lewis, who was just now managing to round up the outfielders. They had a pretty sizeable group and it was pretty clear that the outfield was the area where Nichols was going to axe the most players. Freshman Pete Alger had to beat out red-shirt freshman Jordan Burton for any playing time in left field, Benny was already penciled in to start over junior Brett Vernon in center field, and Paul Varner, William McGee, and junior Timmy Benson were in a three way log jam in right field.

"Okay fellas," Mitchell Lewis said with his hands on his hips. "Grab your gloves and head out to center field. I'm just going to hit some easy fungos.

I want to see how you field before I start teaching you anything. I'd hate to be redundant." Mitchell picked up his fungo bat and a full bucket of balls and started walking toward the right field line. His body leaned to the side on which he held the ball bucket, struggling against the weight of the balls.

A second later he heard footsteps behind him and a voice say, "Need help with that, Coach?" Mitchell turned around to see Pete Alger standing at his side as all the other outfielders jogged by, headed toward the outfield. Mitchell waited until everyone except Pete was out of earshot before handing over the bucket.

"Thanks Alger," Mitchell said. They walked the rest of the way to the right field line together. Pete sat the bucket down when Mitchell gave him the cue and he ran out to center field.

When Pete reached the group Varner was blowing kisses his way. "Not wasting any time kissing ass are we, Sally?"

Pete gritted his teeth and ran to the back of the line behind Benny. Benny leaned over and whispered, "Don't let him get to you," but Pete didn't hear him.

"I might need a few to warm ups, fellas!" Mitchell yelled while Varner waited out in front of the rest of the outfielders for the first fly ball. Everyone watched as Mitchell took a few awkward warm-up swings with his fungo.

"Maybe we should move in a little guys, I don't know if Coach Fruitcake in there can hit it this far," Varner laughed.

Benny gave Varner a dirty look and yelled, "Don't hit 'em too high for Varner, Coach Lewis, he forgot his crash helmet today!"

"Screw you," Varner said over his shoulder as Mitchell hit the first fungo in the air.

"Don't miss it, don't miss it," Benny taunted as it came sailing down and into Varner's mitt.

*****

"Four catchers?" Paul Walker whined while he eyed his competition. "I don't remember the guy that recruited me saying anything about four catchers." He stuck out his pointer finger and pointed at each person around him one more time.

"Quiet, freshman," Bob Stein said. Coach Stein had collected the catchers down the right field line, but he moved the group when he saw the outfielders throwing the balls in to Coach Lewis. "Let's get in the bullpen so we don't get fucking smoked by some dumbass outfielder."

"I heard that, Coach Stein," Mitchell yelled with his bright orange fungo in hand. He smiled at Coach Stein as we walked by, but Stein just grunted, spat on the ground next to Coach Mitchell's foot and muttered, "So what if you did." Mitchell sighed, turned back toward the outfielders, and we continued on.

Once Stein had us in the bullpen and out the way of danger from errant outfield throws, he closed the gate, latched it tight, got us in a line by the plate, and told us to take a knee.

"Catching, men," Stein said with a slight hesitation. He stared us all down before saying, "Have any of you ever made love to a woman?"

"Oh, yeah," Paul Walker said, turning to give the guy sitting next to him a high five. However, Stan Tawas, another of the Wolverine catchers who was known for his uptight attitude, just glared back at him. Paul lowered his hand when Stan didn't complete the high five.

"Wipe that asinine smirk off your face," Stein said. Paul paused a moment before complying with the demand. "Catching isn't anything like making love to a woman. It hurts, it's tiring, you get beaten up day in and day out, and for all the extra effort there is no more reward than playing any other position. People will only notice you when you screw up."

"I don't know B.S., I had a relationship like that once," said Evan Lancaster, a red-shirt freshman that had a knack for annoying tendencies unlike anyone I had ever met. He always laughed at his own jokes, elbowed everyone in the gut after finishing a punch line, and called just about everyone he met by their initials. He also had a bad habit of following up every bad joke with, "You get it? Get it?"

"What I don't get," Coach Stein said while scratching his head, "is how I have four catchers who all managed to get into this university and not a single working brain cell in the group." Stein spat on the ground and we said nothing. "Well, I guess since all we want to do is be funny guys, we might as well move ahead with the torture." He bent down and picked out as many balls as he could hold with his left hand and one in his right. "The first drill we are going to be doing is to get you guys used to being hit with the ball. You're going to get into blocking position, take off your mitt, and put your hands behind your back."

"I'll go first, Coach," I said eagerly.

Stein shook his head and eyed Paul Walker. "No, the freshman goes first."

The rest of us peeled back from Walker, who assumed the position behind one of the two home plates in the bullpen.

"What do you call this drill, B.S.?" Evan asked right before Bob let go of the first ball. It sailed out of Stein's hand at, what I thought, was an unnecessary speed for the short distance between him and Walker. It caught the ground a little too close to bounce up and into Walker's chest protector, skipping instead straight into the freshman's cup. Walker immediately doubled over in pain.

Stein shrugged and looked at Evan. "Let's call this one, 'Ouch, please stop.'" They both looked at Walker, who was in the fetal position making strange gurgling noises, and then back at each other. "Looks like you're up next, loudmouth."

*****

    While the infielders and outfielders took fungos and the catchers did several drills that involved nothing more than the sick inducement of pain, Gene Calloway had the pitchers sitting in a circle on the left field line. The pitching staff had too many to count and I knew I would be sad to see some of them go. I can only imagine how cut throat it was for those guys during that particular Fall Ball.

    "I am a results man," Calloway said. "Which means that I don't care if you bend over and shoot the ball out of your ass," he demonstrated with a sound effect, "if you can get people out, do it. Don't get me wrong, I know a lot about mechanics, weight lifting, running, and all that tired out stuff that is supposed to make a pitcher better, but if you have a program that you are used to and it makes you win, I will let you do it; so long as you continue to win. Otherwise, we are going to be working on power position, stride length, balance point, follow through, and all that horsepucky until I make you puke."

    Merlin, who usually had a tough time staying awake for anything, leaned over to Tucker and whispered, "This guy rules."

Chapter Sixteen
Good Talk

"Bill Dickey is learning me his experience."
     -Yogi Berra

The bullpen bench is special place for pitchers. They can watch the entire game unfold, learn the tendencies of the hitters, plot their strategy, discuss the game, and share their knowledge. However, they usually spend most of their time ripping on the other team, talking about girls, nodding off, or annoying the piss out of me.

At most fields the bullpen bench is located about a hundred feet or so down the line from the dugout, far enough so that the pitchers can talk about or do whatever they want, but still within shouting distance so that when someone needs to start warming up they can hear their coaches or see their hand signals. For one reason or another, while Ray Fisher stadium had fairly nice bullpens, it didn't have a bullpen bench. So the pitchers on our team decided that they would designate the far end of the dugout bench, the portion as far away from where the coaches sat as possible, as their makeshift bullpen. The only people allowed to sit within the designated area were, of course, pitchers and the occasional catcher – although they never usually let me talk much.

The bullpen was a great place for pitchers like Merlin, mostly because he had a difficult time paying attention to anything if he wasn't directly involved, and because the makeshift bullpen was at least far enough away from the coaches that they couldn't tell when he passed out or took a pull off his flask. Therefore, it came as quite annoyance to Merlin when one day during an intrasquad game Tucker started drawing attention with his loud banter.

*****

Tucker clapped loudly from the bullpen bench. "Alright Hum, way to go, keep it up man!" Merlin yawned and shook his head, deciding it was better to ignore the freshman. The other pitchers in the bullpen looked to Merlin to see if he wanted to take any action, but Merlin silently shook his head and passed it off as a one time occurrence. Ten seconds later Bill Hum struck out the batter he was facing on the field and Tucker erupted again, "Yeah, baby! Thata boy! Way to toss that pill, big man!"

Merlin reached over and stopped Tucker in mid clap, inching his face close to the young pitcher. "Look, if you want to be in the bullpen, you need to shut that shit down. I'm all for cheering. I love that rah-rah bullcrap, but most guys can't stand it."

Franklin grunted from the other side of Merlin and said, "Like me."

"Shut up Franklin," Merlin said without turning around.

"So what do you do, just sit here and sleep?"

"Uh," Merlin hung on the sound for a second while thinking, "basically, yeah, I sleep."

"Oh, yeah, check this shit out," Coop said from the top step of the dugout where he was sunbathing with his hat off and shirt sleeves rolled up, totally oblivious of the conversation behind him.

Out on the field Nelson Cruz had just hit a line drive to left field where Pete Alger picked up the ball and fired it eight feet over the second baseman's head. Albert McKinney, who was playing first base, backed up the throw and threw it even higher over the third baseman's head as Nelson was sliding into the bag headfirst. The ball made a loud banging noise as it hit the plywood fence that runs down the left field line, and Nelson calmly got to his feet and trotted home.

"SNOWBALL FIGHT!" Coop yelled, and the bullpen erupted in laughter. "Hey, Shakes, open your eyes next time you throw the ball, it helps." We continued to laugh, but Tucker looked confused.

"So I can't yell for my teammates, but you can make fun of them?" Tucker asked.

"We're just messing with them," I said. "It's pretty harmless. You should see what these assholes say when we're playing someone else."

Out on the field Tex hit groundball to first and Shakes flinched at the last second, causing the ball to go right through his legs.

"There's one for the record books," Coop laughed, "are you guys watching this?" He cupped his hands and yelled toward first base. "I'm swimming laps in your dome right now Shakes, swimming laps!"

"You guys are bush league," Tucker said with a disgusted look on his face.

"Watch it, Tucker," Merlin said with his eyes shut, "you just might hurt my feelings."

"You think that's fucking bush league," Franklin said while pointing back toward the field where McGee was standing in to face Bill Hum. "Check this shit out."

Hummer took his unusually slow windup and then threw a fastball toward the plate. McGee was slow getting started and his late decision made him look terrible as the ball was almost in the catcher's mitt before he started to swing. Tucker looked over toward Franklin and Merlin after the pitch and said, "Okay, trash talk veterans, what would you say here?"

Merlin grinned. "That right there is what's referred to as the 'ol Texas El Paso.'"

"Or the fucking 'Louisiana fastball,'" Franklin added.

Coop jumped in on the conversation. "Is it the 'Louisiana fastball' or the 'fucking Louisiana fastball?'?"

"I don't get the Louisiana part," Tucker said.

Coop winked at the freshman. "It's because the pitch is straight out of the bayou."

"Bayou," Merlin repeated. "As in, he threw it by you?"

Tucker smirked. "Real clever there fellas."

Merlin shrugged and looked back toward the field where Hummer was in the process of striking out McGee. McGee chased the strike three pitch in the dirt and fired his bat toward the dugout.

"There it is again," Tucker said, "the fucking Louisiana fastball."

"Actually," Franklin said, "that was a fucking slider, jackass."

Out on the field McGee was approaching his bat, which he had just violently thrown, and kicked it into the dugout. Coop chuckled and yelled, "I hate my bat!" at the top of his lungs, adding, "Steroids don't help you make contact, meathead." The bullpen erupted in laughter, but Coach Calloway heard everything and quickly shuffled his way toward our end of the bench.

Merlin groaned. "Way to go Coop, you spoiled our fun before it really even started."

"Listen up," Coach Calloway said, walking briskly in their direction, "and you," he pointed toward Coop, "stop your sunbathing and get down here to listen to this." Coop rolled down his sleeves and picked his hat up from on top of the dugout. Then he made his way down the dugout stairs and sat down next to the rest of the bullpen.

Calloway took off his hat, wiped his forehead, and pointed to each player in succession as he talked, "none of you are superstars or prospects. You may think you are, but you are just college ballplayers coming off a crappy season, and the only shred of a career that you have hangs on the chance that we as a coaching staff keep your lame asses around. We're going to cut out that bush league trash talk from the bench and bullpen right from the start. We will talk with our bats and our arms, and nothing else, got it?" Everyone nodded. "Remember, every spot is open. And that goes for you too, Mr. TV star." Calloway spun and returned to his post without another word.

Cooper counted to ten after he saw Calloway sit back down on the far end of the bench before talking. "So anyway, other things you can say after someone strikes out badly like McGee did last inning are, "Thanks for playing," "Swing harder," or my favorite, "Swing now, now, now, now!"

"Aw, c'mon," Coop said after no one laughed, "That's some funny stuff guys, don't get down just because Captain Sweatstain huffed and puffed at us. Do you really think they'd cut us? Get real." Coop stood up, took off his hat, rolled up his sleeves, and climbed the dugouts steps while adding, "Well I guess they could cut you, Franklin."

"Fuck you, Coop," Franklin said under his breath.

Coop turned to respond but Tucker stopped him. "Give me some more examples, Coop."

"The possibilities are endless; you just have to be creative. Trash talk without originality is just meaningless banter and that's easy to block out. You have to come up with something unusual, something they don't hear very often." Coop pointed toward the infield. "Check out that scrub playing shortstop."

Tucker looked. "Simon?"

"Listen and learn." The scrimmage teams had changed positions while Calloway was yelling at the bullpen, and the new infield was taking their warm-up tosses before the inning started. Tex was playing first base now, and Coop waited until he lobbed the ball across the diamond toward short before saying anything. The ball took a couple of bounces before reaching Simon's mitt.

"Skillet!" Coop yelled loudly as the ball bounced off Simon's mitt like it had just hit a spring. Tucker liked Simon, but he couldn't help laughing at him.

"Trade in that waffle iron for a glove," Merlin yelled

"Put a glove on that glove!" Franklin yelled.

Tucker licked his lips. "Yeah, hold the onions on mine!" The excitement stopped and everyone looked at the red-cheeked freshman.

"What was that?" Coop asked through a quiet chuckle. "Hold the what?"

"Onions," Tucker said with wide eyes. "Like on a skillet. If you were cooking something…" He trailed off and everyone tried to hold back their laughter.

"I see you working," Coop said. "That's pretty bad talk, but I see you working."

Chapter Seventeen
Mentors

"You're only young once, but you can be immature forever"
        -Larry Andersen

At this point in the year the freshman appeared to be adapting better than I anticipated. However, with initiation cancelled and a mentoring program put into place, some of the upperclassmen were more aggressive than usual. I guess some of the guys felt like they had to make up for missing out on initiation, so they shunned the mentoring program and dealt the freshman a steady dose of a hard-ass attitude.

Albert, meanwhile, was struggling to keep up with school, baseball, and his long distance relationship – just like Wes had warned him. Therefore, he decided to break off his relationship with his girlfriend before consulting with anyone else on the team. When Albert confessed in his mentor, Tex, about what he had done, he set in motion a series of events that would end up affecting our entire season.

*****

Albert popped on his headphones and bolted out of class as soon as his watch hit the hour. The rest of the class remained seated, but Albert didn't care, he had back-to-back classes located on opposite sides of campus and he would rather leave early than be late to his next class. At Michigan, classes started at ten past the hour and ended on the hour. The buildings on campus were close enough for the students get from class to class in ten minutes or less, but Albert had two consecutive classes on completely opposite ends of central campus, and sometimes it made him late.

The rest of the doors in the hallway burst open when he hit the stairwell and he picked up his pace to beat the rush. He made it from the eighth floor to the fourth before the traffic in the stairwell decreased his gallop to a slow shuffle, but he continued to go as fast as possible without stepping on the heels of the person in front of him. He held his breath for the last two flights of stairs and a slight case of claustrophobia kicked in just before he hit the door that released him from the building and into the brisk fall air.

He took a second to catch his breath before putting his head down and kicking his walk into high gear toward Angell Hall. He broke stride when he saw a large mass of people gathering in the diag, an awkward politically correct war zone that Albert tried to avoid. A few tents were set up offering information from every religion Albert had ever heard of, and some he hadn't. Five people were standing around handing out fliers for every tent, yelling slogans and advertising everything from frat parties to affirmative action.

"Affirmative action rally tonight," yelled a short white woman with glasses. "Please, take a flier!"

"No, thank you," Albert said, trying to be conscious of the volume of his voice with his headphones on.

Tex, who was sitting on a bench in the diag to kill time between classes, called out when he saw Albert ducking through the foot traffic. Albert had his head down and didn't see Tex, so he kept walking. Tex threw his book bag over one shoulder and jogged up behind the freshman.

"Shakes," he said again, this time tapping him on the shoulder to make sure he got his attention. Albert flinched when felt someone touch him and turned quickly, the panic leaving his face when he saw it was his teammate behind him.

"Tex," Albert said with a cracked voice, "you scared the heck out of me. I thought it was the crazy affirmative action pamphlet woman." Albert took the headphones out of his ears and let them hang down on his shirt.

"Sorry," Tex said, his voice muffled slightly by a huge dip. "The pamphlet pushers can be scary sometimes. Where are you headed?"

"Angell Hall," Albert said, pointing with his thumb over his shoulder at the large building behind him.

"Angell Hall? What do you have in there? English?"

"Statistics."

"Statistics, huh? Squat said that class was pretty easy."

Albert's face lost a little bit of its luster. "Yeah, it's not too bad."

"So, how is everything else going? I saw you walking and I just thought I should ask. Nichols wants us to check in with our freshman as much as we can, so I saw you and I thought that's what I should do."

Albert looked at his watch. "Sorry, Tex, can we talk about this later? I think I'm going to be late for class."

"I'll walk with you," Tex said. "We'll talk as we go."

*****

"Wait," Tex said while stopping in his tracks. He put his hand out on Albert's chest in order to halt his advance as well. They stood there for a second before Tex decided to break the silence, "Weasel said what?"

Albert's lip twitched and he raised his hand to scratch his face. "Huh?"

"Repeat what you just said."

"What Coop told me about women?" Albert felt his body start to quiver.

"No, what Weasel told you."

Albert cleared his throat. "He told me college and baseball are too difficult to mix with a long distance relationship. I think he's right - I'm going to be stressed enough without worrying about what she's doing."

Tex looked into Albert's eyes. "Shakes." He sighed and started over. "Shakes, I'm not a man of many words, and I don't like putting my nose in other people's business." He stopped and reached in his mouth to remove the chew from his lip. "You need to realize something about Weasel. Now, I don't like the guy, but he's my teammate. And since he's my teammate, I have an obligation to look out for him and stick up for him. On the other hand, you should know that just about everything that comes out of that kid's mouth is horseshit, and if you want to lead yourself down a sad, cynical, and lonely road, just follow that asshole. He did the same thing to Squat that he's trying to do to you."

"What do you mean, 'He did the same thing to Squat?' All he's been to me so far is my friend. He's been the nicest to me out of anybody, even you."

Tex took two steps forward and Albert's eyebrow twitched uncontrollably. "Hey," Tex said, "don't get in my face, just ask Squat. That's all. I'll talk to Weasel after practice today. We'll see what he has to say for himself." Tex spit at the ground in front of Albert and brushed his shoulder as he walked away.

*****

That day after practice Tex walked up to Wes in the locker room. "Hey Wes," Tex said with a nod of his head. "Let me talk at you."

"You can talk at this," Weasel said while grabbing his package and heading toward the shower room with nothing but a towel around his waist. "Meet me in the shower if you want it, you queer."

Tex muttered under his breath when Wes disappeared around the corner and into the shower.

Lou's head snapped toward Tex. "What was that?"

"Don't worry about it," Tex said. "I just wanted to talk to your butt buddy in there about the mentoring program."

"Mentors," Wilson Jack snorted, "what a joke."

Lou nodded. "No kidding, I can't stand the way my freshman looks at me for advice. It's pathetic."

"I haven't even said a word to Pete except to make fun of him," Varner said, who was eavesdropping on the conversation.

"Well you should probably hop on that Varner," Tex said.

Lou let out a bit of a laugh. "Man, even I've talked to my freshman a few times."

"Really?" Varner frowned and looked across the room at Pete, who was lying on the floor in front of his locker. "Jesus, would you look at that Sally over there?" Varner pointed. "The kid is so scared to get naked in front of the team that he pretends to be tired everyday until everyone is done showering so he can go in alone."

"He's a freshman," Tex said.

"No kidding," Varner said, "thanks for the info fuck-face."

"You know what I mean," Tex replied. "Everyone is a little scared to get in the shower at first; I bet you were, too."

"I'm never scared to get naked with this hog," Lou said while walking to the shower with his towel in his hand instead of around his waist. Tex chuckled in spite of himself when the freshman hid their eyes as Lou walked right in front of them.

"It's a hard thing to get used to," Tex said to no one in particular. "Having naked guys walk around all the time."

"Yeah, I guess," Varner said quietly. He sat in silence for a second before calling out across the room, "Hey Sally, come here," with a beckoning motion. Pete sat up and looked around him, at his freshmen friends, and then back at Varner. "Are you deaf, Sally? I said get your ass over here." Pete sprang from his stool and walked over to his mentor.

"Sit down," Varner said with a sigh. Pete obeyed.

"Be nice, Varner," Coop said from across the room. Varner gave him the finger and took off his shirt before turning to talk.

"Let me make this clear, you little Tina," Varner said while standing and unbuckling his baseball pants. "I don't like this mentor bullshit, and I'm not sure if I care much for your puny pre-pubescent ass, but we can't do anything about it." Varner slid off his sliding shorts and jock and stood in front of the seated Pete while finishing his short rant. "So if you need anything, ask. Otherwise, don't talk to me until you can grow hair on your ass." Varner's nostrils flared in anger when he noticed Pete wasn't even looking at him. "Are you listening?"

"As good as he can with your cock in his face," Benny said from behind Pete.

Varner looked down and then turned without a word and walked toward the shower.

Pete sighed. "I'm glad there's someone like you on the team, Benny."

"Don't say that," Benny said while sliding on his jeans. "I'm no different from anyone in here. I'm just another ballplayer like you."

"Not like Varner," Pete said.

"You just don't know him yet. You'll see. He's a good teammate just like everyone else." He slung his backpack over his shoulder. "I have to get going, the Cubs are playing on TV tonight and I have a lot of homework that I'm not going to do." Benny winked and headed for the door.

"I'll see you tomorrow, Benny," Pete said. Then he stood up slowly and walked back to his locker were he laid down on the ground and closed his eyes. He waited there until almost everyone was done showering, and then he slowly undressed, threw his dirty laundry in the laundry bin, and walked into the shower room with both hands covering his crotch.

Chapter Eighteen
Connections

"If you act like you know what you're doing, you can do anything you want – except neurosurgery."
    -John Lowenstein

    A couple days later after the team stretched, Coach Calloway called Franklin over while he was playing catch. DFF threw the ball back to his partner and held up one finger to let him know he'd be back in a minute. Franklin and Calloway walked a few steps away from the rest of the group before Calloway started talking, "Don, I'm not trying to get on your case, but you came in a little out of shape, and you are going to have to double time it to catch up with the rest of the staff."

    Don looked down at the light bulge hanging over his belt and back at the coach, "What are you trying to say?"

    Gene grimaced. "I'm not trying to insult you. I'm aware of your goals, and what I am telling you is that if you want to achieve them, you need to get into shape."

    Franklin's face turned red. "You don't think I'm good enough to start?"

    "It's going to be up to you and the work you put in this off-season. If you shape up, drop a few pounds, and add a few miles per hour, I think you'll definitely fit in the middle of the rotation. Right now I don't see any reason why you'd get cut this fall, but you never know."

    Don nodded and reassured Calloway that he would do his best. Then he trotted away from his pitching coach frustrated and hurt, but determined not to let anyone see it. He never guessed the new coaches would put him in the bullpen.

    Halfway through the conditioning at the end of practice Franklin grabbed Merlin's sleeve and informed him that they would be drinking that night, and heavily. Merlin was game, as always, and even though he roomed with Franklin to help him conquer his drinking problem, the only fight he put up was by saying, "I'll get the beers."

    After the running was over and practice had ended for the day, Merlin asked Tucker if he wanted to get in on the fun. "Tucker, want to get in on some ruckus tonight? Me and a couple of the guys are going to get shit-faced."

Tucker took a second to respond, still winded from running. "Who's going to be there?"

Merlin blinked. "What do you mean, bro? It's not enough knowing your mentor wants to hang out, you need to know who else is going to be there?"

"No," Tucker laughed. "It's not that at all, it's just that McGee and a couple other of the guys said they could get me into Rick's tonight."

"McGee? What are you going to do hanging around that steroid monkey?"

Tucker tried to hold in a laugh. "He's not that bad, plus he asked me first. Why don't you come with us?"

Merlin made a choking noise. "If you ever see me in that stinkin', sticky floor, meat market again, you'll know something strange is going on." Tucker went to speak but Merlin beat him to it. "No, it's okay. I guess Franklin and I will just have to get on by ourselves."

"Oh, Franklin is going to be there? Hell no, I'm definitely not going now."

"Oh, so, you'd pick McGee and his cohort of male whores over me and Franklin?"

"I like you, Merlin. I just can't stand Franklin."

Merlin shook his head. "You just need to get to know him. He's a little rough on the freshmen because he got it so bad last year."

"It doesn't matter what his excuse is, there is no need for him to act like that to me. We're supposed to be teammates. If I'm around here next year, and I think that's a big if, I'm going to make sure that every freshman feels welcome."

"Tucker. Bro. You're a freshman for Christ's sake. Give it some time."

"Whatever."

"C'mon," said Merlin, "you think I didn't take any crap when I was a freshman? It takes awhile for the dogs to sniff each other out, and here's a little tip, those morons you are hanging out with tonight, if they are being nice to you, trust me, it's just an act to set you up for some kind of bigger embarrassment."

"Yeah, well, it's still going to be better than hanging out with the Master of Fuck over there."

Merlin didn't answer.

They walked into the mudroom together and took off their cleats, putting them in the shoe rack under their names. The shoe rack was one of Q-Bert's organizational additions to the locker room. He also organized the batting helmets by number, and he put the bats in alphabetical order by the name of the company. He built a rack for the catching equipment because, as he said, the catchers were too dumb to be able to stack their bags neatly.

Merlin enjoyed cashing out on the coach and reading a magazine after practice, but today Q-Bert intercepted him before he could make it. "Merlin, what are your plans tonight?"

"Sorry, Pac-Man," Merlin said with a quick side step of the equipment manager, "but it looks like I have a date with a few very important clients of mine, and they don't like to be kept waiting."

Q-Bert shrugged it off and approached Tucker. "Do you like the way I organized the mudroom?"

"Watch it, Frogger, you're under serious homo-suspicion."

Q-Bert sighed. "What? You think I'm gay?"

Tucker sat down in his stool and shot a glance at Merlin, who answered for him, "No Q-Bert, we know you're not gay, it's just a joke."

"I am gay," interrupted the large equipment manager.

Wilson Jack walked into the locker room in time to catch Q-Bert's proclamation. "What? What a joke! A gay equipment manager, what kind of perverts are we hiring around here?"

Q-Bert grabbed Wilson by the arm. "The kind that watches you in the shower with a hidden camera and sells the tapes on the Internet to other gay men. In fact, you are the one I get the most e-mail about, 'Dear Q-Bert, who's the lanky one?'"

Wilson coiled his arm back like he was going to punch Q-Bert, but Q-Bert beat him to it, slapping him hard in the face. After the slap he scampered into the equipment room and locked the door before Wilson realized what happened.

Wilson yelled from the outside. "I swear to God if there really is a camera in the shower I'm going to shove it up your flaming ass!"

"Wilson," Merlin said with a calm voice. "He's just fucking with you, man." Q-Bert's laugh echoed in the equipment room while Wilson twisted at the locked door one more time. When he failed to budge it, he slugged it with his fist before giving up.

"Ouch, damnit," he yelped and held his fist to his face.

"You never punch a drunk with your pitching hand!" yelled Bill Hum when he saw Wilson shaking his hand.

"I didn't, I hit the door with my right hand," said Wilson, deciding to give up and head toward his locker.

"Don't be so dense, jackass," Hum said. "It's from *Bull Durham*."

"I know."

"Oh yeah, sure you know," Hum said with a laugh.

The hitters finished their batting practice by the time the pitchers were done with their showers, and Wes went straight to Tucker to tell him what the game plan was for the night. Tucker mentioned that Merlin asked him to hang out, and what he said about Rick's being a disgusting meat market.

"You're such a pansy Merlin, why don't you ever want to come out and hang with the guys that actually get girls?"

"Nope," Merlin said. "It's like I told Q-Bert, I have some very old friends coming into town tonight and they need a host."

Wes smiled. "Oh yeah, and did you mention their names?"

"I'm not sure our young friend here has had the opportunity to make their acquaintance yet." He looked at the freshman with a straight face, which started to fade as he began listening the names, "Jack, Jim, and Jose?" The locker room, which was close to full by now, laughed together at Merlin's joke.

Tucker frowned. "I don't get it, Jose?"

"Jack Daniels, Jim Beam…" Wes said.

"Jose Cuervo," Merlin added.

*****

"And then what did he say?"

"He said I was getting mixed up with the wrong crowd," Tucker said. A second later a guy with a shirt and tie appeared from the basement that was Rick's All-American Café. He stopped for a second to check his beeper, holding it up to the moonlight before continuing to meet the group.

"What's up guys?" he said, adding, "Who's this?" when he saw Tucker.

"This is Tucker, he's a froshy, but he's cool. He's with us," McGee said. The shirt and tie looked around at Varner, Lou, and Wes for confirmation.

"He's alright, we're trying to teach him the ways," Varner said.

"That's right," Wes added, "and we told him the first place on the tour was Rick's."

"Well, that's true. At least for you assholes, anyway," said the shirt and tie. Tucker laughed because everyone else laughed, his eyes darting around the group. "Hey, Tucker," said the shirt and tie when the laughter had died down, "I'm Miles." They shook hands.

"Miles is a Michigan Man," Wes said with a sly smile. "He had a few pretty good years on the diamond with the Maize and Blue."

"Those years are long behind me, Weasel. Now do you guys want to get in or what? I have a business to run."

"Does a bear shit in the woods?" Weasel said with a grin that said he was already under the influence. Miles nodded and then walked over to the large bouncer who was guarding the door from the long line that wrapped around the side of the building.

"Hell no," shouted a guy in the front of the line as he saw Miles approach the door with Tucker's group in tow. "Don't even think about it!" he yelled as they kept getting closer.

"Quiet!" said the bouncer that was stationed in front of the door. He had an iron grip on the velvet rope with one hand and held the door open with the other.

"Fuck that," the guy in the front of the line yelled as the group began to pass by. Tucker was the last one to go through the door and he got a good look at the angry guy as he passed. He was dressed in a classic metrosexual uniform: faded jeans, a trucker hat tilted to the side and a collared shirt with the collar pointing straight up. "This is horseshit," the guy said as Tucker disappeared inside.

Tucker turned his attention away from the angry mob outside and toward the sticky stairs and musty scene below. Tucker followed his friends down the stairs and up to the table where two bored looking bouncers stamped hands and collected the unreasonably high cover charge.

"Uh-oh," the first one said with a smile. "Here comes trouble right here." The bouncers pounded fists and laughed in slow motion with deep rumblings that shook their chests.

"Are you meatheads serious?" McGee winked and the bouncers stopped laughing and stamped their hands, pausing when they got to Tucker.

"Hold on, guy," said the second bouncer, "let's see some I.D." Tucker's eyes shot back to the group, looking for some help, but only Varner was left standing in front of him. Wes, Lou, and McGee had already disappeared into the crowded bar.

Luckily, Varner turned around to see if Tucker was still following. "He's with us," Varner said. "He's a froshy. We're showing him the sights."

"Froshy?" asked the bouncer jockeying the cash register.

"That's right, we've adopted him as one of our own." Varner smiled and wrapped his arm around Tucker's shoulders. The two bouncers exchanged a laugh and then the one working the register said, "I'd be careful with that crowd, froshy. There's no telling what kind of trouble they'll get you in."

"I'm sure I'll be fine," Tucker said.

"You see that?" Varner added. "He'll be fine, because we're a good fucking influence, thank you very much."

"Alright Varner, get your nappy bearded ass in there, you're jamming up the line."

"I'll show you nappy, fuck-head." Varner made an angry face and pointed his finger toward the bouncer's eye. Tucker got nervous for a second, but the two broke into laughter after a moment of fake tension. The next thing Tucker knew, he was weeding his way through the bar behind Varner until they came up to a table where McGee, Lou, and Wes were waiting.

"Where'd you ladies disappear to?" Wes asked, his voice squealing in a high pitch as he tried to yell over the bar's loud music. Tucker scanned the scene as he sat down. When Merlin called Rick's a meat market, he wasn't kidding. The dance floor was packed with drunken college guys and girls, decked out in their trashiest clothes and dancing like they were in a room alone. There was hardly room to breathe up by the front bar, and it didn't look like anyone was even able to get near the bar in the back.

"I was just introducing Tucker to tweedle-dum and tweedle-dee up there. You morons took off so fast we almost left him."

"Sorry Tucker, I didn't think about it," Wes said with a grin.

"Yeah, I guess it just slipped our minds," Lou said while staring at Varner.

McGee sighed. "Seriously, Varner."

"Oh right," Varner said. "Silly me." He laughed and raised his hand to flag down a waitress who was pushing her way through the table area.

Tucker winced. "You guys were going to let me get kicked out weren't you?"

"Forget about it," Wes said. "We were just going to let you think that. We were going to come back and get you."

"What'd you order?" Lou yelled at Varner, trying to change the subject.

"A couple of pitchers," Varner yelled back while shaking Tucker's shoulders. "We have another one right here."

"You're a douche bag, Varner," Wes said. Varner shrugged and laughed at his own joke. "So froshy, you gonna get some pussy tonight or what?"

Before Tucker could answer, someone bumped the back of his char and he felt some beer splash on his shoulder. "Watch it fuck-wad," said a familiar voice. McGee sprang out of his chair as soon as it happened and when Tucker turned around, he saw the same guy who yelled at him on the outside. He stood there for a second, staring down Tucker with his muscles flexed and fists clenched, looking to fight.

"Take a walk," McGee yelled, taking a couple steps around the table.

"Bullshit," the metrosexual yelled, "I wait in line for forty-five fucking minutes and I watch you guys walk right pass me and you tell me to take a walk?"

"So what do you want to do then, hard ass?" McGee yelled. The metrosexual guy didn't back down until McGee got all the way around the table to get in his face. Once he was able to size himself up to McGee, it didn't take him long to walk away.

"Punk-ass frat boy," Lou said, giving the guy the middle finger with both hands as he walked away. Then McGee shuffled his way back to his seat and sat down. The group drank quietly for a couple minutes before Wes broke the silence.

"So Tucker, what does your dad do for a living?"

Tucker's eyes darted nervously around the group before asking, "Why?"

Wes smirked. "No reason. There are just a few rumors going around that your father has a little clout with the big wigs running the athletic department."

Tucker was slow to respond. He couldn't tell if he was being ridiculed for his father or not. "Well, yeah. I mean, I guess he knows a few people."

"What exactly does that mean, 'knows a few people?'" asked McGee.

"Well, he played football here at Michigan in the 70's, so he's friends with quite a few other big time alumni."

"And Morgan Pulanski?" Lou asked.

"What about him?" Tucker responded while nursing a beer.

"Are they friends?" Wes's voice sounded annoyed, but McGee interrupted before Tucker could answer.

"I'm going to tell it to you straight, froshy. I didn't have a love affair with the old coaching staff, and it wasn't a secret. I wasn't angry to see them let go, but this new staff brings with it a whole new set of problems. When we missed the two mile, Nichols started making all kinds of threats, talking about cutting me, or Lou, or some other guys who have been working their asses off for the benefit of Michigan for years.

"Now, you're cool, Tucker. Not only that but you're cool with Nichols and your father is cool with the most influential man on the athletic campus. Do you see where I'm coming from?"

"No," Tucker said honestly.

McGee looked at Weasel before answering, "Well, it goes like this…"

Chapter Nineteen
Locker Room Chatter

"Last night I neglected to mention something that bears repeating."
     -Ron Fairly

Whenever someone asks me what I miss the most about playing college baseball I say, "Just being in the locker room and hanging out with the guys." Most of the time we were too tired to go home after practice, and we had a big screen TV in the locker room, so we would just sit around and talk. These are some of the most memorable times of my college career; shooting the shit with my friends, and talking about anything and everything.

*****

Coop: "Oh my God, isn't Fall Ball over yet?"
Hum: "*Groundhog Day* was a great movie; I don't care what anyone says."
Albert: "What the hell is wrong with my toe?"
Tex: "It's just filling with blood. You got to take a needle to that sucker and let it drain."
Tucker: "If my arm would stop feeling like it's falling off, practice wouldn't be so bad."
Pete: "The goddamn equipment manager is asleep again and I need some new sliders."
Varner: "Get some extra Vaseline for your vagina while you're at it."
Walker: "I took a ball in the hand today. Hey Squat, does this look swollen to you?"
Me: "You've got to have muscles in order for them to be swollen."
Pete: "So I guess these long practices pretty much takes doing your homework out of the equation."
Wes: "Someone stop that kid from whining for five seconds."
Pete: "What's the secret, Squat?"
Me: "We pray for rain."
Pete: "Funny, but I'm serious. I'm overwhelmed with homework, but practice wears me out so much I can't concentrate at study table."
Me: "I am serious, pray for rain. There's nothing like being stressed out and waking up in the morning to see it pouring outside. Especially when it's

on a day you know you are going to get run into the ground, or the night before you have a big paper due, or a day after you were up late studying. You wake up and see the rain coming down and there is nothing better. It was practically our team motto last year."

Walker: "Speak for yourself, all I've ever wanted to do is play baseball."

Me: "You'll learn soon enough, superstar. All that fire you got in your belly only lasts so long, unless you're Benny, and there can only be one Benny."

Benny: "Knock it off, Squat. I'm sick of it."

Me: "It's true."

Tucker: "Merlin, do you know what we are doing tomorrow for practice?"

Merlin: "Tomorrow? I just want to get to the shower before I pass out, homeboy."

Albert: "Squat, think we'll have a good team this year?"

Me: "Shit, I just want to make the fuckin' team."

Sam: "Cooper, what are you thinking about doing when baseball is over?"

Cooper: "What do you mean, 'when baseball is over'?"

Me: "Can I have three ice bags?"

Merlin: "Can I have two Advil packets?"

Sam: "Can I get a rub down or some heat on my arm before practice?"

Pete: "What's in those bottles you're taking?"

Wes: "Creatine."

Coop: "Joint formula, with glucosomine."

Lou: "Protein powder."

Tex: "This is just a multivitamin."

Pete: "How'd you get so big McGee?"

McGee: "I don't take any of that shit. I'm just naturally ripped."

Coop: "Naturally ripped my ass."

Albert: "Squat, Tex told me to ask you about your girlfriend?"

Varner: "What? Shit-for-brains has a girlfriend?"

Coop: "Yeah, Squat did you ever see that girl again?"

Me: "No, I couldn't find her. What are you talking about Shakes?"

Albert: "Wes talked me into dumping my girlfriend, but now I'm kind of regretting it. Tex said I should talk to you before I did it, but I was pissed and did it anyway."

Me: "Well, I can't tell you what to do, but I did the same thing and I'm still kicking myself. I've never found another girl as good as Beth."

Albert: "That was her name? Beth?"

Me: "Yeah. I don't really want to talk about it."

Wes: "Goddamnit, Shakes, could you stop that face seizure thing for five seconds?"

Chapter Twenty
The Wizard at Work

"You can't hit what you can't see."
   -Ping Bodie

     That Friday afternoon Nichols promised a short practice. The football team was playing Ohio State at home on Saturday at noon, and since Nichols was a Michigan Man himself, he knew how rowdy the weekend could get. Unfortunately, Bill Hum and a red-shirt sophomore named Kelly Summers were the starting pitchers for the day and they were doing a terrible job getting the scrimmage moving. Hum worked his way out of a few jams, but he surrendered six runs in just a few innings. Kelly, on the other hand, was a human rain delay on the mound. He took so long to deliver the ball it was like time was standing still. Then, if that wasn't bad enough, every hitter that swung got at least a double. In the bottom of the third, when Kelly almost got smoked by two consecutive line drives up the middle, Nichols had to take him out for his own safety. I can still remember him muttering, "This kid is going to get killed if I don't get him out," while he was climbing the dugout steps.

     I was happy that Nichols decided to make the change until I saw Sam, the freshman assigned to Coop, trotting in toward the mound. Sam was the tallest of the freshman, but he had the worst arm on the squad, even among the position players. I thought he was going to be the first one on the chopping block when I caught his first bullpen of the fall, but when Nichols gave him a shot in the scrimmage, he surprised everyone.

*****

     "I can't believe that goofy looking bastard just got me out," Lou yelled as he ripped off his batting gloves one by one. Wes was the next hitter, and popped a first pitch bunt straight up. Albert McKinley, who looked very comfortable in the batter's box, was the next hitter. He wasn't having the best fall, but he was doing much better than freshmen usually did. Unfortunately for Albert, Sam had his change-up working, and Albert couldn't figure it out. Sam got a big hint when Albert swung and missed the first one, so he threw him three more. Albert fouled off the first two, popping them up high and straight back over the backstop, but the fourth one stayed fair, and Tex camped under it near first base for the final out of the inning.

"Are we done, Coach?" Smalls asked before jogging onto the field for the next inning.

"We have any arms left, Gene?" Coach Nichols asked.

Gene lifted his clipboard. "One more half inning - I want to get Merlin some work." Gene stood up to the top of the dugout and whistled loudly down to the bullpen. The players on the home team grabbed their gloves and ran back onto the field as Merlin appeared from the bullpen and started to jog toward the mound.

"Merlin's coming in?" Pete asked to no one in particular.

"Looks like it, are you up?" asked someone sitting on the bench as Merlin blistered Paul Walker's mitt with his first warm up pitch.

"Holy shit," Pete said while looking back into the dugout, "he brings it, huh?"

Tom Kindleman and the rest of the players on Pete's team laughed and nudged each other. "First time facing the Wizard there," Tex said before spitting some seeds onto the ground of the dugout, "just swing three times and hope he hits your bat with the ball." The bench erupted in laughter and Tex grinned, basking in his rare moment of humor.

"He can't be that good," Pete said. "He didn't even get drafted last year, right?" Pete looked back at Merlin's imposing figure on the mound while his teammates tried to come up with an answer he would understand. "So, what does he have?"

"What does he have?" Benny said in a mocking tone as he rushed past Pete to grab his bat and batting helmet. "What doesn't he have is the question. I've known the guy for four years and I still don't know what he has." Benny shrugged, took a couple warm up swings, and headed toward the plate.

Pete smirked and watched Benny step into the batter's box and ready himself for the first pitch. Merlin's high leg kick and slow delivery made the first pitch fastball look like it was faster than it really was, although it didn't need much help. Benny took the pitch for strike one, and Pete, who was still standing on the top step of the dugout, couldn't tell if he planned on taking the first pitch or if he was just too shocked to swing.

Merlin gave Benny a closed-mouth smile as he got the ball back from the catcher. "You can't say I didn't give you a chance, Benji."

"I was just giving you a chance by taking that one, hot shot," Benny said while going into his pre-pitch routine.

"Shut up and play ball," Nichols yelled from the bench.

Merlin chuckled as Paul Walker called for a forkball on the second pitch and shook it off. He wanted to go right after Benny. When Merlin coiled and threw a fastball, Benny was behind it and laced it foul down the left field line. With two strikes on the hitter, Merlin could throw anything he wanted, but he decided to finish Benny off with style, so this time when Walker gave him

107

the sign for the forkball, he nodded. The pitch screwed Benny into the ground, and he swung a good foot over the ball for the third strike.

Benny did everything short of dragging his bat back to the dugout. He glanced at Pete on the way by and said, "Just expect a fastball every pitch and try not to look too stupid."

Pete rubbed the pine tar rag on his bat before walking up to the plate, where he stepped in the very back of the batter's box. I saw Merlin laugh to himself when he saw where Pete was standing, and I figured he was about to do something stupid. He closed his eyes half way through his wild up and threw the first pitch four feet over Pete's head. Calloway erupted on the bench after the ball hit the backstop, but Merlin didn't seem to care. He followed it up with three exploding sliders. Pete buckled on all three and took a seat.

Varner was waiting for Pete on the top step when he got back to the dugout. "You need an air bag, Sally?"

"Here," Coop said, handing Pete a seatbelt he kept in his back pocket for such occasions. "Strap it on tight next time." Pete's face turned red, but he didn't say anything.

"It's okay," Albert told him as Nichols brought the team together to conclude practice. "But I have to ask, did you think the batter's box was kind of soggy?"

Pete blinked. "Huh?"

"I was just wondering if you thought there was a lot of water around the plate today."

"Shakes, I don't know what you are talking about."

Albert smiled. "Well, I was just wondering because you were bailing like a madman."

"Yeah, well, your hand is twitching."

Chapter Twenty-One
Scout Day

"I once scouted a pitcher who was so bad that when he came into a game, the ground crew dragged the warning track."
-Ellis Clary

The bathroom mirror in room 117 at the Holiday Inn Express-Ann Arbor fogged up from the steam released from the hot shower as a hairy man with bushy eyebrows and short curly hair pulled back the shower curtain. He stepped out onto the floor mat, and reached for the towel on the rack, and then brushed away the fog from the mirror. After he had uncovered a decent amount of the mirror he dropped the towel to his feet and flexed his chest, turning slowly from one side to the other while trying to keep a smile. *Forty-two and still swole*, he thought. When he finished checking himself out, he picked the towel off the floor, wrapped it around his waist, and opened the door.

The heat from the bathroom rolled out into the room and the man shivered as he moved over to the wall to adjust the thermometer. After he turned up the temperature he walked across the room toward his briefcase. The towel broke loose on the way over, but the hairy man didn't make a movement to cover himself since he was alone in the hotel room. He enjoyed getting a glimpse of himself in the mirror that hung over the desk. He matted down his eyebrows and ran his fingers through his hair before returning his focus to his briefcase.

He licked his finger and rubbed the bronze plate on the front of the briefcase that read, "Cool Cliff." Then he zipped open the front pocket and pulled out a Milwaukee Brewers contact list. Running his finger up the list until he got to a name near the top, he picked up the phone and started dialing.

"Hello," said a wheezy voice on the other end of the phone.

"Ronnie, it's Cliff. You sound terrible."

"It's a goddamn cold," Ronnie said. "How do you get a cold in Arizona?" He coughed violently into the phone.

"Hope you feel better."

"Ah, fuck it, where are you?"

"Ann Arbor."

"Ah Jesus, goddamn hippy country, eh?"

"You know it."

"Who are we looking at there?"

"Nothing serious, just checking the stations. All we have here is a drunk, a wannabe, and an ego that's due to get deflated."

Ronnie grumbled. "Damnit, Cliff, you need to stop scouting like no one is as good as you were."

"What is that supposed to mean?"

"Don't bite back at me like you've never heard it before, Cliff. Not that it's going to do you any good to hear it again. Just brief me on the ballplayers."

Cliff cleared his throat. "Michael Merlin, a right handed closer throwing 94-96, major league fastball and forkball, but he did jail time at the end of last season after repeated drunk driving offenses. Next is Benjamin Marker, but I'm not sure why he's on the list. He's a switch hitting outfielder with a below average arm, speed, and power. Finally, John Cooper, right handed starting pitcher, 90-92, great fastball. The knock on him is his apathy, on and off the field. There are a handful of other guys that won't be draft eligible this year and a couple seniors that might get a look in independent ball."

"Alright, well the new coaches might have a different perspective on these guys so ask around a little if you feel inclined, and like I always say..."

"Never rule anyone out," Cliff interrupted.

"That's right, Cliff, but don't patronize me, goddamnit. It's not my patented scouting line for no reason. I've had that philosophy since you were still in diapers."

"I know Ronnie; I've heard this one before."

"Well you'll fucking hear it again you little prick, remember who you're talking to."

"Yes, sir."

"Don't be such a dickhead Cliff, you might find a prospect once in a while." Ronnie hung up, and Cliff put the phone down on the receiver slowly, staring at himself in the mirror while he did. After he hung up the phone he reached up his left arm and touched the inch thick scar that ran under his elbow, remembering the day he tore his Tommy John tendon. *Some of these guys might be better than I could have been,* he thought while retreating from the mirror, *but I doubt it.*

*****

"Look at Nichols up there kissing ass," said Chase Warner, one of our best starting pitchers, during the fourth inning of the scout day scrimmage. Scout Day was an entire day during Fall Ball reserved for scouts to come in and take a look at some of the squad's top prospects. Nearly every major league organization would have a scout in attendance, but most of them were only authorized to do no more than make a phone call to tell someone else to come take a look.

Scout Day, like most professional tryouts, was set up to measure the five tools that scouts were sent out to rate: speed, throwing, fielding, hitting, and hitting for power. The 60 yard dash was always the first thing the scouts wanted to see, since speed was the major tool that could only be improved, never taught. Fielding and throwing came next. The outfielders went first, getting three throws from right field to third base and three throws from right field to home plate. Then the infielders got their shot to show off their arms, fielding several different ground balls and throwing to first base. Then the first basemen field and throw. Finally, the catchers threw to second base while each scout held a stopwatch to time the throw from when the ball hits the catcher's mitt until it hits the mitt of the middle infielder. This is known as a pop-to-pop time.

Next it was time for the scrimmage, set up for the scouts to measure everything else, and get a good look at the best prospects that the team had to offer. John Cooper started for the squad made up of what Nichols perceived to be the team's first string players, and Wilson Jack started for the other team. Cooper faired well in his two innings of work, striking out four and giving up only one hit, a laser beam off the left center field wall from the bat of Albert McKinney. Wilson had a much more difficult go at things, giving up three runs on five hits in just one inning of work including a massive home run to freshman phenomenon Paul Walker.

"Who cares about Nichols," I answered. I, as usual, was standing next to Chase in the bullpen down the right field line. "If he won't even play all the seniors for their last scout day then he is a worse coach than I thought."

"Seniors?" Chase asked, scanning both benches. "Who hasn't he played?"

I shot him a glare and pointed toward my face.

"Oh yeah, sorry," Chase said with a shrug. "Listen, I need to warm-up because I'm going in next and I have to face that Walker kid. I don't want to give up a yack to him like Wilson did."

"Fuck Walker," I said under my breath as I put on my catcher's mask and jogged back toward the bullpen plate. When I reached the plate I got into a squatting position and Chase started to get loose.

*****

"Nichols," Cliff yelled. He was sitting a few rows above the rest of scouts, who were huddled near the bottom of the seats directly behind home plate. "Coach Nichols," he called again, this time getting the coach's attention.

"Cliff Armstrong," he said while extending his hand. "Milwaukee Brewers."

"Nice to meet you, Cliff."

"Most everyone that knows me calls me Cool Cliff."

Nichols laughed before realizing Cliff wasn't joking. "Nice to meet you Cool Cliff," he said.

"I spoke with Ronnie Mack this morning. He's the national cross checker for our organization"

"I know Ronnie. He was around during my playing days." Nichols put his hands on his hips and squinted into the afternoon sun as he looked back toward the intrasquad. Chase Warner was on the mound now for the Blue team, facing Ben Marker from the Maize. Cliff looked on with Nichols as Marker laid down a drag bunt on the first pitch and beat it out at first by half a step.

"What do you think about Marker?" Nichols asked as he clapped for his team captain.

Cliff grunted. "I don't think about him much. He had a couple people in our organization convinced he was ready for the next level, but I talked them out of it."

Nichols turned to look Cliff in the face. "He just needs a shot, Cliff. Marker is going to surprise a lot of people in pro ball."

"With all due respect, Coach Nichols, there are thousands of draft eligible kids out there this year who are faster, bigger, stronger, and more athletic than him. He puts up numbers, but he has no potential. In the Brewers organization we don't waste our time on guys who will fizzle out in two or three years."

"That's too bad you feel that way," Nichols said. "Because I think someone is going to take him for sure this year. I've talked to three different scouts about his potential just today."

"Don't bullshit me, Coach, and don't act the part of the father figure for this kid. You can't get one past Cool Cliff. I may not get along with the rest of those number junkies down there, but I sure as hell know that Benjamin Marker isn't on their lists. If it wasn't for you putting your tongue in their asses and waiting to pitch the Merlin kid until the end of the scrimmage, they would all be halfway home by now."

Nichols refrained from making a response, sticking out his hand instead. "Nice to meet you Cliff," he said with a fake smile.

"Wait, I have a couple questions about Cooper and Merlin."

Nichols took two steps down the stairs before looking back, "I'm afraid they're going to have to wait until the next time we talk."

Chapter Twenty-Two
Judging Talent

"There ain't much to being a ballplayer if you're a ballplayer."
　　-Honus Wagner

　　The days left in fall ball started to come to a close and the alumni game was just a few days away. Off-season workouts would start soon, and since Nichols was big on developing the team, he scheduled morning lifting for Monday, Wednesday, and Friday at six-thirty in the morning. He knew lifting that early in the morning didn't do much for the body, but it was good for discipline, which was what our team needed the most. Under NCAA regulations, other than lifting, we were allowed two hours a week of individual practice with the coaches. Tuesday and Thursday were conditioning days.

　　Nichols and his staff put a lot of time and effort into our off-season program, but off-season workouts were the least of Nichols' worries, and it was pretty obvious. He wore his emotions on his sleeve, and we could all tell he was feeling the pressure of having to make cuts. I couldn't blame him because when I started to think about who I would cut, I couldn't come up with five names, and he had to come up with eight.

*****

　　"Guys," Nichols said in a meeting late one night, "we've been arguing about this for too long without making any solid decisions. I know it's difficult because we haven't had a lot of time to evaluate the talent, but we can at least narrow things down. I know that you all have a list in your mind about who you think should be the first to go, but let me just preface the discussion with this; let's really try to be objective about this, at least in the beginning. The players that can't contribute to this team, whether in the game or in practice, have to be the first to go."

　　"We can't get rid of Squat," Stein said. "He's the heart and soul of this team. I think we can cut that Alger kid, he's such a pussy."

　　"He's worthless," Calloway snapped. "For Christ's sake, Coach Stein, the other guys call him 'shit for brains.'"

　　"And we're already thin on outfielders," Mitchell said.

　　"We have several infielders who can fill in for an outfielder in case of injury, Mitch," Nichols said. "But I think we can use Pete."

"It's your squad, Nichols. Why don't you give us some names?" Stein asked.

Nichols cleared his throat. "I'll be honest. I'm disappointed with the team's attitude, and I don't think we have done a good enough job fixing the problem. I know we are all a bit slow to react since we are still getting used to our new jobs, but it's time to start cracking down."

Calloway let out a long breath. "What do you have in mind?"

Nichols frowned. "If I had my druthers McGee, Lou, Varner, Wes, Merlin, and Cooper would all be on the chopping block. I don't think there's a single ounce of respect in any of their bodies and they do nothing but bring the team down."

Calloway's jaw dropped. "You can't be serious; Merlin and Cooper are just out of the question, Tom. They're our best two pitchers."

"You cut Varner and you cut all the leadership out of the outfield," Mitchell blurted, his cheeks burning bright red.

"I don't like their attitudes," Tom answered calmly. "They can only hurt us in the long run."

"What can hurt us is fielding a team with no experience and no attitude," Stein snorted, arms folded across his chest.

Tom raised his voice in reply, "I'd rather risk that then have an undisciplined team I can't control. Now, I'm not saying that I'm going to cut them, and trust me, I will have the final say in this, all I'm saying is that we, as a coaching staff, are doing a poor job keeping them under control."

"Okay, Tom, so what do you suggest we do exactly?" Calloway asked.

"Well, there is at least one on my wish list that's expendable."

"McGee is the only outfielder that's on my cut list," Lewis said. "I thought until this meeting it was pretty safe to say that the freshman Pete, Benny, and Varner are our starting three."

Stein grunted. "We can do without Varner and McGee, they are both morons."

"Yeah, but Varner is a pretty good moron," Calloway said. "He gets it done, and that's all I have to say. McGee is a monster of a guy, but he has done nothing this fall. If we are making decisions based on results, then McGee is out. The only reason to keep him is his potential to hit home runs. He is the strongest guy on the team bar none, but I would rather have Varner at the plate than him any day of the week."

"I agree," Tom said. "Is it safe to say that McGee is the first one on the cut list?"

All three assistant coaches exchanged glances. Calloway went to open his mouth but Tom interrupted him, "I know what you're going to say and I don't care. I've heard the rumors as much as you have, but I'm going to keep coaching regardless of what the powers that be might have to say. I'm going to go ahead with the cuts without taking any politics into consideration. If someone higher up has a problem with how I do it, then they can come to me and tell me."

"You're the head guy," Calloway said, looking at Mitchell and Stein. "It's ultimately your decision on the cuts, and I respect that."

Tom nodded and pointed toward Mitchell and Stein. "What about you guys?"

"I don't know," Mitchell said with a blank face. "I can't like and say it doesn't worry me."

Stein licked his lips and said, "I know you aren't questioning whether I'd run and tell on you if you decided to cut a scholarship kid with a bad attitude. If I had it my way I would take his ass behind the woodshed and straighten him out, but those days of coaching are history. Now the players have lawyers, the little pricks."

Mitchell sighed. "I don't mind if this kid isn't on the team. He hasn't exactly impressed me this fall, and he definitely has a bad attitude. The only thing I am afraid of is the scholarship issue. They are going to notice, Tom, even if you don't tell them, they are still going to notice."

"I don't mind if they notice. I mind if they do something about it, but we're finished talking about it. I'm just going to go through with it because it's not a scholarship issue, and it's not McGee's lack of ability, it's his attitude and alleged steroid abuse that I'm concerned about."

"In defense of McGee, I think the steroid thing is just a joke," Calloway said while wiping the sweat off his brow. "You don't really think the guys on the team actually believe he took steroids, do you?"

"Yeah, sure," Stein said. "Have you seen the guy? He's as wide as he is tall. I've been coaching just down the road at Ann Arbor Pioneer for a long time so I know a lot about Michigan teams, and when that scumbag came in here his freshman year he didn't look anything like that."

"And I'm sorry I mentioned it," Nichols said. "It's really beside the point. I've made up my mind about McGee, so let's just talk about the rest of the team. Here's my take on the catching, I like Squat and I really don't want to get rid of him. Plus we really need at least four catchers for bullpens during the winter so I want to keep him no matter what. On the infield I am looking at red-shirting McKinley, and even though I don't like Wes and Lou's attitudes, I might keep them at second and third. Our freshman twins and Nelson Cruz are, if vary narrowly, outplaying the competition and should be kept. What do you think?"

"The infield is your thing, Tom," Gene said. "All I know is that my starting rotation looks like Coop, Jack, Warner, and Hum. My midweek starter as of right now is Franklin, even though I can't stand the kid, and Merlin is my closer. We have a couple young guys that we can easily get rid of, but our starters are set. Right now, if you take out two of the three that you just listed, we are going to have to make a decision between our red-shirt freshman Kelly Summers, who got is ass handed to him in the scrimmage the other day, and the true freshman Sam, who couldn't break a pane of glass."

Tom grinned. "It's an easy decision for me, Gene. What do you think?"

115

Gene shrugged. "It's not going to make a difference, I doubt either of them will make it another year without being cut, let alone be able contribute to the team on the field."

Tom slapped the table. "Okay, it's final then, Sam's on the team. I like the kid's spirit and determination. Plus he just flat out gets it done, and you can't argue with results, right Gene?" Gene chuckled and nodded. "Okay, so at least we're getting somewhere. I think we can make the rest of the cuts fairly painlessly. The only things I'm still worried about are Merlin's record and Coop's hot shot attitude. Keep an eye on them, will you Gene?"

"I'll do my best."

"Stein, Mitchell, anything to add?"

Stein shook his head. "Nope, if you're keeping all my catchers I'm satisfied."

"Mitchell?"

"Nothing."

"Okay," Tom said. "Let me just hit you with the rest of my list then and we can go from there."

Chapter Twenty-Three
A Few Phone Calls

"We live by the golden rule. Those who have the gold make the rules."
     -Buzzie Bavasi

I saw it every year around the end of fall ball; freshman approaching nervous breakdowns. During my senior year, Pete Alger was the worst by far. Pete must have breezed through high school because he never stopped whining about how much homework he had or how he got screwed on a grade by some teacher who "hated him." My guess was that he wasn't used to having teachers who weren't awestruck with his athletic performance. So, when every thing went wrong for Pete, he did the one thing he could think of - he went to his mentor.

*****

"I do what I have to," Benny said when prompted by Pete's question. "I take easy classes and I do the bare minimum to stay eligible. I consider baseball my major, and I need all the time I can to study. If I worked harder in class, stayed up late at night studying, or sacrificed my good eating habits to stuff in time to meet with professors, how would that affect my baseball performance? Not a chance, baseball is my first priority, all the way."
     Pete nodded and walked away from Benny without another word. Benny's answer was not even close to what Pete was expecting, but Pete had been warned by some of the other guys on the team about how he was. Pete had a little more vision for the future, so he didn't share Benny's idea of "majoring in baseball." He went to Michigan for the quality of the education, too.
     Then, on his way back to the dorms after practice, and just when he thought his frustrations had come to a head, he discovered he had three new voice mail messages on his cell phone.
     Beep. "Hey Pete you dickhead, this is Pat, your boy. Just wondering where the hell you've been. But I guess if you're just too cool to hang out with us guys that went straight into the plumbing business out of high school, it's cool. I hope all your high profile rich friends at that liberal asshole school are doing good screwing each other in the ass." Beep.

Beep. "Pete, this is Vince. If you don't call me I'm going to cut your dick off. Pete, did you hear that? I'm going to come to your preppy Michigan dorm room and cut your dick off. It's Vince." Beep.

Beep. "This is Joe. I'm your friend from Saline. We used to hang out, like, three weeks ago. We should do that again. Peace out." Beep.

That night Pete was lying on the vacant bottom bunk of Tucker and Albert's dorm room, when he felt himself starting to suffocate. He was lying on Albert's bed because Albert was off hanging out with Squat and Coop at the movies, and Tucker was up on the top bunk making his nightly rounds on his cell phone. Both of them seemed to be having such an easy time adapting to college life and Pete couldn't understand why he wasn't.

Then, with Tucker talking loudly on the phone in the bunk above him, he quietly opened his cell phone and dialed the number marked "Home."

"Hello?" His Dad's voice was tired and faint.

"Hey, Dad, how goes it?"

"Peter? Is that you?"

"Yeah, Dad."

"What time is it?"

Pete looked at the alarm clock near the bed. "I don't know, about 11:30 I guess."

"Oh yeah. Leno is on TV. I must have dozed off."

"Sorry to wake you up, but I wanted to give you guys a call."

"Of course, you can always call. What's the special occasion?"

"Not much. Just struggling with school and baseball. It's really hard to find time to get everything in. Fall ball is almost over, but we're starting our off-season conditioning right after practice ends; it's like we never stop to take a breather. I'm always tired and I never have the motivation to hit the books."

"Stick with it. New things are always hard at first. You'll be fine."

"I guess."

"Besides, nothing is too hard for Pete Alger - primetime Michigan baseball player and future big league all-star."

"Dad, please."

"Alright. I'm just trying to cheer you up."

"I know, and I appreciate it. I'm just so on edge right now."

"Well, are you still getting your work done? Maybe you should switch up some of your classes if they are too hard."

"It's too late for that."

Tucker, who finished his phone call and had been eavesdropping on Pete's conversation with his dad, remembered he had something to discuss with his dad, too. So he opened his phone and dialed his dad's cell number. "Dad, it's Tucker."

"What's up, Champ, we haven't heard from you in awhile. Your mother and I were starting to wonder if you were alright."

"Yeah, sorry about that, I've just been consumed with all the bullshit that's going on here."

"Bullshit?"

"I didn't realize how political baseball is at this level. It seems like the coaches have their favorites, and they are the only ones that really get talked to, or helped. I'm worried that I'm not even going to play this year."

"Tucker, in all honestly, bud, politics should work in your favor. Coach Nichols recruited you personally, only you and that paranoid kid you are always talking about can say that."

"Pete."

"Yeah, right, Pete. How is he doing?"

"He's paranoid."

"Sounds like you aren't too far from paranoid yourself."

"Yeah, well, now there's a rumor going around that they are going to cut McGee. He's had a really bad fall, but the old coach gave him a fifty percent scholarship right before he retired. It doesn't seem like that matters at all to the new coach."

"Well, Tucker, does this McGee guy deserve to get cut? What year in school is he? Is he any good?"

"I think he's good. He's a junior, and he's a really good guy. A lot of the guys on the team just don't understand him; he's had a tough go at it, just like me."

"C'mon Tucker, no self-loathing, I didn't raise the kind of kid that whines to his parents about how unfair life is. You don't like the way things are going, then go out and do something about it."

"That's what I'm trying to do, Dad. I want you to call Morgan."

"Morgan? Why?"

"Because he can make Coach Nichols keep McGee, just like you said."

"Yeah I know I said that Tucker, but it's kind of unethical."

"I just doing what you taught me, Dad; I'm using my resources."

*****

Across town a party was raging at the South Fifth house, a Thursday night staple. I attended against my better judgment, but I figured it couldn't hurt because it looked like I was facing another year of riding the pine. With this in mind, I decided to put a few down, despite my low tolerance for alcohol.

At one point during the night I scrolled down the numbers in my phonebook until he saw Benny's name, but the alcohol in my system made my reflexes a bit slower than normal and I punched the down button one too many times and landed on another name, Beth.

I looked at my phone for a second, watching the name go in and out of focus through my beer goggles. "Beth," I said out loud, slowly. Then again, this time in question form, "Beth?" *What the hell*, I thought for a second, *maybe I should give the girl a call, just like Coop said.*

I punched the call button before my brain had time to comprehend what was happening. I looked at the phone for a second, reading each of the two words on the screen independently, "Calling," I read out loud, and then "Beth." *Oh fuck*, my brain said to my body, *what the shit have you just done! Hang up, dumbass, oh no, it's too late.* I looked back at the phone, "Connected, Beth."

"Hello?" said a voice from the receiver. The volume was turned up so loud that I could hear it even though I was holding the phone two feet from my ear. *Better say something*, I thought, *I really should say something.*

"Hey," I said, holding the phone to my face and doing the best I could to mask my alcohol induced slur.

"R.J.?" Beth asked. I heard her yawn after asking if it was me. I listened closely, but there was no noise in the background. She definitely wasn't out partying, I had woken her up.

"Sorry," I said.

"Sorry? R.J., that is you, isn't it?" She paused to check her caller I.D. and the time. "It's one thirty in the morning; did you dial the wrong number?"

"Yeah," I said.

"R.J., have you been drinking?"

Beth always hated it when I drank, especially when she wasn't there. "It's not a trust issue," she always told me. "It's just that I like to be around to make sure you are careful."

"I'm always careful," I said, more at the memory than at the person on the other side of the phone.

There wasn't any answer for a few seconds, and then finally Beth said in a very tired voice, "Is there a reason that you are calling me, R.J.? We haven't talked for so long, I'm surprised that my cell phone still holds your caller I.D. number."

*****

Later on that night, Benny found me curled up around a toilet. My head was sunk down so far into the bowl that Benny said he could only identify me by my portly stature.

"Hey Squat, what are you doing? Jesus, are you alright?"

I was too drunk to turn around from my position over the toilet. *Maybe I should answer talk so he knows I'm still alive*, I thought. "Yes, I'm still alive. But I'm caught in the middle of an important prayer of painless death and salvation from another round of puking." I puked as soon as I finished talking, and Benny put his hand on my back because it was the only thing he could do to help.

"Should I call an ambulance or something?"

"No, I just called Beth." I puked again. "Well I drank a lot, too." My voice echoed off of the toilet bowl in front of me as I talked.

"Squat, I hate to ask you something stupid at a time like this but, do you still have Walt's number?"

"Yeah sure, it's under Dubbs in my phone. My phone is in my right pant pocket. I would get it out for you, but I can't really move and my hands are caked with dirt, vomit, and beer."

"It's okay, I'll get it." It took Benny awhile to free my cell phone from my pocket because my jeans were stretched so tight from kneeling on the floor in front of the toilet. As soon as it came free, I puked again, and Benny flushed the toilet.

"Thanks," I said.

"No problem," Benny said. "Thanks for Walt's number. I want to talk to him about independent leagues and whatever."

"That sounds great, Benny, you do that. I always liked Dubbs, that is, besides the fact that he is a negative prick who never stops bitching."

"Like you?"

"Yeah, we hate our own, what can I say."

*****

"Hey Tom, it's Morgan," said the voice on the other side of the phone. Coach Nichols scratched the side of his head and squinted his eyes, trying to prepare himself for what he was about to hear.

"Hey, Morgan," Tom said. "How are you doing?" Tom took the receiver away from his mouth so Morgan couldn't hear him let go of the deep breath that he was holding. Tom gritted his teeth when Morgan's voice came back on the phone.

"I'm fine, Tom, just fine," he paused. "Look, I was cleaning up my office for the night when I received a phone call from a worried parent. That phone call turned into five more phone calls for me and here I am, still at my office. I don't like to be at my office this long, Tom, I really don't. I have kids too, you know."

"Of course, Morgan," Tom said. Morgan didn't respond right away and Tom winced at the thought that he had spoken too harshly.

"You probably already know why I'm calling," Morgan said. "It's getting time for you to start cutting down your team. While we have the resources to fund a baseball team with forty or forty-five players, we, and I mean the athletic department when I say 'we,' are handcuffed by Title IX. Thirty-two is going to be the maximum number of players that you'll be allowed for the upcoming season, and baseball doesn't generate enough revenue to carry eight to ten players over the maximum roster capacity up until the season opener."

"That's completely understood, Morgan," Tom said. "We are planning on finalizing our roster after the alumni game." A tense silence followed Tom's statement. Judging by Morgan's hesitation, he was hoping Tom would infer what he was trying to tell him.

"You know, Tom, I was personally responsible for bringing you here. And I also know that it was a very difficult situation to step into, having to juggle freshmen that were promised things from the former coaching staff with the promises you've made to the two freshmen you recruited personally."

"I don't make promises," Tom interrupted.

"What was that?"

"I said that I don't make promises. I never tell any of my recruits that they are guaranteed playing time, or even a spot on the team. Who was it that came to you about this? Was it your little cousin Mitchell or your drinking buddy Stein? I've heard all about why they were brought in and frankly, I feel like you compromised the ethics of the hiring process by picking two guys that you…"

"Don't get defensive, Tom. I'm not the guy you want to argue with," he paused and Tom gently bit his tongue. "Now I'm going to finish what I have to say and then I'm going to hang up because I'm tired. It's been one hell of a day, I was hoping to read my daughter a story tonight, and I've already spent half the day arguing with people who want to tell me what to think." He stopped and cleared his throat before continuing. "Here is the situation, as dry and as simple as I can put it. You were brought in here to coach, and to coach the way that made you successful before you came in here. Personally, I am willing to give you free reign of the program, to do with it whatever the hell you want as long as the tallies in the win column exceed the tallies in the loss column. I'm on your side here, Tom, I want to make that as clear as possible. However, you have to make sure that you take into consideration the money the university has invested in these individual athletes when you sit down to finalize your roster. In fact, I insist that you do so. Don't put me into a position where I have to defend your ability to manage and coach a team before you have a chance to even put your team on the field of competition. I know how you feel about this, and I want you to know that this is a difficult situation for everybody. You're a smart man, Tom. I know that you understand what I am telling you, and I'm not sure that I have to imply that this is the same reason Coach Witherton is no longer employed with this university. Say hello to your wife and kids for me, I'm hanging up now."

Tom put the cordless phone back on its perch without a word. His wife, Sarah, was curled up in pajamas and reading a book by his side. She took off her glasses when Tom hung up. She smiled for a few seconds, looking into her husband's eyes, glad to have his attention back on her. Her smile faded quickly when she realized something was wrong.

"What is it?" she asked as a worried look crossed her face.

"That was Morgan," Tom said.

"Morgan? Why was he calling?"

"He was calling about the cuts," Tom said, focusing on his wife's eyes. "He wanted to make sure that I wasn't going to cut anyone on scholarship. Apparently someone got wind that I was thinking about it."

"You were going to cut someone on scholarship?"

"Sarah, sometimes you have to cut out the cancer, even if it has already taken hold of some vital organs."

"Gross, Tom. Couldn't you have used a better analogy?" She laughed and poked him in the ribs with her elbow.

"Ouch," he said, wrapping his arms around her so she couldn't hit him again.

"Tom?" she said, struggling against his grasp.

"What?"

"Are you going to do what he says?"

"Well, I think that I have to. I don't think I have an alternative," he said. "But it makes me want to do it even more."

"You would," she said, trying to wriggle a hand free so she could tickle him. "You're such a man."

"Stop it, I'm serious. I'm worried I'm just going to become a puppet for these people, you know? Doing whatever they tell me."

"I think you're overreacting," she said, pulling free from his grasp and starting to walk away. She stopped at the edge of the living room, turning her head over her shoulder to face her husband, who was still on the couch with his eyes pointed toward the ceiling. "Tom, this is an adjustment year for everyone. This is the kind of thing that happens when people get promised things just before power is transferred," she sighed. "Now I'm going to bed, are you coming or what?" She winked suggestively and disappeared around the corner.

Morgan and McGee were the furthest things from Tom's mind as he scrambled to turn off the lights and made a beeline for the bedroom.

Chapter Twenty-Four
The Alumni Game

"Old-timers' weekends and airplane landings are alike. If you can walk away from them, they're successful."
     -Casey Stengel

The alumni weekend was always an awkward time of the year, but it was much worse my senior year worse because Coaches Nichols and Calloway were both alumni themselves. They had a funny glow about them all weekend, and it made everyone on the squad a little uneasy. It was strange to watch them reunite with old teammates that they hadn't seen in awhile, and we found ourselves feeling sorry for them because their time was over. The stories they shared were set in all the same locations as our stories. It was the first time I started to realize that it wasn't going to be long before I was in the same situation, the next year it would be me coming back to Ann Arbor only one weekend a year to relive my greatest memories with my best friends.

On the other hand, the alumni game was revitalizing at the same time because we got to personally see the Michigan pride in the hearts of famous baseball alumni we had watched on TV as kids. There was a lot of gawking involved because even the alumni with no professional experience in baseball had professional experience in the business world, and the alumni game weekend was always the best time to make an impression on the people that could help us out after graduation. We knew the alumni themselves were always looking at the players, trying to give opportunities to Michigan Men like themselves, because only those inside the select club really understood what it meant.

So you can imagine why my hands started to sweat when I saw a familiar face approaching me at the golf outing. Nichols assigned posts to all of the upperclassmen, more for our own good than for a punishment. Nichols knew as much as anyone else how powerful some of the alumni were, and since the freshmen weren't in position yet to capitalize on their rich brethren, he gave the jobs to juniors and seniors. I was working on the ninth green, handing out free beverages to the alumni who passed through when a man with a blue polo shirt and khaki pants approached with his putter in tow.

"R.J. Hansen, right?"

I rubbed my hands together. "That's right."

"I'm Matt. I think I met you at a party at the South Fifth house this fall. I was a real mess; I made a fool of myself. I came over to apologize."

I just stood there with my lips quivering until I spat, "Actually, I think you met my roommate John Cooper and one of our freshman, Pete Alger." Matt nodded and turned to watch the rest of his scramble group try to chip in from just outside the green.

"Shit," a tall guy in khaki shorts said after chipping the ball over the green and into the rough on the other side. "This shit sure isn't as easy as it looks. It's your turn Matt, and the pressure's on. We all fucked up pretty bad."

"Okay, one second." Matt reached into his pocket and handed me a business card. "I don't know what your situation is, R.J., but here is my card. If you're interested in the kind of stuff I do, or if you know anyone on the team that is looking for a job, just let me know. I'll be around for the rest of the weekend and then you can reach me at the number on the card." Matt slapped me on the shoulder and walked away.

I took a look at the card while Matt chipped and knocked the ball a foot away from the pin, prompting the rest of his group to cheer and give him high fives. The first guy in the group easily putted the ball in the hole and before I knew it, Matt and his group were driving on to the next hole. I took a look at Matt's card as soon as the group disappeared. "Matt Slydel," it read, "Professional Sports Agent."

*****

The next day was the day of the alumni game. Coop was starting for the varsity squad and Gene Calloway was starting for the alumni. There were a couple of alumni that were better pitchers than Gene, one of whom played in AAA for the Tigers, but Gene told him sorry, he got to start because he was the coach. "Besides," Coach Calloway told Nichols when the game was approaching, "I've been waiting to rattle a couple of these guys' cages for awhile."

Gene had to face Benny as the first batter of the game, and he lobbed the first pitch over the middle for a strike, knowing full well that Benny would take because he was the prototypical lead off hitter. Calloway got a pretty good read on Benny during Fall Ball and he knew Benny's tendency to go the other way when he was behind in the count, so Gene busted him in with the next two fastballs, but they both missed for balls.

Ed Masters, a long time Big Ten umpire, agreed to work behind the plate for the alumni game and Calloway wasn't too happy when he called the two inside pitches balls. "Try not blinking when the ball is crossing the plate," Calloway said under his breath. Calloway threw a 2 and 1 change up on the next pitch and Benny was way out in front, grounding out to the shortstop Quinton Diggs, who fielded it perfectly and fired it over to first base.

"Good pitch, old man," Diggs said after firing the ball around the horn.

Gene snorted after he got the ball back. "Old man? Aren't you about ten years older than me, Diggs?"

Diggs' smile was as broad as he voice was deep. "Not in the way I play, baby."

Calloway smirked and stepped back up on the rubber. Wes was the next hitter, and he challenged him right away with a fastball. Wes swung and hit it on the ground between Diggs and the third basemen for a base hit.

"Dive, Diggs!" Calloway yelled as the ball scooted through.

"Shit," Diggs said rubbing his knees. "Don't you know I'm ten years older than you?"

Gene chuckled and went back to work. The big Texan was in the three hole for the varsity team, and Gene knew he had some speed on first base with Wes. Gene was pretty sure that no one was trying to play strategy in the alumni game, but he threw over to first base a couple times just to keep Wes honest. When he finally delivered the ball to the plate it was a slider and Tex took a big hack and missed.

"What are you doing swinging at the first pitch?" Calloway asked as he caught the ball thrown back from the catcher.

"First pitch slider?" Tex asked. "You must be scared."

Calloway huffed and scraped the mound. I'll show you scared.

That's right, Tex thought, *get mad and give me that fastball.*

Calloway did and Tex took a huge hack, banging the ball off of the right field fence. Tex went into second base standing up as the throw from the outfield took a long time because the legs of the alumni were a little slower than usual.

"Unhitch the trailer, Nichols," Coop yelled from the bench while Nichols chased the ball around the outfield. Wes scored easily on the play and chuckled as he crossed home plate. This infuriated Calloway, who watched as Wes gave Lou a high five and told him that Gene had nothing that could get him out. Then Lou stood in the box with a grimace and whiffed at three straight change-ups.

Calloway stared down Lou on his way back to the dugout. "I don't hear you chuckling now, tough guy." Lou stared back at the mound while he walked to the bench, looking like his head was about to burst. "Don't say anything," Calloway warned. "Don't say anything or I'll cut you."

Gene settled in after giving up the early run. He finished up the inning by getting Smalls to fly out to center field. Then in the second inning he took down the bottom of the line-up in order, finishing off the side by striking out Pete Alger. Coop, on the other side, only gave up a few fouls tips, and was pissed when the last batter he was scheduled to face in the second inning flew out to Varner in right field.

After Coop and Coach Calloway gave way to their respective bullpens, the offenses for both teams started to show up. Nichols and Diggs both hit doubles in the bottom of the fourth to tie the score at one, but we got four runs in the bottom of the inning to claim a lead the alumni would not recover from.

Walt Williams, nicknamed Dubbs by his teammates while at Michigan, was the talk of the game for the alumni squad after finishing three for four at the plate and making two great catches in the outfield. Walt sat behind Benny for the majority of his career at Michigan, but he signed with an independent team in the Frontier League after graduation.

Coach Stein, who had assumed the head coaching position for the varsity, gave me an at-bat in the last inning when we had a healthy six run lead. I had to face Ronnie Derby, a submarine pitcher that was only two years off of the team. He got ahead in the count with two straight fastballs that tailed hard in on me. I took them both and gave Ed Masters a glare after each one.

"Inside again, Ed," I said after the second strike call.

"You're up four runs and this is the goddamn alumni game, R.J., shut your mouth."

"That doesn't give you an excuse to screw me."

The next pitch was a huge Frisbee slider, starting behind me and breaking back into the strike zone. I buckled at first, but when I realized it was going to be a strike, I flung my bat in the general direction of the ball and missed badly. I pouted on the way back to the dugout, pissed that I'd missed another opportunity.

"Don't worry about it, Squat," said Merlin, who was about to go into the game for the ninth inning.

"I can't believe Derby got me out," I said. "I only caught about five hundred bullpens for the guy."

"Yeah, I thought those first two were inside," Merlin lied.

"Fuck Ed Masters," I said with defeat in my voice. "I knew those balls were inside."

*****

At the end of the game I was walking over to say hi to Coop's parents when I got intercepted by Wes's sister. "Hey, R.J.," she said with a smile. She threw her arms around me and I did the same out of reflex. She let go after a couple seconds, looking me straight in the eye before saying, "What's wrong? How come you only got the one at-bat at the end of the game? Are you hurt? I saw you playing catch with the pitchers in the bullpen."

I sighed. "No, I'm not hurt. To tell you the truth, I don't play much. I thought I would get some solid playing time this year, but it looks like the coaching staff is all about Evan and this new stud freshman we have."

Cassie smacked her lips, pretending to feel bad for me. "I thought you were a senior?"

"I am. I just..."

"John!" Cassie yelled over my shoulder, and then looked back at me and said, "I have to go say hi to John." I watched Cassie gallop down the steps of the stadium and run up to Coop, throwing her arms around him with twice the enthusiasm she did to me. Not even five seconds passed before I saw Wes climbing the stands and coming right for me.

"What in the hell do you think you're doing?"

"I met your sister the other day, I was just saying hi." Wes's eyes got bigger. "I gotta go shower now."

Wes slapped me in the face. "Stay the fuck away from my sister, fat ass."

"Don't touch me, douche bag," I pointed toward where Wes's sister was practically molesting Coop in front of his parents. "Besides, it doesn't look like you're going to have to worry about me anyway." Wes peeled away and made a beeline for Coop, but I didn't want to stay and watch. Instead I headed back to the locker room, showered quickly, grabbed Tex, and left without waiting for my all-star roommate.

Part III:

The Off-Season

University of Michigan Baseball
Final Cuts and Opening Day Depth Chart

Catcher
1. Paul Walker
2. Evan Lancaster
3. Steve Tawas
4. R.J. Hansen

1st Base
1. Tom Kindleman
2. Albert McKinley
3. ~~Brad Kelly~~

2nd Base
1. Wes Roth
2. Eli Kleinfeldt
3. Tyler Bowers

3rd Base
1. Lou Whitley
2. Nelson Cruz
3. ~~Dean Shively~~

Short Stop
1. Glen Schmalz
2. Simon Bowers

Left Field
1. Pete Alger
2. Jordan Burton

Center Field
1. Ben Marker
2. Brett Vernon

Right Field
1. Paul Varner
2. William McGee
3. ~~Timmy Benson~~

Starting Pitcher
1. John Cooper
2. Chase Warner
3. Wilson Jack
4. Bill Hum
5. Don Franklin
6. ~~Kelly Summers~~
7. ~~Zach Anderson~~
8. ~~Sam Weir~~

Relief Pitcher
1. Tucker Howard
2. Nick Elston
3. Clive Hunter
4. Oliver Press
5. Sander Utley
6. Quinn Marchowski
7. T.J. Regan
8. ~~William Kingston~~
9. ~~Mike Stevens~~

Closer
1. Michael Merlin

Chapter Twenty-Five
Remis

"Whether you think that you can, or that you can't, you are usually right."
    - Henry Ford

      Coach Nichols made the final cuts the morning after the alumni game and there were only a couple big surprises. Freshmen Albert "Shakes" McKinley, Pete Alger, and Tucker Howard all found themselves moving up on the depth chart after beating out some pretty stiff competition. The Bowers brothers somehow made the team while Sam, the freshman pitcher that Coop had been mentoring, found his name on the chopping block after having a pretty good fall. McGee, on the other hand, was still on the squad even though he was doing everything possible to piss off the coaches. I didn't think Nichols was the kind of guy that would put up with so much crap from a marginal player like McGee, but it looked like I was wrong. Anyway, morning lifting started the next day after cuts so I didn't have any time to focus my energy trying to figure out the thought process of our new staff. Besides, I was just happy that I made the squad, there was no way I was going to ruffle any feathers.

      Morning workouts were the worst part about playing collegiate athletics. My job still requires me to get up early in the morning, but as a collegiate athlete, you don't wake up in the morning to sit behind a desk, or talk on the phone. Instead, an early morning wake up call as an athlete meant a couple very different things: dry heaves and the complete uselessness of your body for the rest of the day. Oh well, it came with the territory. There were a million people that would pay to go through morning lifts and workouts just to be where I was, and that was something I tried to never let myself forget. However, despite my best intentions, I was known for throwing the occasional temper tantrum.

      I remember the first day of lifting my senior year. I woke up still pissed at Coop and said, "Ah shit," at my alarm clock as it went off. I groaned and slowly lifted my torso so I could sit up in bed. Now in a sitting position, I closed my eyes just for a second, trying to squeeze another moment of rest out of a terrible night of sleep. I glanced at the alarm clock, hoping I didn't see it right, and that I really had another hour to sleep before lifting, before I had to face Remis. But just before I could fall asleep in the sitting position, I heard Tex and Coop's alarm clocks blare out in unison.

I stood up and pulled on my baseball issued shorts and t-shirt. I always put my workout clothes on the floor of my room so I could just wake up and throw them on. I did this, like so many of my teammates, to try and squeeze every last second out of my sleep deprived life. I noticed my shirt was a little dirty from wearing it while working out the day before so I licked a couple of my fingers to try and rub out the stain. After a few unsuccessful attempts, I decided I didn't really care since only about one percent of the population of Ann Arbor was awake at this hour anyway. In these early morning hours I found myself becoming jealous of the regular students who didn't need to worry about athletic performance and early morning attendance in order to keep their scholarships and stay in school, but I quickly snapped out of it and stumbled into the living room.

"Hey!" I yelled. "Hey guys! We got lifting! Let's go!" I started tying my shoe laces when I heard my alarm go off again, followed by a flurry of activity from behind his closed door. Before I knew it, Tex was standing above me, ready to go.

"Coop up yet?" Tex asked.

"No, can't you hear his alarm?" We both turned and looked at Coop's door with tired sighs. Tex finished tying his shoes, stood up, and grabbed his things. "Well," he said, "I'm heading down there."

"Alright," I said after Tex had already bolted out of the apartment, leaving Coop as my responsibility. "Coop," I said while tapping gently on his door, "get up, ya bastard, we don't want to be late on the first day of lifting, you lazy fuck."

"I'm up, I'm up," Coop said reassuringly as he opened the door dressed in a disheveled manner.

"Jesus," I said, "you sleep in your clothes again?"

"C'mon man," Coop said, pushing past me and toward the door. "You know I always sleep in my workout clothes. I gots ta get my sleep, man."

*****

Remis was a walking, talking, grunting stereotype. He was in his low thirties, with shaved head, and a thick neck. He never showed any emotion except anger or confusion toward the pathetic weaklings he had to get into shape. Forget greetings, once Remis punched the time clock, he was all business, and his business was the business of inducing pain for the betterment of the university sports programs.

"There is no way," he was yelling as the baseball team hit the weight room door at 6:30 sharp. "There is no way you are giving up on me, no way, no way." The women's track team had an earlier appointment with Remis, and the baseball team got to witness the end of that session. Remis was standing over a tall skinny girl who was jammed into a leg press machine with a few forty-five pound plates on each side. Tears were welling up on the sides of her eyes as Remis yelled at her.

"Remis is in rare form today," Benny said with a chuckle. The team went over to the coat rack and hung up their sweatshirts and sweatpants, keeping one eye on Remis and the track girl while they did.

"Poor Tonya," Coop said, "Remis is going to kill her."

"You know that girl?" Pete asked.

"Coop knows every girl on campus in one way or another," I said.

Coop shrugged. "You know it."

Tonya finished her set and the weight crashed back down to the supports. Remis walked away without saying a word and headed straight for the members of the baseball team, who were still standing huddled by the entrance.

"It's nice to see a men's team in here," Remis said once he reached Nichols and the squad. "I'm sick of babysitting these ladies, you guys ready to get huge or what?" There were already beads of sweat on top of Remis's head and the only people who were more nervous than the freshmen were the upperclassmen who actually knew what they were about to endure.

Pete looked over Remis's shoulder at the women's track team, who lay scattered in the weight room like someone had just thrown a grenade. Tonya was still panting in the leg press machine and several others were sprawled out on their backs by the benches, the free weights, and the pull up bar.

"What are you looking at?" Remis yelled when he saw Pete looking over his shoulder. Pete shook his head furiously, unable to get a sound to escape his throat. The upperclassmen had purposely forgotten to tell the freshmen the proper way to avoid being singled out by Remis. He was part of the initiation tour, in a sense. If you didn't know how to talk, walk, act, or lift the "Michigan Way," you were going to hear about it.

"I'm Tom," Nichols said, extending his hand and introducing his staff behind him before continuing. "I'm sorry we've only just spoken on the phone, but I've had a pretty hectic transition over at the Fish, trying to get everything the way I like it."

"The real question is, are you going to work out with your team? It looks like you could use a little meat on your bones, too, coach." Remis folded his large arms across his chest and wore a smile only until he saw Wes standing behind his coaching staff holding his mouth to keep from laughing.

"Something funny, Weasel?" he yelled louder than necessary. Wes straightened up and shook his head, which was the only correct answer. "Good, let's go get acquainted, men."

It wasn't long before freshmen were running to the bathroom with dry heaves and the upperclassmen were doing their best to hold them back. All of their credibility would be gone if we joined in the puke session because we couldn't make fun of the freshmen if we threw up too. Although I was feeling ill, I couldn't get my mind off Coop and Cassie. Midway through my workout, I cornered Coop and starting firing questions at him.

"You had to do it, didn't you?"

"What are you talking about?"

"You had to take her from me - I told you that I liked her."

"Squatster, it's too early for this shit, what are you talking about?"

"Cassie. Wes' sister. I saw her first."

Coop groaned. "Dude, she practically tore my pants off, what am I going to do?"

"Maybe you should tell her to respect her prior arrangements?"

"Jesus, Squat, what were you, engaged to the girl? Did you even go on a date with her?"

"I invited her to South Fifth, that's close enough."

"Dude," Coop said with a flourish. "Too damn early for this, it's not my fault if she didn't want anything to do with you. Let's get back to the workout before Remis…"

"Hey jerk-offs over there in the corner," Remis yelled from across the room. "Are we lifting this morning or pulling each other's dicks? Meet me at the pull up bar you pussies!"

"Son of a bitch, Squat," Coop hissed as they walked.

"Blow me."

Chapter Twenty-Six
Dubbs

"If the human body recognized agony and frustration, people would never run marathons, have babies, or play baseball."
    -Carlton Fisk

When Benny finally worked up the courage to give Walt a call, he wasn't even sure if Walt would still be in Ann Arbor. I knew Walt had a semester left of school, but I didn't know his plans after graduation. He was always a bit unpredictable, and he wasn't close to many people on the team. He preferred to keep to himself.

Walt was a die hard Michigan Man, something for which Benny had always admired him. However, the circumstances of their relationship never allowed them to grow close. To put it lightly, Walt hated Benny ever since they met. You see, Walt was a sophomore with a big scholarship when Benny came in as a freshman walk-on, just looking for a chance to play. They were the two hardest working guys on the team and were always in competition to out hustle each other. Benny won. Benny always won when it came to hustle, and it was a game that Walt wasn't used to losing. No one had ever worked harder or loved Michigan more than Walt, and here was a freshmen walk-on, taking his spot on the field and the admiration of his teammates.

Walt and Benny never talked in the years they played together. They didn't know anything about each other except what was evident on a baseball field. Benny always regretted that fact, but Walt would never let him get close.

"I'll be your friend when we aren't competing for the same spot," Walt told Benny several times. "Until then, we don't talk, got it?"

After a short phone conversation, Walt reluctantly agreed to meet with Benny. When Benny got to Walt's apartment, he stood at the door for a couple minutes before knocking; trying to prepare what he was going to say. When he finally worked up the courage to bang on the door, Walt answered in workout clothes and he was breathing heavily as he said, "I just got done working out, have a seat while I change clothes."

Benny walked into the apartment and sat down in the living room. Walt was living in a small studio in a nice apartment building off campus. Benny was shocked how the quality of living increased as he got farther off campus; he had never been in an apartment building that wasn't within walking distance of his classes.

Dubbs took about five minutes to change, and when he walked back into the room he was wearing the t-shirt of the independent team he played for and an unfriendly look on his face. He sat down on the couch opposite of Benny and made a motion with his hand for Benny to talk.

"How'd you do it, Dubbs?" Benny asked. The question flew out of his mouth more by force than by choice. He felt upset just sitting in Walt's presence, especially as he wore that t-shirt.

"I'm not sure I know what you mean, Benji," said Walt with a cold stare.

"Cut it out, man. You know it was never personal."

"It was personal for me," Walt interrupted, his eyes beating down on Benny like the hot summer sun. "It still is."

"Look," Benny said with a sigh, "I came here because I'm coming to the end of my college baseball career and it scares me. I want what you have, and I just want to know how you overcame the odds. Now, if you are still pissed about the shit that went down when we played together, I can't do anything about it." Benny stood up and headed for the apartment door after muttering a frustrated, "Fuck it."

"Wait," Walt said as soon as Benny's hand hit the knob. Benny waited, but he didn't want to turn around. "Sit down, Benny."

Benny turned his head, his hand still on the doorknob. "No, Walt, I think maybe I should just…"

"I said, sit down."

Benny obeyed. His desire for the information outweighed his uneasiness.

Walt leaned back against the couch and put both of his hands behind his head before speaking. "I never liked you, Benny, it's no secret. I didn't allow myself to, and the fact that everyone loved you made it even worse. I couldn't vent to anyone, I couldn't tell anyone how I really felt. I always got the same answer, 'Man, why are you so hard on him, he is great,' or 'Leave him alone Walt, he just has more heart than you do.' I was the one who was supposed to be the underdog Michigan Man, school pride poster boy and all that bullshit. But I started hating all those principles when you stole them from me. For awhile I was defeated. For a long time, really." Walt took his hands off his head and leaned toward Benny. Benny retreated a bit as Walt started to talk. "You want to know how I overcame that?"

Benny swallowed and muttered, "Yes."

"First of all, I never stopped believing how good I was, that I just needed to be seen by the right guy at the right time, in the right place. I didn't let myself believe that my place was on the bench, or that my role was always going to be the guy who gets the last inning pinch-hit. I was the star, and I had to make myself believe it before I could make anyone else believe it.

"I used all that energy and anger and I turned it into motivation. I was determined to make everyone who saw me be surprised that I didn't play in college, I wanted to make them ask the question, to make the statement, 'This

136

guy's been screwed in the past,' and 'He deserves a chance because he can play at this level.' And it took me a really long time, a dozen or more tryouts, but I finally found someone to take a chance on me, and I haven't let them down. I hit .256 last summer with 5 home runs and 29 runs batted in. Not unbelievable numbers but I proved that I belonged. They've extended my contract for next year and I should get even more playing time."

"I'm happy for you, Walt."

"Spare me. I know you don't like me as much as I don't like you."

"That's not true. I've always felt bad about the way things went down."

Walt sneered at the thought. He stood up and stuck out his hand. "Don't tell me that. Just shake my hand and leave."

Benny stood up, shook his hand, and looked him right in the eye. "I'm serious Dubbs; I never meant anything personal. Every time you got in I was pulling for you. You were my teammate no matter if we competed against each other for a spot or not."

"Yeah, well, I was hoping you would fail so I could get in. And to tell you the truth, I would rather you wouldn't try and make friends with me, I'm afraid I would lose my edge. All I have is the hatred for how I got screwed. It's the only thing that keeps me in the game, to prove everyone wrong."

Benny sighed and walked toward the door. "Good luck next year. I hope I get a shot in the Frontier League, too."

"I hope you do, too," Walt said just before Benny closed the apartment door. "I can't wait to kick your ass in pro ball."

Chapter Twenty-Seven
Memories

"This is a game to be savored, not gulped. There's time to discuss everything between pitches or between innings."
    ~Bill Veeck

Most years, I could last until Thanksgiving before I started to struggle with the urge to bitch about everything. My body could only come close to vomiting fours times a week for so long before it started getting pissed. However, Thanksgiving vacation wasn't completely free of stress because it meant that I had to deal with my parents, who never failed to find ways to embarrass me. Lucky for me I got to bring home a few teammates for the break, although one of them was a bit unexpected.

*****

"And then I said, 'All I want to do is talk,'" Bill Hum said, "'and get you sloppy drunk.' She got all pissed and wouldn't listen when I tried to tell her it was from *Doc Hollywood*." He chuckled and took a sip from his beer. "And that was how Michael J. Fox broke me up with my last girlfriend."

"You know what?" I said after taking a long drink from the unmarked plastic cup filled with an unidentified cheap beer. "There is something special about this dirty, shitty-ass, South Fifth porch, isn't there?"

"What do you mean?" Varner asked. Then he unzipped his pants and walked over to the edge. "Like how easy it is to piss off of?"

"Well, yeah," I said. "That's a pretty handy, but I'm talking about something else. Hey - smart guy, help me out here."

Q-Bert sighed and replied with an annoyed and sober tone, "Beats me, all you degenerates do is get drunk and share your lame ass stories about baseball and getting laid."

"What's wrong with talking about baseball and getting laid?" Varner asked.

"I love getting laid," Coop said.

"Baseball isn't so bad either," Benny said.

"The only thing better than those two things might be telling stories about them on this here porch," Tex said.

Q-Bert rolled his eyes and tightened his already white knuckled grip on his broken down chair just before an alarm on his digital watch went off and he slumped over in a dead sleep.

"Fuckin' A," Merlin said before finishing off his beer. "Who wants a refill?" Varner and I raised our hands so Merlin grabbed our cups and hobbled over to the keg.

"Alright, I need to hear something funny," Coop said. "Someone start us off, who has a good story?"

"I got one about a groundskeeper," Varner said. He set his beer down between his feet and leaned forward. "One time we were playing in a tournament up in Toronto on this gem of a field. I mean really nice. It was obvious that whoever took care of it kept it in tiptop shape. I've never seen anything else like it."

"One time, at band camp," Bill Hum said with a laugh.

Varner sneered at Bill and said, "Fuck off, movie queer."

"Get on with it," Coop said, rolling his eyes.

"Well, we found out that despite how great the field looked, there was only one guy who looked after it. He drove everywhere around the field in a golf cart, really unfriendly, and a complete drunk. He knew everything about field maintenance, but he was dumb as a box of rocks after that. He sat right behind home plate during every game, alone, in his golf cart, with a case of Milwaukee's Best Ice." Varner paused while everyone made gagging noises.

"What we didn't know was that this guy had a history of yelling at the umpires, especially when the calls went against the home team, but the umpires were able to shake it off most of the time because they all received a warning before they took the field. Well, this night there was an umpire crew who wasn't warned about the groundskeeper, and after the home team started getting ripped in the first inning, he would yell after every pitch.

"Ball one," the umpire said.

"Horseshit," the groundskeeper said. The umpire turned to see where the voice came from and there he was, sipping a beer and just staring back at the ump.

"Ball two," the umpire said on the next pitch.

"Fuck you, eh," the groundskeeper said, louder than the first time.

"Wait a second," I said, "he didn't really say, 'eh,' did he?" Most the time you couldn't tell that Varner had a Canadian accent, but I always liked to call him on it when it came out.

"Don't interrupt, fat ass," Lou said with an open mouthed stare. There was an awkward silence that lasted a second before Varner continued.

The umpire didn't turn after the second ball, but he sure did after the third.

"Ball three," he yelled on a pitch way off the outside corner, almost too far for the catcher to reach.

"Circus!" the groundskeeper yelled after the pitch, "this is a fucking circus."

"Quiet," the umpire yelled back at the groundskeeper, unaware of who he was. "I'm warning you, buddy. Keep it clean or you're outta here."

"Maybe you should bend over and look out your good eye," the groundskeeper fired back, unable to finish the sentence before the umpire tossed him from the game.

"That's it," the ump yelled. *"You're outta here!"*

"Bullshit, I'm outta here," the groundskeeper said. *"There's no fucking game without me!"* He stomped on the gas of his golf cart and tore around the first base dugout and onto the playing field.

"Then he drove straight across the outfield, almost ran over the kid playing in center, and drove right up to the box that controls the lights. He jumped out of his cart, opened the box, and turned around to yell at everyone to get off his diamond before he turned off the switch and the place went dark. Then the groundskeeper hopped back on his cart and we all squinted in the dark and watched him tear back across the field and leave."

Hum laughed. "No soup for you."

"Pretty funny, Varner," Coop said. "You're not as bad at telling stories as I once thought. Congratulations, you've just earned one cool point."

"Gee, thanks," Varner said.

"No problem," Coop said.

"Hey," Merlin said, but no one really listened and a few side conversations struck up. He looked around, his eyes a bit hazy from the alcohol and repeated himself with the same result.

"Hey," he said a third time, this time with the loudest voice he could manage, startling most of the people on the porch into silence.

"Hey," Coop said.

"Hey," Varner said.

"Hey," Merlin said. "I got me a story." He smiled, looking toward Tex.

"What are you looking at me for?"

"Merlin, stop it," Wes said. "If you have a story, just tell it."

"I am," Merlin said. He paused for another second and everyone leaned in to hear. "Okay, so here it goes. I was in high school, pitching well, when my catcher gets hurt. But our backup catcher was our second basemen and we didn't have a backup second basemen so we just threw some random kid in off the bench to catch for me. So here I am, throwing around ninety, or whatever, and here is this guy behind the plate who had no clue.

"I thought I broke his thumb during the warm up pitches because he caught the ball so bad, but he didn't make a noise. So the inning starts and he doesn't even get a mitt on the first inside fastball I throw and it smokes the umpire right in the armpit." Everyone erupted in laughter, dissolved into painful faces as they put themselves in the shoes of the umpire. "Yeah, it gets better," Merlin said.

"After the game is delayed like twenty minutes while both teams' trainers checked the guy out, I didn't think I wanted to throw another fastball because I seriously doubted this kid would touch it. On the first pitch, he calls for a forkball and I let one fly. Only he squeezes his mitt near his chest and the pitch darts down in between his legs and comes straight up and drills the umpire on the inside of the thigh." The crowd let loose another fit of laughter and grimaces, and Merlin couldn't help but laugh himself. "Just wait, there's more. He misses a third pitch, another fastball, this one must of taken a chunk off of the ump's shoulder, and when he stands up he yells, 'That's it, you're outta here!' at the catcher and throws him out of the game. Then he turns to our bench and starts yelling at our coach, 'You're gotta get someone out here who can at least draw leather, or I'm gonna get killed!'"

Coop turned around and spit the beer out of his mouth and into the bushes, and I tried to talk over the group laughter, "Speaking of umpires, I have a couple great stories."

The laughter continued and as people wiped tears from their eyes. Then Merlin said, "Man you guys are wasted, it wasn't that funny."

"Shut up," I said. "Let me tell my stories."

"We're listening," Coop said while covering his mouth, trying to get under control.

"Okay," I said while rubbing my hands together. "I lived by myself my sophomore year in college, but there were two guys that lived across the hallway that I always hung out with. They were both really cool, and one of them was the sports editor for the Michigan Daily. He had a photographic memory, and he had a ton of stories from his days umpiring seventeen-year-old travel baseball in Novi."

"Wow, really exciting Squatster," Varner laughed. "Leave it to shit for brains to follow up a good story with a dud."

"I'm not done asshole, shut up." I waited until everyone was quiet before I continued, "Anyway, one time he was umpiring in the field in a really close game. Like the team in the field was up by one run in the second to last inning of the game. There was one guy on and a one ball, two strike count on the batter. The pitcher throws a pitch that is really close to the outside corner, and my friend's umpiring partner behind the plate calls it a ball. The catcher holds the ball for a long time, trying to show up the umpire but it doesn't matter…"

"The next ball is out of the park, isn't it?" Coop interrupted, half laughing. I gave him a glare. "What? That shit always happens to me."

"Yeah, well you guessed it. The guy hits the next ball over the fence and starts to round the bases. But when the home plate umpire hands the catcher a new ball, instead of throwing it back to the pitcher, he steps away from the umpire and fires it straight over the backstop and out of play." There were a few chuckles in the group, more from my pantomime than anything else.

Merlin walked back from the keg with a plastic cup in each hand. "Gotta love you Squat," he said while handing Coop a fresh beer.

Coop laughed. "Love? I like you, Squat, but my definition of love is the girl who goes home afterwards without having to call her a cab." Coop chuckled and took another pull off of his beer.

"You're such a scumbag, Coop," Benny said.

"I was just joking," Coop said. "Take it easy, Benji. The definition of love for me is a girl that doesn't even wake me up before leaving." Everyone within earshot laughed this time, save Benny and I. We just rolled our eyes and exchanged a glance.

"Anyway," Merlin said loudly, "who wants to watch me do a keg stand?" Most of the group agreed enthusiastically and Merlin was upside down in less than a minute, chugging cheap beer. When Coop saw that Varner remained behind he decided to ask him what was wrong.

"Don't worry about it," Varner said.

"You sure? You looked pretty pissed."

Varner cleared his throat. "Well, my parents always go down south once the cold weather hits the Upper Peninsula and they don't bother to break their pocket books to get me a plane ticket to Florida for Thanksgiving. Which is no big deal, screw them, I usually go home with Wes for the holiday but this year he says that he already asked that freshman pitcher Tucker."

"Ah, you mean Daddy's Boy?"

"Yeah, that's the one."

Coop thought for a minute, and then watched as Merlin triumphantly fell to the ground after his record breaking keg stand. "Hey, I have a great idea, why don't you come up to Squat's parents' cabin for Thanksgiving? He has another seat in the car."

Varner made a face before asking, "Are you serious?"

Coop chuckled. "Who are you, McGee? Where else are you going to go?"

Varner sighed.

"Sweet," Coop said. "Hey Squat, Varner is coming up north with us."

I stopped cheering for Merlin, who was back up on the keg for round number two, and turned to look at Coop with death in my eyes.

"Yeah, I know," Coop said, slapping Varner on the back. "I'm excited, too."

Chapter Twenty-Eight
The Hansen Family

"People ask me what I do in the winter when there is no baseball. I'll tell you what I do. I stare out the window and wait for spring."
-Roger Hornsby

I couldn't stand anything about Varner and I couldn't stand that he was going home with me for vacation – a time that was supposed to be soothing and relaxing. My anxiety over Varner's presence, however, didn't last much longer than it took us to get to our cabin up north. Why? Well, that was when Varner finally met his match.

*****

The car swerved and Varner let out a blood curdling scream. "Gas pedal's on the right, asshole!" I yelled toward the driver's side window.
"Wow," Coop said from the backseat. "You scream like a girl, Varner, really nice,"
"Fuck off, Cooper," Varner said, and then he reached out and smacked me on the head. "Jesus Christ, Squat, what's with the road rage? Is that gut of yours clogging your brain?"
I shrugged and raised my voice in a defensive tone. "He passed me and started going slower. I'm not going to put up with that shit."
"You yelled at him through the closed window," Varner said. "You realize they can't hear you, right?"
My face turned red. "I'm not even sure why I'm bringing you along, so just shut your mouth and let me drive." Varner shot Coop a look, but he did as I told him, and kept his mouth shut until we reached the cabin.
"Now Entering Hansen Country," read the green sign outside of the dirt driveway that disappeared behind some trees.
"Where are we again?" Varner asked after the bright red light on his cell phone turned on. No service. "Have they heard of cell phones here?"
I ignored him and drove the car around a couple curves. With the house still not in view, Varner scanned the surroundings nervously and said, "If we take a wrong turn in here we'll end up meeting the real life cast of *Deliverance*."

Coop laughed and Tex slapped me on the shoulder from the backseat. I returned the gesture with fake smile.

"Don't look at me like that," Tex said with wide eyes.

"Wait. Squat, I thought you went to high school in Ann Arbor," Varner said. "What are we doing way up here?"

"My father's a bit of an outdoorsmen. Since he retired he's been spending as little time as possible around civilization."

"You still have the place in Ann Arbor, though, right?" Coop asked.

"We still have it, but its deserted most of the time. My parents are thinking about selling it." I turned the car up another steep hill and the wheels skidded a bit on the gravel road. As the car broke over the top of the hill we arrived in front of the main entrance of the house. The four guys jumped out of the car and stretched their muscles before grabbing their gear and heading inside.

"R.J.!" yelled a loud, high pitched voice as soon as the door shut behind us. Seconds later a short woman in an apron appeared from out of the kitchen area and galloped up to embrace me.

"Hi, Mom," I said, muffled by my mom's strong hug.

"It's like Squat with a wig," Varner whispered to Coop, who smacked him as an answer.

"Manners," he whispered. "We're working on your manners on this trip."

"Mom, you remember my roommates Tex and Coop."

"Hi, guys," my mom said with a warm smile.

"And this is Paul Varner. His parents had business during Thanksgiving, so I said he could come home with us."

"We're glad to have you, Paul, I hope you enjoy your stay here. I know we kind of live in the middle of nowhere, but we have a lot of entertainment for such a small place. Mr. Hansen will have to show you around."

The main floor of the cabin was wide open with a set of stairs on the left that led to a second story loft. Varner could see it was just big enough to hold four beds. As they were exchanging greetings with my mom, a short bearded man with a dark tan walked up to the railing on the second floor and watched from above.

"Holy shit, is that my son? I hardly recognize him anymore!"

"And that's my dad," I said toward Varner.

"I see where you get your sarcasm, Squat."

"Hold on there, R.J., I'ma comin' down." My dad started to limp his way down the stairs and I felt the need to explain.

"My dad doesn't get around so good." I glanced back at my dad, who was still making his way toward the group. "Take what he says with a grain of salt, okay? Some of the things he says…"

"Some of the things I say, what?" My dad laughed as he embraced me. It was a loving embrace that I felt lasted a few seconds longer than it needed to, especially with company present.

"So who's da Yooper, eh?" My dad said after releasing the bear hug.

"That's me," Varner said, unusually short.

"Well," my dad said, "this guy is probably going to take all my money on the rifle range then, eh?"

Varner laughed, stopping abruptly when he noticed no one else was. "What do you mean, 'on the rifle range'?"

"I mean in my underpants," my dad said. "What the hell do you think I mean, I mean on the damn rifle range we got out back. You never bet on shootin' before? R.J., what kind of Yooper is this guy?"

"Apparently not the kind you'd imagined, Dad," I answered, amused at the expression on Varner's face. It was the first time Varner was getting a taste of his own medicine.

"I reckon you ain't getting none of my money, Mr. Hansen," Tex said with a grin.

"Oh, you slow Texan, you've known me long enough that you can call me Wayne." Mr. Hansen winked and Tex and Coop chuckled while I rolled my eyes at my dad's antics.

"Wayne?" Varner asked. "Is that your first name?"

"No, it's John," Mr. Hansen said with a wide-eyed stare, waiting for Varner to get the joke. A few long moments passed and Varner's expression never budged. My dad turned to me and said, "This boy lied to you when he said he was a Yooper, R.J., I hate to break it to you," and then to everyone else, "Let's head into the TV room here guys, I'm sure the Mrs. has something to munch on while we shoot the shit."

"It's on the table," my mom yelled from the kitchen as my friends and I sat down and grabbed at the trays of food in front of us.

"Coop," Varner said under his breath when he was sure no one was listening, "why was everyone laughing?"

"Wayne," Coop said. "As in John Wayne."

"Yeah, so?"

"Yeah, so? John Wayne, dude. You know? Famous spaghetti western star." Varner shrugged and Coop went into an impression of the old west star, drawing the attention of the rest of the group.

My dad, who didn't catch anything but Coop's facial expressions, said, "Are you choking, Coop?"

"Funny, Dad," I said.

"No, Mr. Hansen, just giving Varner my John Wayne impersonation." Coop chuckled and tore off a sweet roll from the bunch that was sitting on the table in front of him.

"Thank God," my dad said grabbing at his heart. "I thought maybe you were shitting your pants over there or something."

I rolled my eyes again and my mother yelled out from the kitchen, "Behave yourself, Rodney."

"That *is* behaving myself," my dad snorted and stood up, pointing at Varner. "New guy, can I get you something to drink. A Diet Coke, or maybe a beer?"

"I'll take a Coke," Varner said.

"Yeah, no, we don't have it; we have Diet Coke and beer."

"Well," Varner said, "I guess I'll take a beer. What do you have?"

"Hell if I know," my dad said, with his back already toward Varner and on his way to the mini fridge in the corner of the room, "I don't touch the devil juice." He opened the fridge, reached inside, closed it, and then spun, tossing a bottle into Varner's lap.

"I've never heard of this brand," Varner said, popping the top and taking a long drink.

"That's because it's made of deer piss," my dad said, doubling over in a fit of hysteria. Varner made a choking noise, and then spit the liquid back into the bottle before examining the label.

"Real nice, Dad," I said, holding my hands over my face.

Varner gulped. "This really isn't deer piss is it?" Coop and Tex laughed harder.

"Yeah, but it's no big deal," my dad said, walking over to get the bottle. "Just make sure you scrub really good before we take you out in the woods tomorrow or you might get raped by an elk."

My mom appeared in the doorway with her hand over her mouth, "Oh, Rodney, you didn't!" She rushed over and grabbed the bottle out of Varner's hands and gave my dad a smack on the back of the head on her way out of the room. My dad chuckled and stumbled over to the couch.

"So welcome to our humble home, Varner; it looks like we are going to have a great time together." My dad grabbed for the remote and flipped on the television.

Coop poked Varner in the ribs and I overheard Varner whisper, "Don't tell anyone about this, okay?"

I smiled on the inside. As much as I was embarrassed by my dad, he finally gave me a reason to feel like I had something on Varner.

Chapter Twenty-Nine
Slowly Moving Fast

"I majored in eligibility."
    -Tim Laudner

When we got back from Thanksgiving break, I started seeing little changes in Varner. I don't know whether it was my dad making fun of him, or whether he was just finally getting tired of being such a dick, but I saw more and more improvement in his attitude every day. The only people who didn't like the new Varner were Wes, Lou, and McGee. Varner started coming up with excuses for why he couldn't hang out with them, and once in a while I would catch one of the three giving me a dirty look or saying something under their breath. However, I didn't really care what Wes, Lou, and McGee thought, and I still didn't really like Varner, even though he stopped hanging out with the rest of those idiots.

I kept my distance from those guys anyway, and with only three weeks between the end of the Thanksgiving break and the start of Christmas break, I was too concerned with studying for exams to worry about them. The class I stressed out about the most was my poetry class, not because I didn't like the subject, but because I talked Coop and Hum into taking it with me, and I never knew what they were going to do to embarrass me.

*****

"By the way," Coop whispered through the side of his mouth one day in class, "thanks for talking me into taking this class. Our teacher is a real bitch and a half, but man, there are some serious ladies in the English department. Is it too late to change my major?"

I squeezed his eyes shut. "It bothers me that you don't take this stuff seriously. You know you're supposed to have an epic poem done today, right?"

"Seriously? I've learned more in this class than I have since I got to college. I mean, besides the fact that there are a million girls that are English majors, I also learned that the pen is mightier than the sword." Coop stopped to think, and snapped his fingers when he thought of something else. "Oh, yeah, I learned that the rain in Maine falls mainly..."

"It's the rain in Spain, jackass."

"Whatever." Coop looked around the room for a second before slapping me on the shoulder and continuing his list. "Oh yeah, I learned that that girl Jessica over there always wears pink panties because sometimes she wears skirts and..."

"Okay, Mr. Cooper, that means it is your turn," the teacher said with a grimace.

Coop flashed a smile while he stood up and walked to the front of the class. "You bet, Ms. So-and-so." Bill Hum, sat on the other side of Coop from me, covered his eyes, trying his best to dissociate himself from his rebel friend. I covered my mouth a second too late, allowing a small laugh to pierce through the silent classroom. Ms. Soranso's fake smile deepened into a full out glare as she began to cradle her grade book in a threatening manner.

No one was sure what Coop was going to do next, so all eyes were on him, and he always thrived in that position. When he reached the front of the room he turned around, cleared his throat, and announced the name of the poem as, "Jersey Chaser."

Put on the lip gloss
and thong underwear
Shake your hips as you walk
And watch the guys stare
Take a seat with your skirt
On the edge of the bleachers
Bend over in your tank top
And show off your features
Bat your eyes to wipe away
One night stands like an eraser
It won't be long before I
have a go with you, jersey chaser

A vision of the apocalypse appeared in my mind while hearing Coop read his "epic" poem out loud. I closed his eyes and imagined the women in the class throwing chairs and screaming obscenities. I pictured Mrs. Soranso jumping on Coop's back and clawing out his eyes. I waited for a reaction; thinking I should jump through the eighth story window in order to escape the cannibalistic liberal minded women of the poetry class. But then I heard clapping, an actual applause. I opened my eyes and frowned, they liked it!

"Yeah, I'm pretty fucking cool, huh?" Coop said, immediately turning to face the Ms. Soranso. "Did I say that out loud?"

*****

As Coop, Hum, and I walked out of class that day, we spotted Q-Bert darting out of the computer lab and hurrying down the hallway. We exchanged a glance and picked up the pace of our walk a bit so we could get within shouting distance.

"What do you think the genius is doing in the hippy neck of the woods?" Coop asked. Cooper called Angell Hall a 'haven for hippies,' because, well, it was.

I mumbled a little before answering. "I don't know, maybe he was feeling bad about himself and thought he would do some social experiment by hanging around with the lower type people or whatever, I don't know."

"Yeah, nice try, wasn't funny."

We kept following Q-Bert up the stairs to the second story of the building. He walked in a classroom and the three of us followed him.

"Burtinski, you sly dog, what are you doing in hippy land?" Coop asked as he walked through the door.

"Excuse me, are you guys supposed to be in here? I'm sorry but the class is starting." The man in front of the class didn't look much older than me, and we were struck with a bit of confusion as a sheepish grin crossed Q-Bert's face.

Coop chuckled. "Of course we're supposed to be here, we roll with Q-Bert."

"Wait," I said. "What class is this?"

"This is a discussion for Psychology 111. Now if you are friends of Carl you can talk to him after class, otherwise I imagine he needs the time to ask questions before the final."

"Dude, you're taking Intro to Psych?" Coop yelled. "Man, I barely passed that one, it was really hard!"

"Intro to Psych?" I said while looking over to make eye contact with Q-Bert, who was sinking in his chair more and more by the second. "That's a freshman class."

"Yes, that's right, and I believe Carl is a freshman. Thanks, you two, for the status check, now get out of my classroom."

"Freshman," I said. "Well, I'll be."

"Oh, Lucy," Hum yelled with a smile, "you got some splainin' to do!"

Just then Q-Bert's watch went off and his head smashed into the table.

Chapter Thirty
Executive Decision

"There's been pressure on me since I was born. My parents wanted a girl."
   -Lee Smith

     I have to admit it, Q-Bert had us all fooled. I was pretty shocked to find out that he was actually just some ultra-smart, pathologically-lying freshman. Hum and I didn't care that much when we found out that day in Angell Hall, but Coop went through the roof. Q-Bert's condescending, wiseass routine had started wearing thin on most of the guys in the locker room, including Coop, so he was furious to find out that Q-Bert was a fraud. Q-Bert was terrified that we would tell the rest of the team, or even worse, the coaches. He didn't think they would keep him around if they found out he had been lying to them about his resume, but it was never clear why he was lying in the first place. For some reason or the other we let it slide without asking many questions, and we would come to regret it.

     Hey, no one could blame me for what happened after the season ended, because you can bet that I wasn't going to say anything. I was still riding on cloud nine because I made the team and I wanted to stay under the radar. The last thing I wanted to do was go into the coaches and tattle on our equipment manager and give the coaches another hassle they didn't need. I wrestled with the idea of getting it off my chest during Christmas break, but judging from Nichols' attitude once we got back, and how terribly practice went during conditioning, there wasn't a chance I was going to tell him.

     To make things even more awkward, McGee came back from the break weighing fifteen pounds more than he did when he left, and his gains were all muscle. He was so bulky now that he had a hard time running and throwing. Even his hitting was being affected by his size. His muscles looked so tight that I thought he could burst at any moment. It was clear to everyone that McGee's gains weren't natural, and everyone was holding their breath and waiting for the coaches to do something about it. Then Nichols' got an unexpected visit from the biggest name on campus.

*****

     Tom was in his office one day, nervously eyeing the schedule, when he there was a knock on his door. The door opened before Tom could get out of his chair, and a tall man with square shoulders and a flat top walked into the room.

"Coach Nichols," the man said as he sat down in the chair in front of Tom's desk.

"Coach Harnick," Tom replied, "to what do I owe this pleasure?"

"I am here concerning some players of yours." Harnick looked down at the clip board and read off their names. "William McGee and Tucker Howard."

Tom's heart sank. "Have they done something?"

"You could say that," Coach Harnick said with a grunt. "I don't want to lecture you, Tom, but I have a couple more years in this business than you do. I understand that baseball and football are two completely different sports, but the principles of coaching are the same. There needs to be trust, communication, and commitment between players and coaches."

"Coach, why don't you just tell me what this is about."

Harnick pursed his lips hard before speaking. "The football equipment room in the Hall of Champions is where all varsity letter winners pick up their letters each year. The first year the athlete receives a jacket, the second year a watch, then a blanket..."

"And a ring for the fourth," Tom interrupted. "I was a four year letter winner at this university, too. I know the process, what happened?"

"This William McGee and Tucker Howard were caught stealing from it," Harnick said with a point blank tone. Tom groaned and leaned forward to put his head in his hands. Harnick didn't saying anything until Tom leaned back in his chair and looked at him. "They told my equipment manager that the younger one had just earned his first varsity letter and when he went to check the list of letter winning athletes, our assistant equipment manager walked into the room to find them stuffing watches and rings into their pockets. Now, I don't have the power to tell you how to deal with this..."

"Don't worry," Tom said forcefully. "I think I know exactly how I'm going to handle it."

*****

They finished their conversation and Tom was on the phone the instant the door shut behind Coach Harnick.

"Morgan, it's Nichols."

"Tom, I heard."

"Then you probably know why I'm calling."

"I probably do, but let me warn you if you go down this path you can't just get rid of one of them; you have to get rid of both."

"No," Tom said, "just McGee. He is causing more problems than he is solving, and he is a cancer on my team. For Christ's sake, we have reason to believe he has been abusing steroids, and now..."

"You can't prove that," Morgan interrupted.

"One of my players confirmed it," Tom lied.

Morgan sighed and said, "I don't know, Tom. This is really weak. This is a big move, and you're putting me in a difficult position. How would you explain to our alumni and athletic administration tight wads that their scholarship money is being wasted by a first year coach? Your sport doesn't generate any money as it is, and it's not like you can't use the scholarships. You know that it's this university's policy to honor scholarships for all players who get cut. Why can't you just rag this kid into quitting so we can get the money back to use elsewhere?"

"We've been over and around all this bullshit, Morgan."

"Watch your mouth, Tom."

Tom ignored him. "You brought me in here to win, Morgan, and win my way. My way is to cut out the cancer, no matter the cost. Scholarship money doesn't mean anything if you can't win ballgames. And this is not Tucker, this is straight from McGee's bad influence."

"It will look too irresponsible."

"The only irresponsible thing is to let this kid stay on my squad."

There was a long pause on the other end of the phone. "You better win, Tom."

"What?"

"I said you better win. You've made your point, and now you're going to get what you want. But this is a double-edged sword your dealing with here, and there isn't any looking back. If I give you this, your job security plummets. Your five year plan is going to vanish when his name goes off the roster."

"What are you telling me?"

"I'm telling you that you're going to get what you ask for, but you need to know the consequences."

"Which are?"

"If you get what you want and you don't win, you're history. Jesus, Tom, you're going to piss off some people that have the power to erase your name from the fucking log of this university. If you cut this kid and don't put out a good year, you might open the program next year and find out that you aren't even listed as a former player, let alone coach. We have alumni to please, and," Morgan paused and came back on the line a second later. "Tom, we have parents threatening to transfer their kids if McGee gets cut. These parents have deep pockets and long lists of connections. I hope you realize the magnitude of this – you aren't just playing for you job anymore, you're playing for mine, too." The phone went dead.

Tom put the phone down and leaned back in his chair. He wasn't sure how he should feel, but he knew he did the right thing. It was going to be painful, but the team would recover.

Chapter Thirty-One
The Making and Unmaking of McGee

"Don't cut my throat, I may want to do that later myself."
    -Casey Stengel

McGee was a small kid when he came to college, far too small to compete at the Division I level, and the coaches immediately started to get on him to gain weight. That's when he met Tommy. Tommy worked at a local nutrition store and was the kind of guy that had to get elastic sleeves on all of his shirts because his biceps were too big to fit into plain cotton. Tommy suggested several supplements to McGee over the time they knew each other, but McGee still wasn't satisfied with his body, and old man Witherton's decision to red-shirt him his freshman year made him more determined to get big. That was when Tommy introduced him to anabolic steroids. After all, McGee's goal wasn't just to play for the University of Michigan, but to sign a pro contract and make it to the Major Leagues, and to McGee, the ends justified the means.

Now, a few years later, I witnessed McGee walking into Coach Nichols' office after being caught stealing from the football equipment room. He looked nervous, and personally, I hoped his spot on the team was on the line, but the rumor was his connections made him untouchable. Despite everything, McGee disappeared into the room with his head held high and his chest puffed out as far as it could go.

*****

Coach Nichols told him to have a seat and took a few seconds to gather his thoughts and said, "McGee, I'm not good at sugar coating these kinds of things, so I'm going to put it to you straight." Tom figured McGee was the type who would appreciate the honest approach. The look in McGee's eyes, however, said otherwise. "You've become a liability to the team. Your actions have shown your lack of dedication to the goals we've set as a squad, and I can't allow your behavior to prevent this team from going where I want it to go."

"Where you want it to go? Just where is that exactly, coach?" McGee's lips quivered and his face started to get red. It wasn't going to matter what Tom's justification was for cutting him, he was going to be in for a fight.

"Excuse me?" Tom asked. He had prepared himself for a nasty confrontation before McGee arrived in his office, but now he felt physically threatened. He suddenly regretted not allowing the rest of his coaching staff to be present.

"Admit it, Nichols, this is a personal vendetta." McGee gripped the arm rests of his chair, his knuckles turning white as he talked.

"Vendetta?" Tom asked with a surprised look. "Look, I'm not sure what you're implying, but…"

"I'm implying," McGee interrupted, "that you've had it in for me since the very start."

"You're wrong," Tom said, tired of being a nice guy. "First of all, you don't have a position. Secondly, you aren't that great of a hitter, and I don't have room on my roster for a third string DH."

"I thought you said this was about disciplinary problems."

"Your off the field behavior was the last straw. I've given you way too many chances already. Right now there are a lot of kids that we cut ahead of you who would kill to be in your position, and you go out and steal watches? I won't have that in my program."

"Make up your mind, Coach."

"I have," Tom said. "And that's all I'm inclined to tell you. I don't have to justify my decision making to you, McGee, no matter how important you think you are."

"You're right," McGee fired back, "but there are some pretty important people who are going to want to know why a scholarship athlete is being cut to make room for some scrub walk-on named Sam." McGee got out of his seat in a rage, and turned to leave the office.

Tom was a little startled when he heard Sam's name; he didn't remember telling anyone that Sam was his choice to replace McGee. But with McGee's hand on the doorknob, Tom had to say something.

"Morgan already knows," Tom said, causing McGee to stop in his tracks. "He authorized it, and just for the record," Tom waited to finish until McGee turned around to face him, "if it wasn't for him in the first place, you would have been gone a long time ago. You're the one who is the scrub, McGee, not Sam. Sam is the kind of kid that makes a program better – you, on the other hand – aren't even worth the breath." McGee slammed the door shut before Tom finished his sentence.

Tom regretted his tone as soon as the door shut behind his former player. He sat at his desk for the next half hour, staring at the blank paper in front of him and replaying the scene with McGee. All he could picture was Shane rounding third, and the memory made him vow to smooth things out with McGee when he noticed he had written Shane's name on the notepad in front of him and underlined it three times, the last one ripping the page.

Chapter Thirty-Two
A Time to Fight

"When I began playing the game, baseball was about as gentlemanly as a kick in the crotch."
    -Ty Cobb

      I hate to bash anyone, but the team got an enormous boost after McGee was cut. There weren't many secrets in our locker room because all we did in between seasons was sit around and gossip. Word had leaked out about Morgan's threats and how Coach Nichols' job might be in jeopardy if we didn't put out a winning season. Nichols wasn't very popular with the guys after the first cuts, but there was no way around that; however, we grew to like him in the days after Fall Ball and we couldn't help but feel a little sense of responsibility for protecting his job.

      Tom used the open roster spot to bring Sam back to the team. Nichols told Sam that he was going to be red-shirted, but that he should to work his hardest to get back into shape because you never knew when someone was going to get hurt. I was glad to see Sam was back; I didn't think that he should have been cut in the first place.

      Wes, Lou, and Tucker were the only people that had a problem with McGee's dismissal, and from the stories they told, McGee wasn't doing a good job of handling it. He had started drinking more, and his steroid use hadn't stopped. By the end of winter practice, his friends had given up trying to help him, deciding it would be better for McGee to just work it out with himself.

      The weekend before the team was leaving for Florida for the spring trip we decided to throw a party. The usual crowd showed up, and everyone was outside on the couches in front telling stories, even with the freezing cold weather. Around midnight Wes, Lou, and Tucker got tired of dancing with the sorority girls and came out on the front porch.

*****

      "Varner, let's hit the bar," Tucker said while walking down the front steps to the house with Lou following closely behind. Lou stopped at the top of the stairs when Varner didn't move at Tucker's suggestion.

"C'mon beard boy," Lou said, "train's leaving." Lou walked down the stairs and started back around behind the house where Wes was waiting with the car running.

"Where the fuck is Varner?" Wes asked when only Lou got in the car.

"He's coming," Lou said, sitting down in the passenger seat and shutting the door behind him.

Back up on the porch, Varner was trying to decide if he wanted to go to the bar or sit and keep telling stories with his teammates. "I have an idea," he said, "how about you guys come out to the bar with us?"

"I'm not really the bar type," I said.

"It's too dark to pick up chicks there," Coop said.

"I can get way drunker for way cheaper right here," Merlin said with a loud belch that caused some laughter.

Varner stood up with a sigh, "Well, I need to go with those guys, they're waiting for me."

"Just say no, Varner," Benny said. "You don't have to give into peer pressure."

"It's not peer pressure, fuck-head," Varner said. "No one pressures me into doing anything, but those guys are my friends, and I like to go to the bar with them."

"Well, tell me how it goes," Coop said. "I'll be here hooking up with a few of sorostitutes." Coop pointed his thumb back over his shoulder, toward the front window of the house where four scantily clad women danced provocatively in front of a group freshman.

"Yeah," Merlin added, "my drunk ass is staying right here."

"This place is disgusting enough for me," Q-Bert said. "Besides, I don't think my mind would allow my body to be enveloped in the combined stench of sweat, alcohol, urine, and puke without first being altered by some powerful drug."

"Who the fuck said you could talk, smart ass?" Varner asked, starting to back pedal off the porch and down the steps. "It's okay, I see how it is anyway. I take the leap to try and be friends with you assholes, and you won't even return the favor. 'Try stepping out of your comfort zone,' remember that shit? Give me a fucking break." Then Varner disappeared around the corner, and Wes's car pulled out of the driveway a few seconds later.

"He was pretty pissed, huh?" Tex said after Wes's car disappeared out of sight.

*****

McGee went straight up to Varner as soon as he saw Shakes walk through the door with me, Coop, and Tex.

"What the fuck is the handicapped kid doing here?" McGee asked, wiping the beer from his lips and then bringing his plastic cup back up to his mouth while Varner answered.

"I don't know, I didn't know they were coming, relax."

"You can't be serious, Varner. You bring that asshole into my fucking bar?" McGee was starting to get red in the face and his voice became more and more elevated with each word, but the noise of the bar drowned out his words so that Shakes and the rest of us were oblivious to the impeding danger. We stood at the entrance, joking, searching for Varner, and scooping out the girls on the dance floor.

"Wow, look at that one," Coop laughed. "Sorry to ditch you guys, but duty calls."

"Coop," I yelled at Coop's back, but Coop was already enveloped in by the crowd and couldn't hear me. "Ah shit," I said to my three remaining friends. "Same old Coop. I sure hope he doesn't keep me up all night this time."

"Earplugs, Squat, that's my secret," the giant Texan said about the same time Albert spotted McGee weeding his way through the crowd.

"McGee," Albert said in a choked up voice, but no one heard him.

"Earplugs aren't going to stop the damn apartment from shaking," I said. "I guess I better just get wasted so I pass out. Let's go to the bar."

"McGee," Albert said again, a little bit louder this time, but no one heard him. A man with two long necked beers in each hand passed by Albert with an, "Excuse me, Chief," and separated Albert from Tex and I for just an instant, the same instant that McGee reached him.

"Get out of here, fuck-face."

Tex followed me a few steps toward the bar before he realized Albert wasn't behind him. The tall Texan shot a glance over his shoulder in time to see McGee shove his pointer finger into the middle of Albert's chest, making him back up a step.

Tex turned around and yelled toward me, but I had already been swallowed up by the crowd. Tex quickly weeded his way back toward Albert. He was only about ten steps away from Albert, but it took him a good two minutes to get to him. Tex almost started a couple of fights on the way; one when he spilled a beer from the hand of a guy who was sporting a frat sweatshirt and another with a guy who had four of his toes smashed under the pressure of his cowboy boot.

Shakes looked at Tex and then back into the face of his potential assailant. *Have you ever noticed how big you are, Albert?* Tex had told him once, *For God's sake you are at least four inches taller than McGee.* Albert stood up straight and looked down into McGee's red face. *Yeah, he's intimidating with his big steroid built muscles and mean attitude, but look at you.* Albert wiped McGee's spit from his face and wiped it on McGee's shirt.

"Don't touch me, motherfucker," McGee said, closing within inches of Albert's face. "You're a second away from getting beat within inches of your life, right here in front of all of your girlfriends."

Albert leaned in toward McGee even more, until their noses were almost touching, "You know what? You're not going to do anything, because all you ever do is talk." Albert's voice was strong and true with no hint of a stutter. *No one your size should ever be afraid of someone like McGee.*

"Watch your mouth."

"Do something about it."

McGee leaned back to swing and Albert jabbed him in the face with his right hand, knocking him off balance for a second, and then hit him with a roundhouse left across the side of the face, sending him straight to the ground. Tex was on Shakes in the next instant, holding him back so he couldn't do any more damage.

Wes, Lou, and Varner all appeared in time to see McGee fall to the ground. Lou rushed over to get McGee to his feet, and Wes immediately got in the freshman's face. "What the hell is your problem? Why did you hit him?"

"McGee was the one making the threats," Tex said. "Albert just defended himself."

"Shut up, Tex, why the hell are you even here?"

Varner grabbed Wes's shoulder. "Take it easy, Wes, they came with me."

Wes shook his hand free and said, "What the hell is your problem lately, Varner? Why are you even sticking up for these pussies? The one with the nervous twitch isn't even man enough to break up with his bitch high school girlfriend who lives two hours away."

Tex stepped in front of Albert. "Take it easy, Wes."

"Who the hell are you to tell me to take it easy?"

"Walk away."

Wes gritted his teeth and stepped into Tex's face. "Make me."

Chapter Thirty-Three
Locker Room Chatter Part Two

"The doctor's X-rayed my head and found nothing."
        -Dizzy Dean, after getting hit in the head in the 1934 World Series

        I missed all the action, like usual, which sucked because I would have
loved to give McGee a few kicks in the ribs while he was down. Anyway, Wes
attacked Tex after Albert knocked out McGee. The only problem is Tex broke
his hand defending himself. I knew Wes and his group of idiots would fuck up
our season somehow, but I didn't quite anticipate a fight like that.

                                        *****

        Coop: "Wes, you moron, what are you doing starting fights?"
        Wes: "Don't worry about it – coach is sitting me down for the first
fifteen games."
        Me: "That's a pretty nice black eye you got there. Tex is going to miss
the first three weeks of the season because of you."
        Albert: "Speaking of Tex, where is he?"
        Me: "At the doctor getting a cast for his hand. He broke three bones
in his hand on Wes's face."
        Wes: "Like I said, don't worry about it. Nichols straightened me out
already, so stop your yelling. I don't need everyone on the team giving me
crap."
        Hum: "That's like in *Office Space*, where he's all like, 'Did you get the
memo?'"
        Wilson: "Hey Varner, I forgot to ask you. How was it visiting with the
in-breeders up in hillbilly country?"
        Varner: "You won't believe this, but I actually had a pretty good time
at shit for brains' place."
        Pete: "Hey, is it true? Albert knocked out McGee?"
        Me: "Hell yeah he did, I was there."
        Smalls: "You guys shouldn't give Franklin so much crap about the way
he cusses."
        Wes: "He just makes it so easy."
        Coop: "God I hate fucking classes, make them stop!"

Varner: "Yeah, I almost feel like we would be doing the world a disservice if we didn't rip on him."

Smalls: "Yeah, well, all you guys do is piss him off. You know, we are sophomores now, all that crap is supposed to end."

Wes: "Okay, okay, we'll try to lay off."

Lou: "You can lay off. I'm sure as hell not."

Smalls: "Get back in your cage, Lou. No one is talking to you."

Lou: "The equipment manager is out cold again, anyone want some free stuff?"

Wilson: "Fucking Remis kicked me off of the bench press today. He said the hockey team was coming in for strength testing. You know what? Remis thinks he is so tough, but he's really just a big pussy."

Me: "Calm down, Wilson. You gotta learn how to let shit slide."

Wilson: "Fuck off, Squat."

Me: "See what I mean? It affects your pitching, too. You never have bad control until someone boots a ball behind you."

Varner: "Coop, now that I think of it, I have a rumor to confirm."

Coop: "What's that?"

Varner: "I heard something about Q-Bert. Someone was trying to tell me that he really isn't a med student? He's really just some punk freshman?"

Coop: "No, someone just made that up. They were probably just screwing with you."

Tucker: "Pete, what's up man, how are things going?"

Pete: "Better, I got to hang out with some of my friends from high school over Christmas break so we're cool now. I passed all my classes so I am cool there, too. I don't have such a hard load this semester and I'm loving it so far."

Tucker: "Yeah, man. It looks like you're probably going to get some serious playing time this year in left, too, huh?"

Pete: "I hope so, what about you? Think you'll get a get a few starts?"

Tucker: "I think so. I know the coaches really want to red-shirt me so they can get me for another year, but we all know that this team in going to need me this year. I will probably start out as the first guy out of the bullpen. I'm guessing that I'll end up in the starting rotation by the end of the year."

Wilson: "Deflate that head, Daddy's Boy, you're not taking my spot."

Tucker: "Oh yeah, of course not. Never."

Wes: "Shakes, I bet those women just love that finger twitching shit, don't they?"

Part IV:

Pray for Rain

University of Michigan Baseball Schedule

Date	Opponent
2/25	Stetson
2/26	Stetson
2/27	Stetson
3/1	Central Florida (DH)
3/2	South Florida
3/3	South Florida
3/5	Jacksonville (DH)
3/6	Jacksonville State
3/11	Oklahoma
3/12	Oklahoma
3/13	Oklahoma
3/18	Kansas
3/19	Kansas
3/20	Kansas
3/25	Texas – San Antonio
3/26	Texas – San Antonio
3/27	Texas – San Antonio
4/1	**Ohio State***
4/2	**Ohio State* (DH)**
4/3	**Ohio State***
4/5	Notre Dame
4/6	**Central Michigan**
4/8	Penn State*
4/9	Penn State* (DH)
4/10	Penn State*
4/12	**Eastern Michigan**
4/15	**Iowa***
4/16	**Iowa* (DH)**
4/17	**Iowa***
4/22	Illinois*
4/20	Illinois* (DH)
4/22	Illinois*
4/23	**Western Michigan**
4/24	**Bowling Green**
4/29	**Northwestern***
4/30	**Northwestern* (DH)**
5/1	**Northwestern***
5/4	Eastern Michigan
5/7	**Indiana***
5/8	**Indiana* (DH)**
5/9	**Indiana***
5/13	Michigan State*
5/14	**Michigan State* (DH)**
5/15	Michigan State*
5/20	Minnesota*
5/21	Minnesota*
5/22	Minnesota*
5/25-29	Big Ten Tournament
6/3-6/6	NCAA Regionals
6/10-6/13	NCAA Super Regionals
6/16-6/23	College World Series

Home games (bold) at Ray Fisher Stadium
Big Ten Conference game
Schedule is subject to change

Chapter Thirty-Four
Go Time

"A hog dog at the ballpark is better than a steak at the Ritz."
    -Humphrey Bogart

Practice flew by and before we knew it we were receiving our travel itinerary instead of practice plans. When the front wheels of the plane hit the ground in Florida our first opponent already had twenty games under their belt. The Stetson University Hatters were ranked 19th in the nation and sported an intimidating 18-2 record to boot. More importantly, they hadn't spent a single day practicing inside during the winter, and they gave Coop a rude awakening.

In fairness to Coop, he pitched well considering it was his first outing of the year, but Stetson's pitcher already had thirty innings and three wins. Not to mention it was the first time our hitters and fielders had been outside since the fall, and our depth perception was so far off that we didn't even need our bats at the plate. When all was said and done, the Hatters handed us a 7-0 loss. It was a humiliating defeat, but Coop still joked around in the locker room after the game.

"So much for an undefeated season."

"Hey, we still have fifty-five more games on the schedule and we played a pretty good team tonight," Coach Nichols said.

We had high hopes coming into the season, but the moral was low after our first loss. The rest of the spring trip was the same thing over and over; we couldn't field, we couldn't pitch, and we couldn't hit. Our fielders were used to taking balls off of the Astroturf in our indoor facility, so they had a difficult time with the bounces off the grass. The outfielders hadn't had to deal with the sun in their eyes for six months, and the pitchers apparently didn't know what to do with their arms feeling good in the warm weather because none of them could come close to the strike zone all week long. Bill Hum gave up so many runs I think we would have lost count if they didn't have a score board, and I don't think Wilson Jack threw a single strike in his outing. By the end of the trip we had a 2-8 record and a bruised ego.

Pete and Albert were the only highlights of the trip, surprising everyone with their hot gloves and bats. Pete made several diving defensive plays in the outfield and Albert, who was filling in for Tex at first base, slugged two home runs and came back to Ann Arbor as the leading hitter on the team with a .412 batting average.

During the practice after our Spring Break thrashing, Nichols reminded us that the true season started with the Big Ten. Unfortunately, we still had a few weekends on the southern swing before conference play started. To my surprise, we went 5-4 in our remaining games to raise our record to 7-12. It wasn't great, especially after the goals we set for ourselves, but it was respectable considering the awful start. Benny led the team by hitting a scorching .612 during the last nine games of the road trip, raising his average to .402 overall.

The team was starting to come together. Albert McKinley was filling in well for Tex, Merlin was lights out, Smalls was gobbling up just about everything that came his way, and Coop was getting more and more dominant with every start. Franklin was the only question mark on the pitching staff, and Nichols' quickly demoted him to the non-conference, midweek starter's role with the conference season approaching.

It wasn't a very popular decision with me, but it didn't take me long to figure out the reason for it. I had caught in the bullpen for each and every pitcher on our staff about a million times, so I knew their stuff, and Franklin had some of the best stuff on the team. That meant there was only one reason for his demotion, and that was Coach Calloway. Coach Calloway had been riding Franklin ever since practice started; there was always something wrong with the way he pitched. I was pissed because I knew how much pride Franklin had in the University of Michigan, and with our first Big Ten opponent being our arch rival Ohio State, there was no one I would have liked to see out on the mound more than Franklin. Well, except for Coop that is.

*****

"Hello, Wolverine fans, and welcome to another day of Michigan baseball. I am your radio broadcaster, Don Archie, here with your play-by-play. It's a cold March day here at the Fish and Michigan will say hello to the Buckeyes from Ohio State in the opening series of this year's Big Ten conference schedule. With me this year, as you know, is Harold Frank. Harold, your thoughts?"

"I'm ready for some baseball."

"It looks like the Wolverines are, too, Harold."

Harold snorted. "They better be."

Harold shook it off and said, "As you and I and so many Michigan fans know, only three real opponents matter for the Maize and Blue and those are Michigan State, Notre Dame, and these, the buckeyes of Ohio State. Harry and I will be right back with your starting lineups after this message from Crazy Eddie's Buffalo Wing Palace."

*****

"And we're back. Once again, a blustery Friday afternoon in Ann Arbor and the fans are just starting to pile in here at Fisher stadium. Ohio State is the opponent. Big Ten regular season championship is what's on the line. Your thoughts Harry?"

"I think you nailed it, Archie."

"You bet I did. If there's one thing I know best, it's the hatred these teams have for each other. But that's another story. Harold, hit me with those starting line-ups."

"Okay, for Tom Nichols and his Wolverines today we have Glen Schmalz leading off playing shortstop. Wes Roth hits second and will play second base. The hot hitting Ben Marker will hold down the third spot for the Michigan nine today. He's in center field. Lou is hitting fourth and playing third while Albert McKinley is playing first and hitting fifth in place of injured senior Tom Kindleman."

"Boy, we'd like to get him back as soon as possible."

"Yeah, but I tell you what, Albert's been hitting the ball pretty darn good."

"That's true; the young man has really filled in well. Let's hear the rest of the line-up."

"Okay. Paul Walker hits sixth while catching. Evan Lancaster is the DH in the seventh spot. Then Paul Varner hits eighth in right field and freshman Pete Alger will bat ninth and play left field. Hitting today for the Buckeyes will be…"

"John Cooper is on the mound today," Archie interrupted, "and we have a fresh bullpen to back him up against the Buckeyes in the series opener."

"Should I read the Ohio State line-up, Arch?"

"They're all Buckeyes, Harold, what more do you have to say? Stay tuned as we pause a moment for station identification and we'll be back with the first pitch after this."

*****

Coop grunted loudly as he threw the last fastball of his pre-game bullpen. Then he threw his jacket over his throwing arm and started to walk toward the dugout. I got up from my stance and opened the door of the bullpen so Coop and Calloway could get through.

"Light 'em up today, Coop," I said as I gave Coop the game ball. "Don't forget I'm your agent, and the better you do against the Buckeyes, the more money I can get you."

Coop completely ignored me as he blew into his pitching hand. "These fuckers are going down today, Squatster." Coop nodded toward their dugout. "Just look at 'em." The entire Buckeye bench was out in front of their dugout, swinging bats, playing catch, or playing flip. "They walk around here like they own the place, well not today."

I blinked. "What are you thinking, Coop?"

"I'm thinking it's my job to set the tone."

"Well, just be yourself. You don't need to do anything extra-special; you're already the best pitcher in the league."

"Everything I do is special." Coop flashed a grin at me. "Did I say that out loud?"

*****

"Walker sends the ball down to second and we're ready to play ball. Jonathan West is the first batter of the game for Ohio State, and he will step in opposite the All-American Wolverine pitcher, John Cooper. Okay, folks, here comes the first pitch… the rivalry has begun with a fastball, and Jon West is down! First pitch fastball and West is down. West takes one in the back of the helmet and Cooper doesn't appear phased."

"Yeah, he smoked him alright," Harold said. "West has to be seeing starts after that shot. I'm not sure the mules he raised back home in Indiana kicked that hard."

"The team trainers go to West's aid," Archie said, "but it looks like he's getting up and will wave them off, walking gingerly down to first base. And just like that the first batter of the series is on for the Buckeyes, but it came at a cost. Well, Harold, big game and lots of emotion, it appears the adrenaline just got the best of Cooper on that one. You hate to have the first batter on in a series like this, but nevertheless, here is Brian Miller, the 2nd hitter for OSU."

"The first two guys are speedsters for the Buckeyes," Harold said, "so look for them to put on some type of bunt, steal, or hit and run here. Ohio State is a small ball team, and against a dominating power pitcher like Cooper, you can bet you're going to see Miller bunt here, even if it is the first inning."

"That's a good point, Harold. West at first base already has twelve stolen bases on fourteen attempts in this young season. But now it's batter number two and pitch number two for John Cooper, who, coming into this game, had only hit four batters in 26 innings of work. Miller will square to bunt like we anticipated; looking to move an early runner into scoring position. Coop takes a long look at him before rocking and firing and, oh man! Miller will take this one in the shoulder and that will send the Michigan pitching coach to the mound. Two quick runners on base, and I'm surprised the home plate umpire is not warning both benches. Cooper looks dangerously out of control with his pitches today, Harold. If you're Tom Nichols you might be thinking of getting someone else up in the bullpen and letting Cooper come back for the game on Sunday."

Harold rubbed his shoulder and said, "You'd think he would, but it looks like these balls are just slipping out of Cooper's hand, Arch. I don't think Nichols is going to make a move just yet, and I'm not sure that Cooper would let him anyway. Right now he looks like he's about to kill and eat the pitching coach for coming out to the mound as it is. You know, Coop does like to eat raw meat, maybe that is having some kind of effect on his pitching today."

Catcher Paul Walker took a stiff jog to the mound in order to beat Coach Calloway to the punch.

"Dude..."

Coop interrupted him. "Shut up, Walker. Just sit behind that plate, squat down, and put down the old number one. We're right on schedule."

"Coop?" Coach Calloway asked when he hit the mound. The sweat was dripping down his face, and he couldn't get anything else out of his mouth so Walker and Coop just stood there and stared at him for a couple of seconds before anyone said anything.

"I'm fine, Coach."

Calloway rubbed his hands together. "Well, you just hit the first two batters of the game and we were all kinda wondering..."

"Gene."

"Yeah?"

"Get your ass back in the dugout or you're the next one who's going to wear a ball in your back."

"Well," Calloway paused, "alright." He turned and walked back toward the dugout, causing the freshman catcher to crack a smile.

"Wipe that shit-eating grin off your face, Walker."

He did as he was told and waited for further instructions.

"Okay, you can get your dumb ass back behind the plate now."

Walker nodded and sprinted back toward home.

Chapter Thirty-Five
Mentors Part Two

"I never had a bad night in my life, but I've had a few bad mornings."
    -Lefty Gomez

      I would be lying if I said Coop had an amazing performance that cold day in March against the Buckeyes, because it was much better than amazing. After "unintentionally" hitting the first three batters of the game, he struck out the next seven he faced. Our offense was led by Lou's fourth inning three run home run and Smalls' bases-loaded triple in the sixth. Coop pitched a complete game two-hitter to seal the 6-0 victory. Coop wasn't kidding when he said he was going to set the tone, because none of Ohio State's hitters looked like they wanted to step in the box all weekend, and it was a big reason for our 3 games to 1 series victory. The most thrilling victory was our game two win in a 13-11 slugfest. Neither team could find a pitcher on their bench that could get anyone out until we got to Franklin. Calloway almost had a fit on the bench when Nichols decided to get him up in the bullpen, but we were running out of arms and Nichols didn't have much of a choice. Franklin surprised us all and earned the victory by pitching two shut out innings and giving way to Merlin, who earned the save with a perfect ninth.

      After the Ohio State weekend we had our annual showdown with the Notre Dame Fighting Irish in Grand Rapids, Michigan, home of the Detroit Tiger's single-A affiliate, the West Michigan White Caps. The game against Notre Dame was always one of the biggest nights of the year because, if we won, it proved to recruits and alumni that we were on our way up. However, it was easier said than done, because Notre Dame was perennially in the top twenty-five teams in the nation. It was the one night of the year that I always had a blast whether we won or lost. It was a great experience to play in a minor league stadium and in front of a substantial crowd of Michigan faithful.

      Going into the game none of us were sure who Nichols was going to start. Franklin's success against Ohio State put him back into the bullpen, and Nichols didn't have many fresh arms that could carry some solid innings. Coop, Wilson Jack, Chase Warner, and Merlin were all available to pitch briefly in the game, but since it was early in the Big Ten conference race Nichols was hesitant to give them more than one inning apiece because he needed them to be healthy for the next weekend. I don't know who else he could have picked besides who he did, but I was still a tad leery with his decision.

"I want you to start against Notre Dame tomorrow."

Tucker gulped. "Really?"

"I recruited you to pitch in big time games, do you feel up to it?"

"You bet," Tucker said, trying to disguise his shock. "But I have to tell you that I didn't see it coming. You haven't exactly given me much of a chance up to this point."

"Much of a chance? You have almost twenty innings, including two spot starts."

"I realize that, but it's not like I've been in the rotation like we talked about before I came."

Nichols blinked. "What are you saying?"

"I'm not saying anything, I just thought that we discussed how much I playing time I was going to get as a freshman and I remember you making it clear to me that you thought I could step right in and contribute."

"You are contributing, you have the sixth most innings on the staff and you're a freshman. We still have about a month to go in the season, what's the problem?"

Tucker started to open his mouth but cut himself off, "No problem, Coach. Thank you for the opportunity, I'm going to get after it tomorrow with everything I've got." They said their goodbyes and Tucker turned to leave, kicking himself for having said anything at all.

*****

The bus ride to Grand Rapids was a relatively short one, and Tucker was out on the mound before he had time to make himself nervous. His arm felt better than it had all season, and he didn't waste any time showing it off. He knew that he wasn't going to be able to go deep into the nine inning game, so he treated the start like a relief appearance, not saving anything.

He got out of the first two innings without giving up much more than a one out double in the first and a swinging bunt single in the second, but the third inning proved to be a tougher challenge. Calloway could tell that Tucker was tired, and he had Hum up in the bullpen before Tucker toed the rubber to start the inning. The Notre Dame starter hadn't allowed a hit yet and their bullpen was clear of any activity. Tucker took a deep breath before looking in for the sign, but he couldn't quite get his focus, and he walked the first batter on four straight pitches. He got behind the second hitter too, but just when he thought he was getting back on track, The Irish executed a perfect hit and run on a 2-1 count, sending the ball past Wes who was streaking to cover second base.

With runners on first and third and nobody out, Tucker peeked down toward this bullpen to see Hum waving his hat in the air toward the dugout, telling them he was ready to go in the game. *No way, Hummer,* Tucker thought, *I haven't even given up a run yet.* But he thought too soon, because the next batter sent a deep fly ball to left center field. Benny made a good run, catch, and throw to keep the runner at first, but the runner at third scored easily on the sacrifice fly.

"One pitch away," Walker yelled from behind the plate.

Tucker pulled his hat over his eyebrows and tried to focus on nothing but the mitt. He used the fastball grip three times in a row to start the next hitter, but his aim missed just low of the strike zone on two out of the three. Confident that the hitter had his fastball timed after three straight, he shook off to a change-up on 2-1, thinking he could catch the hitter by surprise to force a ground ball double play. But he hung the change-up and watched the ball sail high over the left field fence for a homerun.

He got a new ball from the umpire and he could tell the coaches were talking about bringing him out, so he got on the mound and delivered the first pitch as fast as he could. The new batter was sitting on the first pitch fastball, and dented the right center field fence with a ferocious swing. This time Nichols was on the mound before the ball got back to Tucker, slapping him on the butt and telling him that he pitched better than the score looked.

Tucker ran straight past his teammates who came out of the dugout to shake his hand and up into the tunnel. He was throwing everything he could get his hands on when Merlin appeared in the doorway to the locker room.

"I don't know what the fuck happened," Tucker said, almost on the verge of tears. He hadn't realized how much this outing meant to him until he saw Nichols standing beside him, telling him he was out of the game. "I was blowin' ched in the bullpen and I started out on the mound like a baby. Like a fucking pussy." Tucker took off his glove and threw it into his locker where it ricocheted back just enough so he could give it a kick into the bathroom area.

"Hey," Merlin said, "don't worry about it. You're a freshman and you're starting. You're a stud." Tucker turned around and looked into Merlin's eyes.

"No way, man. I have no fucking talent. I'm not going to make it."

"Shut up. Don't talk like that. What if some of the other freshmen heard you saying that shit? How would it make the guys on the team feel that never touch the field? Don't be such a bastard."

"They already know."

"You're wrong, Tucker," Merlin said. "Besides, you're missing the point. We have juniors and seniors on this staff that have had a hell of a lot worse outings than you just experienced. A lot worse. Damn, one time Hummer gave up four homeruns and hit four batters before he got an out. It was awful - even the fans were yelling to take him out."

"They were yelling to take me out tonight, too. I could hear them."

"Yeah, but they were concerned with Hum's health, not the score of the game. We all thought he was going to get smoked with a line drive and die."

Tucker laughed and Merlin smiled. "Look," Merlin continued, "the only time you feel shitty is if you go out there and baby your stuff. If you go out and give it your all, you can never feel bad if you get your tits lit. Sometimes hitters get the best of you, you can't control that. You can only control what's going on between your ears."

"Bullshit, man, it's all bullshit," Tucker said quietly. "Someone else should get my innings; the only reason that I'm playing is because of my dad."

"What do you mean?'

"What do I mean? I mean that if my dad wasn't such a big shot alumni I wouldn't be here right now."

"How do you figure?"

"C'mon Merlin, do you honestly think that I'm that much better than the older guys that I should be getting their innings?"

"Actually, yeah, I think…"

"Don't patronize me, Merlin," Tucker interrupted. "I should transfer to some rinky dink school were they have never heard of my dad. That way at least I will know when they play me it's because I earned it."

"You know, Tucker, I hate to break it to you, but…" Merlin trailed off.

"What?"

"Yeah, well, like I was saying I hate to break it to you but everyone already knows about your dad or whatever. And everyone also knows that you used him to keep McGee on the team, but look what happened. I'll tell you want happened, we have a badass for a coach and he told that Morgan guy to blow it out his ass, he was going to cut whoever the hell he wanted. So if he went through with cutting McGee against the wishes of your dad and Morgan Pulanski, do you really think that he would still favor your sorry ass because he was scared of the same thing?"

"Wait," Tucker said, his cheeks blaring with the red tint of embarrassment. "How did you know about all that?"

"What do you mean, how did I know? I'm the Wizard." Merlin smiled and Tucker pressed him for a better explanation. "Okay, McGee told his buddies Varner, Wes, and Lou and they spread it around to most of the senior class. A few other guys might know, but I think it's just the seniors. Can we go watch the fucking game now?" Tucker nodded and they went back down the tunnel.

Michigan was able to score a couple runs in the bottom of the fifth inning, and Hum held off the Irish bats. The score stood at 3-2 going into the sixth inning. Hum's night was done and Michigan was looking pretty solid since Coop, Wilson, Warner, and Merlin all told the coach they were good for an inning instead of just throwing a bullpen. All they needed were a couple more runs. Coop, Wilson, and Warner all did their jobs to perfection, not allowing a runner past second base in any of their innings. Merlin made things interesting in the top of the ninth inning, walking the first two batters before inducing a double play and then striking out the next man he faced, but the Wolverines were still down by a run heading into the bottom of the ninth.

Wes led off the inning with a bunt single, and then the Wolverines took a page out of the Irish's play book, executing a perfect hit and run with Wes and Tex, which moved the tying run to third and the winning run to first base. Notre Dame brought their corner infielders in but kept their middle infielders at double play depth, conceding the tying run and instead playing for the double play. Lou was the next batter, and he used his fly ball swing to hit a ball deep into the air to right field. The right fielder panicked and tried to throw the runner out at home, over shooting the cut off man and allowing Tex to take second base. The winning run was now in scoring position with one out, so Michigan had two chances to get the run home. Varner was the next to hit, and even though he quickly got behind in the count, he took a huge swing at an 0-2 pitch, looping it over the second basemen's head and allowing Tex to score on the play, ending the game.

Some men in suits stood smoking cigars when we exited the locker room and when I recognized Matt and his friends from the alumni golf outing, I walked up to them with no fear. Matt congratulated me on a job well done and mentioned the possibility of a job opening up at his office at the conclusion of the season. Matt's friends didn't seem to be really happy about the idea, giving me a look up and down. Most of the team was on the bus at this point, so I backpedaled, said goodbye to Matt and his friends, and boarded the bus.

"Who are the suits?" Wilson Jack asked as the bus started to pull away.

I had to take a deep breath in between bites of pizza before I could muster an answer. "One of the alumni guys we met at a party this fall and then again at the alumni game. He has some business, or works at some business, I'm not really sure, but he has been all up in our nuts every since he saw us. I might find out more about it and try and work for him when I'm done."

"What?" Varner said from a few rows behind me. "You mean you aren't going pro, Squat?"

"Shut up and eat your pizza, asshole," I said, doing the same.

Chapter Thirty-Six
Bus Ride

"I ain't afraid to tell the world that it don't take school stuff to help a fella play ball."
    -Shoeless Joe Jackson

    The next weekend we had our longest road trip of the year to College Station, Pennsylvania, to play the Nittany Lions of Penn State. Most of the guys on the team hated riding on the bus, but I didn't mind. Flying took just as long as driving if you add up all the time you have to sit around and wait to load and unload your luggage. Besides, we got to listen to Tex play his guitar on the bus.

    The Thursday morning the bus was leaving for Penn State, Tex arrived a few minutes late and Nichols gave him an earful for delaying the start time of our eight hour bus ride. Tex told Nichols he was sorry and made his way down the aisle toward the back, making a half-hearted attempt to avoid hitting his teammates with his guitar as he walked.

    "Ouch."

    "Watch it."

    "Pardon me," Tex said with a laugh. When he finally reached the back of the bus, he found three freshmen taking up the last few rows.

    "Guys," Tex said, setting down his guitar for a rest. "I'm not about jumping on freshmen, but when it comes to the bus, get the hell out of our seats." The freshmen reluctantly retreated to the front of the bus. "And don't be afraid to double-up," ordered Tex as they squeezed by.

    "Good work, Tex," Merlin said when he heard the story of Tex's backseat ejection. "You can treat the freshmen nice, but they still need to stay in their place."

    "Yeah, buddy," Varner said with a smile when he saw Tex's guitar sitting next to him in the seat. "You going to sing us a couple tunes, Tex?"

    "I was thinking about it," Tex said. "After we get down the road a little I'll take some requests."

    A couple hours later everyone was wide awake and already bored. "I can't believe we have to play the day after we sit on a bus all day," Pete whined from the front of the bus. "I guess this is the kind of thing you guys are always talking about when you say, 'pray for rain,' huh? Man, what I would give for a rainout."

Coop smiled and leaned back so only the upperclassmen could hear, "We're teaching these young guys early." A few people in the back chuckled and then Coop yelled toward the front, "Hey, Pete, I think Tex has a song that might make us all feel better."

"It's too early," Tex said.

I grunted. "Dude, eight hour bus trip, Penn State, boring countryside, sore arms. It's time for the song."

"Okay, okay," the big Texan said, reaching over and pulling his guitar onto his lap. He started to tune it as everyone inched closer.

"I'll have to dedicate this one to the freshmen," Tex said, making the upper classmen laugh knowingly. "Because there isn't a cloud in the damn sky, and they're getting their first taste of the college baseball grind."

Tex started strumming his guitar as soon as he finished his dedication and I watched those who had never seen him play hold their mouths open in awe due to the gracefulness of Tex's fingers. His voice was low and rich, but he only used it in the chorus. The song he played was sung to the rhythm of, "A Boy Named Sue," by Johnny Cash.

Here at Michigan we've got a team
We're kind of tough, we're pretty mean
but there's one thing that makes us not want to play

We've got a lotta games, we play through the pain
But when clouds are in the sky, we'll be praying for rain
Thirty percent chance? Boys, lets just bag it

There's no chance our coaches would let us do it
They tried to stop us, but we said screw it
and left the sprinklers on all night long

That's the great thing about our staff
They're good for a joke, great for a laugh
Mitchell and Stein were the cheapest they could find

As for Nichols and the man named Gene
They came over from the Grand Valley scene
And I guess they're okay because they're Michigan men

You've still got our dirt bag players to meet
Who leave trash in the wake, and pee on their feet
That's disgusting - I don't care what it cures

First there's this fat hillbilly catcher named Squat
And there's no end to the bullpens he's caught
Which's made him one ornery S.O.B.

Coop's the man now, there's no doubt about that
But on the mound freshmen year he shit in his pants
And became a legend for miles around

Walker might get Big Ten freshmen of the year
But between you and me I think he might be queer
Because he stares a long time at those hitters' butts

I don't want to tell our right fielder Varner
But no amount of pulling is going to make it longer
You just have to live with what you get

Benny and Pete, two peas in a pod
They dive for balls and come up eating sod
But we all love to watch them play

Wes and Lou, well, they love to pick fights
They'll fight you, and every man in sight
As long as they get the first shot, and a sucker punch

Wilson Jack had a pretty nice date to his prom
Some called her Mrs., but he called her mom
I guess that's how they do it in Tennessee

I forgot about McGee, the poor steroid monkey
Wanted to get bigger, but turned into a junky
Took his roid rage out on the man they called Shakes

Speaking of Shakes, the fill-in first baseman
Has a freshmen year home run record he's chasin'
And before the season he thought he'd never play!

Then there's the handsome first baseman named Tex
He asks for a kiss, the ladies give him sex
But he punched Wes in the face and broke his hand

I almost left out Franklin, he's pretty fucking good
He thinks he belongs, the coaches aren't sure if he should
And he still shoves every time he touches the mound

That's our squad, like it or not
We're a damn good team, but we still keep Squat
and he's in the back praying for rain

"I haven't really thought of a way to finish it," Tex said with a laugh, still strumming the chords as if trying to think of another verse.

All of the freshmen got a kick out of Tex's song, but even after they made him sing it a few times the long bus ride started to wear on them and everyone either shifted their attention to the movie or to sleep. Bill Hum always loved the bus because he was in charge of movies, and for this bus trip he had selected *Fight Club, Monty Python and the Holy Grail,* and *The Evil Dead.*

"Put in *Forrest Hump,*" Wilson Jack, who always had a tough time with bus trips because he could never sit still, yelled from the back, causing a dozen guys to break out in requests for more movies.

"Put in *Terms of Enrearment!*"

"Put in *Poca-hot-ass!*"

"Put in *Intercourse with a Vampire!*"

Wilson didn't like Hum, let alone the movies he picked, so the only options Wilson had left were to sleep or read because everyone else was asleep. Wilson wasn't much of a reader and he never slept well on buses, so he made bathroom trips every fifteen minutes or so, just to see who was awake. During one of his typical bathroom runs, climbing over people who were sleeping across the aisles and under the seats, he saw Benny reading a book in the back seat. Wilson sat down next to him with a thump and asked Benny what the special occasion was.

"The man who struggles to get through his classes every semester is reading a book ladies and gentlemen," Wilson announced to his silent audience of snoring baseball players.

"It's probably one of the best baseball books ever written," Benny said.

"What is it?" Wilson grabbed the book out of Benny's hand, not even thinking about keeping his spot for him, and examined the cover. "The Natural?"

"Don't tell me you've never heard of it."

"Of course I've heard of it," Wilson said. "I'm just surprised that, out of all people, you are reading something that isn't related to class work."

"I study enough to get by," Benny snapped.

"Don't get your panties in a bunch. I just thought it was unusual to see you reading."

"I only read baseball books, if anything."

"Hey, I remember now, *The Natural* is that movie with Robert Redford where he hits that home run in the end and the lights blow up into a million pieces and shit." Wilson nodded his head in excitement, proud that he remembered the movie.

"Yeah, but the movie is a lot different than the book."

"Like how?"

"Well," Benny said, starting to get annoyed, "for starters, the Robert Redford character strikes out in the end and blows the game. And that is the only at-bat in the game he really tries, because in the movie he throws away the first three at-bats because he took money to throw the game. Then he hits his girlfriend in the stands with a foul ball, and finds out later she's pregnant. It ends before it really tells if he gets kicked out of baseball for good or not, but I'm pretty sure he does."

"That's pretty fucking depressing. Why would they make the ending so different in the movie?"

"I don't know, I guess no one likes a sad ending."

"But you do?"

Benny shrugged. "I guess not, but it's kind of like every time I read it I'm still rooting for Roy to not strike out, like if I read it again maybe he won't blow the game. Maybe this time when I get to the end he will hit the home run just like in the movie and everyone will be happy. It's kind of refreshing to read about a lead guy in a story who is flawed, who makes wrong decisions, and screws himself at the end."

"Sounds pretty weird to me," Wilson said. "I know I always make the right decisions, I guess they can't write a book about me."

"Shut up, dumbass," Benny said, giving Wilson a punch in the shoulder. Wilson yelped in pain, but shook it off when he thought of another question.

"Wait, how do you know the ending of the book if you are only about halfway through it?"

"I've read it before."

"You're reading it again? Why? Don't you remember it from the first time?"

"You watch movies that you like over again, right?"

"Yeah, but that's different."

"How?"

"It's hard to read books, it takes too much effort."

Benny grinned. "Too much thinking?"

"What are you trying to say, that I'm stupid? I bet my GPA is better than yours."

"I don't have a girlfriend that does my homework for me."

Wilson made a shushing noise. "Not many people know about that, be quiet."

Benny shrugged and went back to his book, but Wilson refused to leave, staring over his shoulder as he read. Benny only lasted a few minutes before he felt the need to say something. "Fuck off, Wilson." Wilson smiled, stood up, and climbed his way back to his seat.

Chapter Thirty-Seven
Win the State

"You can lead a horse to water, but you can't stick his head in it."
        -Paul Owens

The state of Michigan has two Big Ten conference schools, Michigan and Michigan State, and three Mid-American Conference schools, Eastern, Western, and Central Michigan. The University of Oakland also has a Division I sports program, but outside that, there weren't a lot of choices for midweek non-conference games. Midweek games are tough all around; it's hard to get up for them because you're spent from the weekend series, neither team has any pitching left, and some of the overworked position players are usually given the day off. In other words, the games can get a little sloppy.

The coaches tried their best to get the team up, giving us a speech about how important it is to "win the state" for recruiting purposes, but Nichols' words fell on deaf ears. At this point, we had been beaten up pretty consistently since the season started, except for the games against Ohio State, and it didn't look to be getting any better since this week's opponent was Eastern Michigan. EMU always sacrificed their conference games to throw their best pitching at us. We, on the other hand, were coming off a weekend thrashing at the hands of Penn State, where we were lucky to salvage one win out of four games.

We played Eastern on a rainy Tuesday afternoon after we got back from Penn State, and our bats were just as bad as our pitching. We didn't get a runner past second base until late in the game, and then we had to face Eastern's All-American closer, which shut down any hope of a comeback. Franklin, who was a late scratch for a start against Penn State, started for us and did a pretty good job working around several errors. Nichols and Calloway publicly argued about Franklin's talent, and even though he was out pitching several guys on our team, Calloway still thought his place was as a midweek starter.

*****

"Have you guys heard about this douche bag Vandendrich?" Coop asked, his arms folded tight to keep heat from escaping. He was talking about

Eastern's pre-season All-American closer, whose six foot eight inch frame was sitting like a man amongst boys down in the visitor's bullpen.

"No," Merlin said at the same time I said, "Of course, the guy's a complete stud."

"Well, I'm sure he's not that good," Coop said, his breath steaming up the cold air with each word. Coop coughed after he got done talking, but he refused to cover his mouth.

"Baseball America says that he's the best closer in the nation," my words slowed down as my I finished. I shot a glance at Merlin, who just smirked. "I mean, I think that's complete horseshit, anyway. Everyone knows you're the best, Merlin."

"That big goon couldn't spell All-American let alone be one," Merlin said as Franklin struck out the last batter in the seventh inning. Merlin glanced up to the stands where half a dozen radar guns gave way to pencils as scouts wrote down their readings. "DFF is throwing hard today, must be that Michigan blood that allows him to perform in this suck-ass weather."

"Yeah, us guys from Michigan are cool like that," I said with a sheepish grin. The players that were on the field ran into the dugout, followed by Franklin, who did his trademark slow walk from the mound to the bench.

"I'm going to take a jog in case our hitters get their heads out of their asses," Merlin said, taking off down the right field line toward the outfield wall.

I watched Merlin run out of the dugout by himself and then I turned my attention to Franklin, who had resumed his post at the far end of the bench near the coaching staff. I heard the coaches talking to Don, but for some reason it didn't register that I shouldn't interrupt.

"Way to shove it up their butts, DFF," I said with a smile that faded into a grimace as Coach Calloway shot back a glare that said, 'We're kind of busy here dumbass.'

"Thanks," Franklin said, wrapping a towel around his pitching elbow in order to keep it warm between innings. Then he turned the back of his head to me as he and Coach Calloway continued their dialogue.

*****

Vandendrich's first pitch whizzed past Varner's ear and I thought I saw Varner show fear for the first time since I'd known him.

"He's throwing fucking gas," I said under my breath. "We have no chance."

Jesus, thought Varner at that very instant, *I have no fucking chance.* Vandendrich stared down Varner as he got the ball back from the catcher. Vandendrich's eyebrows burrowed into a 'V' shape and the look on his face said the last pitch wasn't a mistake.

"'To announce my presence with authority,'" Bill Hum said on the top step of the bench, the allusion more of a reaction to the situation rather than an attempt to be funny.

"Bull Durham," Benny said from behind Hum. Hummer turned, pointed at his nose and then back at Benny before returning his attention back to the game, where Vandendrich was blowing another fastball past Varner.

*****

Up in the booth, Archie had the call on the final play of the game, "Tex swings and hits a towering pop up that heads over to foul ground behind first base. The second basemen Yurich and the first basemen O'Conner give chase and Yurich will call off O'Conner and catch it easily in this early evening sky to give the Wolverines their fifth loss in six games. That moves Michigan's record to 14-15. Well, you have to give it to the Eagles pitching staff today, holding the men in blue to just four hits on their way to a shut out.

"Edwin gets the win for the Eagles today, he improves to a record of four wins and two losses, and propels the Eagles to a recent record high of twenty eight wins against only nine losses. Franklin is the hard luck loser today, going all eight innings for the Wolverines, surrendering five hits and only one run as the blue nine loses, one run to nil."

*****

"Franklin, come here for a second," Coach Calloway said as the team was loading their equipment into the bus and getting ready to take the ride back to Ann Arbor. Franklin, who was talking to his parents at the moment, told them to hold their thoughts while he had a quick word with the coach. Franklin turned from his parents and walked over to where the coach was standing by the team bus, holding the ice bags on his shoulder as he walked to make sure they didn't fall off.

"What is it, Coach?" Franklin asked. The game had only been over for about fifteen minutes and Franklin was still sweating from his gutsy performance, but talking to Calloway made him sweat even more.

"I think you're throwing too many fastballs, Don," Calloway said, stunning Franklin for a second.

"What do you mean?" Franklin asked, his voice shaking while he tried to control his frustration.

"There are situations in the game, Don, where you need to pitch around some people," Calloway said, moving his hands in the air as he talked, trying to emphasize his point. "For instance, you have to know from the first couple innings tonight that our offense just wasn't clicking. That means that when you get runners in scoring position, you have to be more careful than you usually would."

"Coach, with all due respect…"

"You know what? Save it Franklin, I don't want to hear your excuses this time. I am the coach and I am telling you that you lost the game for us tonight by throwing a fastball to that four hole guy with a runner in scoring

180

position and a base open. If you don't want to be coachable then fine, I'm just not sure when I can throw you again. I won't have pitchers on my staff that aren't willing to learn from their coaches." Calloway turned and climbed the stairs on the bus, leaving Franklin in a stunned silence, unable to move.

Feeling defeated, Franklin walked back over to his parents and thanked them for coming. Then he got his stuff out of the dugout, and mounted the bus. All of his teammates congratulated him on his performance, but it just made Franklin feel worse. On the bus ride home he informed Merlin that there was definitely going to be some drinking going on at the University Towers that night.

Chapter Thirty-Eight
Rain Dance

"[D]on't pray when it rains if you don't pray when the sun shines."
    -Satchel Page

Iowa came into town that Friday night and gave us an old fashioned ass kicking. Coop gave up five runs on seven hits in just an inning and two thirds. The forecast for the overnight hours was cloudy with a seventy percent chance of rain, and no one was complaining. Coop had a hard time that night, he got his ass handed to him by the worst team in the league on Friday, and even though he had no chance of seeing the playing field for the rest of the series, he still didn't want to sit through a double header. As soon as he saw there was a good chance of rain during the night, he made a phone call.

*****

Merlin, Coop, and I were already standing out by the dugout when Benny got to the field. He went straight through the locker room and out into the stadium, surprised to see the three of us at the field so early. The early morning sun was starting to burn off the dew that had formed overnight, and Benny noticed we were staring at the cloudless Saturday morning sky as he approached.

"What the hell are you guys doing here so early?" Benny asked before we knew he was walking up on us. None of us answered right away, and Benny took the opportunity to scan the field in silence, taking in the scenery of the well groomed surface meeting the morning air.

"60% chance of rain," Cooper snorted, breaking the serenity of the moment. "What kind of a bullshit job is the weatherman anyway? Bastards never get it right."

Merlin smirked. "Oh and how they play with our emotions." Benny looked at me, waiting for me to comment, but I said nothing.

"You amaze me," Benny said while letting his eyes drift over the field.

"I know," Merlin answered, "I amaze myself too."

"Shut up, Merlin," Coop said, turning to walk back to the locker room.

"Don't be bitter, all-star," Merlin responded to Coop's back. "You've already made your start." We watched as Coop disappeared down the tunnel and inside the locker room.

I sighed. "He's just pissed because he has a date tonight and he was banking on a rain out."

Benny had a disgusted look on his face. "I can't believe you guys," he said. "All this pray for rain bullshit has gotten out of hand."

"It's just a joke, Benny," I said. "It's not like we literally sit around and pray to God for it to rain so we don't have to play."

"It's no joke to me," Benny snapped. "It's insulting. No, it's more than that, it's tragic. It's over after this season, don't you see that?"

"Fuck off," I elevated my voice louder and louder as I talked. "You think I don't know that?" I stared at my feet after speaking, trying to get a hold on my temper.

"Whoa, guys," Merlin said while backpedaling. "It's obvious you two have some unresolved outside issues affecting your moods. Look, it's a sunny Saturday morning and…"

"Quiet, Merlin," Benny snapped.

Merlin blinked. "Yeah I know." He retreated into the locker room without another word, leaving Benny and I by ourselves.

"So what's up Benny?" I asked. "It's not like you to act like this."

"Sorry," Benny said, the anger gone from his voice. "This attitude you guys have just wears on me. It's so opposite of what I believe in, it just kills me that my teammates, guys that I would lay it all on the line for, would rather spend the waning moments of their baseball careers at home watching it rain than playing baseball."

"We can't all be like you," I said.

"Don't start that shit."

"No, really. I know it's hard to believe, but it isn't always a love affair with this game, or the coaches, or the university. We all have outside issues that wear us down, but not you. It's hard to live up to your standards, the great infallible Benjamin Marker, whose entire focus is strictly confirmed to athletics. It's minimal in school, and absent in social life, except for front porch stories. You have no other focus, but we do. Not to mention the fact that I've seen 99.9% of my games here from the end of the bench we call the bullpen."

"Stop it, R.J."

"You stop it, Benji." I turned and went back into the locker room, leaving Benny alone out on the field. When I disappeared from the Benny's sight, I hid in the mudroom and watched Benny go over to the visitor's dugout and sit down on the bench. As he sat there I wondered what it would feel like if Benny was on a different team. What it would be like to come to play against him knowing U of M had turned him down as a player out of high school. I wondered what would have happened to Benny if he wouldn't have played baseball or what if he wouldn't have made the squad his freshman year.

I knew Benny had spent every drop of his energy on baseball during his four years at Michigan. Benny pushed everyone to be better, but while that made our team stronger, it brewed up a lot of hostility toward Benny, and I knew that that made him sad.

"Super Doppler 9000 my ass!" yelled a voice from the tunnel. It was Wes, yelling at no one in particular, upset like everyone else that it wasn't raining. *We're going to get our asses kicked today*, I thought.

I was wrong, however, and from the very start of the double header it was clear that either Iowa had been up all night boozing or they had wished that it would rain even more than we did. Wilson Jack got out of the first after surrendering only one hit, a harmless two out blooper over Lou's head at third base. Benny led off the home half of the inning with a double. He was pissed that Nichols held him at second base, so he stole third on the first pitch to Wes. Then Wes hit a deep fly ball to center field and Benny scored easily on the sacrifice fly to make it 1-0, and we never looked back. Walker and Tex, hitting three and four in the lineup, had back to back doubles, and then Lou hit a towering opposite field home run to make it 4-0 in the first, en route to the offense providing nine runs in the short, seven inning game.

Wilson held off the Iowa bats for most of the game, surrendering only two runs on three hits until he lost his control and starting walking the house in the sixth. Nichols decided to bring Merlin in a little early, and the stands exploded with radar guns. Merlin had a little trouble getting out of the mess that Wilson made, giving up a double to the first batter he faced, which scored a run and left runners at second and third. But he struck out the next hitter and made quick work of the Hawkeye hitters in the seventh as we won 9-3.

After we tasted victory in the first game of the doubleheader, there was no holding us back in the nightcap as Chase Warner went seven strong innings on the mound and Iowa threw their entire pitching staff at our lineup but still couldn't manage to hold us under doubled digits. When the final out was recorded, we won 12-1, and the team went screaming into the locker room and sang the fight song louder than any other day during the year. The two wins gave us sole possession of fourth place in the Big Ten standings, and we were only three games out of first place in a very close conference race.

"Great wins today, guys," Coach Nichols said after the game. "But we really need to go out and win tomorrow. I know it was tough to lose that game on Friday night, but it is important that we continue to stay focused and win tomorrow. Iowa is having a tough season this year, and we need to take advantage of that in order to secure our spot in the conference tournament, because we all know that Ohio State and Minnesota will probably wax the floor with them. Great wins guys, but come out fired up tomorrow."

We came out fired up to play on Sunday, but so did the Hawkeyes, and we were neck and neck in the top of the ninth inning, tied at three runs apiece. Benny wasn't having a particularly good game that day, and he started to wonder if he used all his luck up the day before. Just then a Hawkeye batter ripped a ball deep over his head to lead off the ninth. As he chased it back he peeked toward the wall and saw it he was approaching it quickly.

"Wall! Wall! WAAAALL!" Pete yelled from left field, desperately trying to warn Benny. Benny kept running anyway, picturing the ball landing in his mitt before he crashed into the fence, still believing he could reach it. But at the last second, before he extended his arms, he hesitated, and I know he saw nothing but the doctor's face. He slid to a stop on the warning track and the ball bounced off the wall an arm-length over where his head would have hit. It ricocheted over Benny's head and back to where both Pete and Varner were backing up the play. Varner took control of the situation, grabbing the ball and firing it toward the infield. It was too late to prevent the damage, however, and the Iowa hitter was able to take third on the play.

Iowa had no one out and three solid tries to plate the go-ahead run, so Nichols pulled the infield and outfield in to cut the runner off at home. Benny crept in to a distance where he knew he could throw out the runner at home. Benny didn't have the greatest arm for college baseball, but he wanted the chance to throw out a runner at home more than ever. Unfortunately, he didn't even get the chance to be tested. After the next hitter popped up behind the plate for the first out, the next batter hit a single up the middle. We failed to get any offense going in the bottom of the ninth and ended up losing the game 4 runs to 3.

"I got scared," Benny confided in me after the game. He knew no one blamed him for the play. There aren't many outfielders with the guts it would have taken to make that play because it would have required nothing short of a head first dive into the wall. But at the same time, it was a play that Benny usually came up with. "I can't let it happened again, I just have to suck it up next time."

"Bullshit you do," I said. "You've been hard nose all your life, Benny, but smashing your head into the wall doesn't really prove anything. For Christ's sake, are you going to tell the coaches, or should I?"

"You can't, Squat," Benny said. "I may not ever play again after this season."

I laughed. "Well, don't worry about it Benji because I definitely won't be playing anywhere after this season."

Chapter Thirty-Nine
The Wizard at Work Part Two

"The most important things in life are good friends and a strong bullpen."
  -Bob Lemon

How can I even begin to describe Michael Merlin. Well, he was a bit of a drinker, a very good guy, but an even better pitcher. Unfortunately, alcohol always seemed to get in the way of his promising baseball career. Even Franklin and Smalls weren't doing much to help him kick the habit. For example, an entire year after losing hundreds of thousands of dollars in signing bonus because of a drunken driving offense, and during a game with a ton of scouts just begging for the chance to see him pitch, this happens...

*****

"Holy shit, Mike, get the fucking ball down. You're gonna get hammered out there," I yelled from underneath my mask. I lobbed the ball high in the air back to Merlin, intending to give a few more seconds for his words to sink in. To my amazement Merlin just stood there and squinted at me, still holding his glove at his side like I had not thrown the ball back yet.
    "Christ, Merlin, look out!" I yelled as the ball bounced off the shoulder of his throwing arm. He grabbed his shoulder as if he wasn't quite sure what happened. Then, realizing he had just been hit by the ball, he stood there for a second, then walked over and picked up the ball. After picking up the ball, he slowly walked back to the mound. I continued to look on as Merlin took off his mitt, put it under his arm, and then bent over to grab some dirt and rub up the ball. After putting his mitt back on, he looked at me for the first time.
    "You gonna catch," Merlin said, "or just stand there with your mouth open." Merlin started into his motion, reached back, and fired the ball five feet over my head. I tried to jump to catch the ball, but it was out of my reach. I watched as the ball sailed completely out of the bullpen and into the stands. I pulled my mask off my head and yelled out a half-hearted "heads-up," but I knew it would probably do more damage than harm. I always thought it was better for someone to take it in the back of the head than to yell "heads-up" and have them take it in the face. I watched as the ball drilled a spectator square in the arm, and as everyone around him rushed to his aid, Smalls popped the ball up and the air and made the third out of the inning. As soon as the second

baseman from the other team caught the ball, the Police's "Every Little Thing She Does is Magic" blared over the loudspeakers.

"Well," Merlin said, "that's my cue." Merlin put his glove down on the ground in order to tighten his shoe laces. Before he ran onto the field, he paused for a second to reach in his back pocket and tossed something toward me. I caught the bottle in my mitt and checked out the label, which read, "Jack Daniels."

"Oh God," I said out loud.

"What did he throw to you?" Tucker asked when I got back to the dugout.

I swallowed hard and ran my fingers through my hair. "An empty bottle of whiskey."

"Oh God," Tucker said.

"Holy shit," Wilson said, jumping off the bench to get a look at the bottle. "Did he drink it in the bullpen?"

"We're going to find out," I said.

The Padres scout who talked to Merlin that morning was sitting in the stands behind home plate, his radar gun pointed right at Merlin's right shoulder, but Merlin wasn't worried. *Here goes nothing*, thought Merlin with a laugh, the alcohol preventing him from being serious. He peeked up at the scoreboard. Michigan led 8-7 in the bottom of the ninth, and Merlin had the game over before he knew what was happening.

The first batter of the inning tried to bunt the first pitch, but popped it up behind home plate, giving Walker an easy play for the first out. The second batter jumped at the first pitch too, but this time with a full swing, grounding out weakly to Wes at second base. Merlin threw the first pitch to the third hitter behind the guy's back. He shrugged toward home plate when the batter looked at him with anger, and mouthed the words, "It slipped." The next pitch was inside too, but for some reason the batter swung at it, more in self-defense that anything and popped up to Smalls.

The crowd cheered and our bench cleared, running out onto the field to congratulate each other after the win.

"Good job, Merlin," Smalls said.

Merlin flinched. "Yeah, you, good job, too."

"Way to make quick work of them, Merlin," Coach Calloway said.

"Of course quick work I did, yup."

"Merlin," I said, grabbing him after the team finished giving each other high fives and holding him on the field for an extra second until most everyone was out of earshot. "Are you drunk?"

"I am drunk."

"Honestly? You weren't just fucking with me with the Jack Daniels, right?"

"Why? Do I have any left?"

I smirked. "Shit, I better give you a ride home."

"Yeah," Merlin said, "you better."

187

Chapter Forty
Home Plate Rendezvous

"Experience is a hard teacher because she gives the test first, and the lesson afterwards."
    -Vernon Law, Pittsburgh Pirates pitcher

We traveled to Champaign, Illinois, the next weekend, looking to move up in the Big Ten standings against a struggling Fighting Illini squad, but we laid an egg and kissed sisters after winning the first two games. So I didn't blame the rest of the guys when they decided to fire it up Sunday night after we got back, but I had other plans. I had been in contact with Beth over the few weeks leading up to that Sunday night, trying to talk things out and apologize for the way I had acted. I played it as smooth as I could, pretending I just wanted to mend my ties with her and be friends, but I knew Coop was right when he told me I was still in love with her, so I kept plotting day and night, trying to figure out a way to win her back. I recruited Benny to help me with Beth, and I invited her to the party Sunday night at South Fifth. I gave Benny the job of redirecting her to the field, and I personally placed him on the couch on the front porch of the South Fifth house, leaving him with strict instructions: remain sober long enough to spot her coming.

*****

It only took Benny a few hours before he started drinking and getting into the stories. Paul Walker, who wasn't very good at talking in the first place, tried his hand at a story, causing uproar.

"Jesus Christ, Walker. You've got to be the worst goddamn story teller I have ever heard."

"Yeah, no shit," Wes said. "It's time to shut that shit down." Drunken laughter erupted around him and Walker looked around him as everyone laughed at his expense, trying to think of a comeback. When he looked behind him and into the living room of the house, he got all the ammunition he needed.

"Yeah, well, I got a pretty funny story," he said, "how about Weasel's sister and every guy within three city blocks." Walker pointed over his shoulder and through the front window of the house. The guys on the porch, including

Wes, followed his finger to see Cassie dancing on the stripper's pole with a group of guys around her cheering.

"Well I gotta go," Benny said, sensing a fight in the forecast. Wes pushed Benny back into his seat as he started to stand and Benny decided it was time to verbally intervene before something bad happened. "Ah, c'mon Wes, not that many people have been with her, Walker is just kidding. We've all been looking out for her ever since her John Cooper experience, just like you said."

"Well, Lumberg fucked her," Hummer said.

"*Office Space*," the group said in between laughs.

"Lumberg?" Walker said, lining up the knockout punch, but just before he did, Benny saw Beth poke her head into the group and he remembered me talking about how she might show up. He knew what Walker was about to say, and he knew how it would affect Beth, but his reflexes were too slow from the alcohol to stop Paul. "Lumberg? That's nothing compared to Squat," Benny stood up and pushed his way out of the group when he saw Beth turn and run off the porch. As he ran after her down South Fifth Avenue he could still hear laughing on the porch and Walker continuing the joke, "Am I right? Am I right? Squat and Cassie, boy is that a disgusting mental picture."

Benny squinted through the dark as he chased her, fearing he would lose her before he could explain to her what Walker had meant. She took a sharp left into a church parking lot, a place that people who partied in the area often used to put their cars for the night. She had to pause to shuffle for her car keys and it gave Benny just enough time to reach her.

"Beth," he gasped while grabbing her shoulder. She turned with a shriek, tears staining her cheeks and ruining her make-up.

"Benny," she sobbed, turning back to her car and opening the door. "I was just leaving." She jumped into the driver's seat and started to shut the door. Benny grabbed the door the same time she did and help it open.

"Wait," he said, "you're making a mistake."

She let go of the door and wiped the tears from her eyes. "I made a mistake just coming here." She stretched to look at the condition of her make-up in the rear view mirror. "I can't believe I let him talk me into coming."

"I know you heard what we were talking about." She sniffled and looked him in the eye. He continued, "Wes's sister showed interest in Squat in the fall, he said he told you that."

"Vaguely."

"Nothing happened, Walker was just trying to make fun of Wes. Cassie talked to Squat a couple times, but that's it; they just talked. When she found out he never played she started ignoring him and hooked up with Coop."

She sighed, "Really?"

"Yeah, really. I swear."

"You're one of R.J.'s best friends, how do I know you're not just covering up for him."

"Do you really think I'm the kind of guy that would do something like that?" Benny asked.

"No."

"Alright then, Squat is waiting for you at the field."

"The baseball field, why?"

"He wanted it to be a surprise. He wanted me to set it up somehow, like he forget something down there and needed you to meet him there before coming back to the party. I was supposed to grab you as soon as you got to South Fifth and tell you."

"I don't understand."

"Okay, look, I don't want to ruin the surprise, but he has this whole picnic thing set up for you at home plate. He has really put a lot of effort into it. Don't tell him I told you, he really wanted it to be a surprise."

She reached for the door. "I won't tell him."

After she closed the door, Benny knocked on the window and she rolled it down. "He still loves you, Beth. Just give him a chance to talk tonight." She nodded, rolled up the window, and drove off toward the field. Benny watched the back of her car until she drove out of sight, and then he started to walk back toward the party, saying a little prayer for me as he did.

*****

"You know, I wasn't even going to come," Beth said, appearing out of the darkness. She took a look around to see what I had set up. A giant blanket covered up home plate and both batter's boxes, and I had candles all along the edges and two in the middle for light. There was a wicker picnic basket by my side filled with food wrapped in saran wrap, and two large plates in the middle. For a moment I couldn't even hear what she said because I was mesmerized by the way she looked and how much I had riding on the moment.

When my brain finally woke up I replied, "Why?"

She was silent as she contemplated her response. I saw pain in her face through the candlelight and I felt a twinge of panic.

"Who's Cassie?" Beth asked and then bit her lower lip.

"Cassie?" I had a tough time coming up with much else besides a mumble.

"Yeah, Cassie," she pulled her skirt down to cover her ankles and then sat down and hugged her knees. "I overheard someone at the party tonight say something about you and Wes's sister. They said her name was Cassie."

"Beth, you have to believe me…"

"I will, Squat. Just tell me what I want to hear."

"I wouldn't say it just because you want to hear it," I pleaded. "She was the first girl that paid attention to me since I'd been in college. The first girl since you, but she tossed me aside for Cooper when she found out I was a bench warmer."

"Did anything happen?"

"No," I spat. "I never even talked to her on the phone." Beth raised her eyebrows, probing me for a lie. "I swear to God. I met her this fall and…"

"I wouldn't care R.J...."

"...I didn't see her again until the alumni game where..."

"...it really makes no difference..."

"...she ended up making out with Coop. That was the night I called you."

"So you thought of me when you were rejected by the only girl who talked to you since we went out. Thanks."

I adverted my eyes.

"R.J.," she said while staring at me, refusing to give me any ground. She had been hurt too much by me already. There was no way she was going to make this easy.

"I'm not sure what else I can say," I said softly. "I've spent every day of the last four years regretting the decision I made. I've missed you every second. I didn't call you that night because she passed me up for Coop, I called you because I was never so sure I screwed up the best thing I ever had. Baseball, my social life, school, my family, all of it was in the shitter, but I had you. You made all that stuff seem better, you made me feel better about myself, and since we broke up it's just been one day after another that I wake up hoping it's raining so I don't have to leave my apartment."

"Don't be so dramatic, R.J." Beth rolled her eyes and I felt like screaming; I didn't know how else I could tell her how I felt. "Don't give me the manic depressive routine," she said. "I know you better than that. I haven't even talked to you for the last four years, but I still know you better than that."

"I love you, Beth." The words burst out of me before I knew what I was saying and then I cringed as I waited for Beth's reaction.

"I don't even know why I'm here," she said under her breath while she brushed herself off and stood up, her face disappearing from the candlelight and taking my hopes with it. "I think I better just go. You broke my heart when you left me, R.J., and I was just starting to get over you. Now I get drunk phone calls in the middle of the night and everyone that you know trying to tell me that you still love me, but I can't just go back to the way it was. I'm different now and I think that you're different now, too."

"Wait," I said. "You can't leave; I did all of this for you."

"And it's very sweet," she said. "But I just can't put myself out to be hurt again. This was a very sweet gesture, but I'm sorry." She kept backing up until she left the candlelight, then she turned and ran out of the stadium, leaving me by myself in the soft glow of the candles and cloudy, moonless night.

Chapter Forty-One
Pick Me Up

"There's only one thing bigger than me, and that's my ego."
-Dave Parker

There was about a month left in the regular season when Beth walked out on my attempt to reconcile our relationship. Northwestern was coming into town, but I couldn't have cared less. I sat on the bench and watched Coop pitch on that Friday night thinking of Beth and how messed up things had gotten. Coop pitched seven innings, allowing two earned runs and striking out nine. By that time, the fifteen radar guns in the stands had reduced to four, even though Merlin came in to pitch the ninth inning.

We won the game 5-2, Coop picked up his eighth win of the season and Merlin got his ninth save. We sang the fight song loud and proud in the locker room after the game, but I couldn't put my heart into it. Coop's constant success made matters worse. Some people have some weird gift with luck, my dad always told me when I was little, and they always fall in shit and come out smelling like roses. I was starting to understand what my dad meant.

After the team had breakfast on Saturday morning Coop was on his phone with scouts before we got back to our apartment. There was about an hour downtime before we had to be at the field, and Coop didn't put his phone down once. When I tapped my watch with twenty minutes left Coop shushed me with a finger to the lips and I lost it.

"Don't shush me, shit-head," I said with clenched fists.

"Jerry, are you going to be at the game today?" Coop asked into the phone, waiting for an answer while looking into my eyes. "Great, I'll talk to you after the game." He hung up and said through gritted teeth, "I was on the phone with the Mariners. Besides we still have twenty minutes, what's your problem?"

"Do you even have to ask?"

Tex looked up from the kitchen table where he was reading the morning newspaper. He sighed when he saw me standing off with Coop.

"I don't understand why you're blaming me for this," Coop said. "It seems to me that you did your best and she made her decision, just live with it, and move on."

"Fuck you, Coop," I said with a quivering lip. "You're part of the reason I'm in this mess."

"What are you talking about? It's my fault because I stole Wes's sister from you? If I hadn't done that then you wouldn't have even tried to get back with Beth, which was my fucking suggestion in the first place! Why don't you blame Walker? It was his big mouth that started it." Coop cleared his throat, trying to settle himself down. "This is a really important time for me, Squat. I'm putting all my time and effort into baseball right now and I can't be distracted…" he trailed off as I took a step forward, getting right in his face.

"You're such a selfish prick," I said. "Don't you care about how I feel?"

"Get the fuck out of my face," Coop said, pushing me in the chest with both hands. "Of course I care how you feel, that's why I was at the field that night, watching from the tunnel to see if you could pull it off. I know how much she means to you and I'm sorry about what happened, but if she can't be persuaded by what Benny told her, and what you said that night, I say fuck her. You're shouldn't have to beg, you shouldn't…" he trailed off again, shook his head and stormed out of the apartment, slamming the door loudly behind him.

"Squat," Tex said, looking up from the paper, "what's going on?"

"Don't worry about it." I turned away from Tex and headed off to my room while saying over my shoulder, "I'm going to get my stuff. Can you give me a ride to the field?"

"No problem."

"Alright, give me a second."

*****

"Have you seen Squat today?" Benny asked when he saw Coop in the locker room. "You have to help me do this Coop, you're his roommate for Christ's sake, think of all the shit he has done for you."

"First of all," Coop said with a confrontational glare in his eye, "that fat little fuck has never done anything really substantial for me. Second of all, what the hell am I going to tell her that she doesn't already know? 'Hello, Beth? Yeah, this is Coop. Listen, I fucked Cassie Roth so I think you should get back together with R.J.' Yeah, that would help."

"How could you turn your back on him like that?" Benny raised his voice and Coop took a step back.

"You need to relax, Benji." Coop's cell phone rang and he picked it up without hesitation. "Hello?" Benny stormed out of the locker room, leaving Coop alone. The phone call was from the Rangers, but Coop decided he would rather stay in the locker room and talk about draft scenarios than go on the field and shag flies for batting practices.

"What if we drafted you in the third round and offered you three fifty?"

"We'd have to see." It was Coop's default answer, and he just put it on repeat for situations like this, trying not to give the scouts much information.

"What if we drafted you in the fourth round and offered you three seventy?"

"We'd have to see."

"What if we drafted you in the first round and offered you one point two?"

"We'd have to see."

"What if we..."

Coop was hearing the words, but he wasn't listening.

"What if we drafted you in the second round and offered you one point three?"

"We'd have to see."

*****

When the doubleheader was over and we'd taken two games from the Wildcats of Northwestern, Benny found Coop standing by his truck in the parking lot and talking on his cell phone.

"Yeah, that's right," Coop laughed. "Yeah, he still does that sometimes, too. Yeah, I can't believe the smell, either." Coop held up a finger to Benny when he approached. "Hey, Benny is here now and he said that he really wanted to talk to you. Okay, talk to you later. Yup, here he is." Coop handed the phone to Benny.

Benny held his hand over the receiver. "Who is it?"

"Just talk, okay, I fixed everything."

Benny put the phone up to his ear. "Hello?"

"Hi, Benny."

"Beth."

"Coop called me and told me the whole story. He's right, I overreacted."

"So can I talk you into coming down to give Squat another chance?"

"Maybe. I might be free in a couple weeks."

"Well, I'll tell you what, I might be able to convince Coach Nichols to start Squat in our last midweek game of the season against Eastern Michigan. But whether or not he plays, I would really like to get you two together. Would you be up for it?" Benny looked at Coop, who slapped Benny on the back.

"Are you happy now, Benji?" Coop mouthed.

Benny nodded and shook Coop's hand.

"Okay," Beth said after a long silence and a few sniffles. "Hey, Benny?"

"What?"

"I have some single girls that I live with, would you be interested?" she laughed into the receiver. "I mean, I told them how great of a guy you are and I thought that maybe I could help you out the same way you've helped Squat."

Benny grimaced. "I'm kind of married to baseball right now, Beth, thanks anyway." He paused while his college life flashed in front of his eyes. He'd been focused on baseball for so long that he didn't even remember what it was like to be on a date. "I'll tell you what, if we get to the summer and I don't get picked up, I just might take you up on that offer."

Chapter Forty-Two
Squat's Grand Finale

"I'm the only man in the history of the game who began his career in a slump and stayed in it."
-Rocky Bridges

I had just finished warming up Tucker before the last midweek game of the season at Eastern Michigan when I saw her. She was sitting just above the dugout, right next to my mother, her face beaming with the most beautiful smile I had ever seen. My heart stopped for a second and I had to swallow hard in order to get it going again. I looked from her face to the sky, where there wasn't a cloud around, just the bright sun fading on the horizon.

The game started a few minutes later, and everyone got a little annoyed at my unusual enthusiasm, but I didn't let anyone know where it was coming from. We were down 2-0 early after Tucker had a difficult time getting out of the first, but he started to cruise after that and the game went into fast motion. But I could care less about the game, and I turned to get a glimpse of Beth whenever I could. Soon the game was in the eighth inning and the guys on our bench starting looking pretty grim when we saw Earl Vandendrich's six-foot eight inch figure get up in the Eastern Michigan bullpen.

"Fuck," Franklin said when he saw Vandendrich starting to get loose, "they got that fucking giant up."

Coop looked down the bench, taking note of the slumped shoulders and frustrated expressions of the coaches and the bench players and said, "Well, this one's over."

"Don't be so negative, guys," I said while fidgeting with my chest protector. "We're only down by one run."

"Earth to Squat," Franklin said, pointing down toward the Visitor bullpen. "The All-American closer who blows absolute fucking cheddar is up to close out the game. It's not like we had a lot of fucking success against him last time, he struck out all three batter's he faced on three pitches for Christ's sake."

"He's not that good," I said.

Coop reached up to feel my forehead but I knocked his hand away. "What's with the positive outlook, Squatster, it's not like you."

"Get your hand off of me," I said.

"Don't get so worked up man, I'm just screwing with you."

"Hey, Squat!" Nobody heard Coach Nichols the first time he called my name, but the entire bullpen turned their attention to the coaches' end of the bench the second time he yelled my name. "Squat!"

"Yeah, Coach?"

"Get that gear off, son. Get your bat ready."

I immediately started peeling off my shin guards and chest protector. I got two steps toward the bat rack before I heard the pitchers starting to buzz behind me.

"Holy shit, Squat is going to hit."

"Well, we're giving this game away now."

"Shut your mouth, he's your friend."

"Friend or not, it's over."

Tucker struck out the batter he was facing just as I picked my bat out of the rack.

"Lead off," Nichols said as he walked past me and up the dugout steps, "I want you to hit for Pete."

"For Pete?"

"That's right," he said. He paused at the top of the dugout stairs, walked back down to where I was standing with my helmet and bat in hand. I imagine that I looked as white as a sheet because Coach Nichols threw his arm around me and walked me out to the on deck circle. Vandendrich was taking him warm up pitches, and I glanced up in the stands to see over a dozen radar guns pointing toward the mound. I saw Cool Cliff standing near the net, and Beth sitting a few rows behind him.

"You're coming off the bench, you're cold, this guy wants to be a first round draft pick," Coach Nichols said.

"Okay," I said, my heart beating fast.

I pulled on my batting helmet and Coach Nichols continued his instructions, "He's going to come right after you, Squat. It's going to be ninety five miles per hour, right down the middle. You know how I say you should never swing at the first pitch, right?"

"Yeah."

Nichols leaned in even closer, almost whispering. "Well, forget it. This asshole is all yours, and he is all yours on the first pitch. Go get him. Go get that douche bag." He released his grip on me and he ran the rest of the way to the coach's box by third base. I glanced up in the stands again, over the head of Cool Cliff, across the sea of scouts, and back into the eyes of Beth, who smiled. I was too scared to smile back, but when my eyes drifted back into the dugout, I saw that everyone was on the top step, including Coach Calloway. I turned my attention back toward the mound and started trying to time Vandendrich's fastball, but I could hardly see it.

Meanwhile, Merlin, Franklin, Cooper, and the rest of the players on the bench were yelling their lungs out for me. It's something I'll never forget.

"Get his ass, Squat!"

"You can do it, Squatster!"

"Relax, baby, no problem."

"You got this!"

"Rip this fucking meat!" Merlin yelled, causing everyone to stop for a second, turn their attention toward Coach Calloway, and wait for a reaction. Coach Calloway, mouth full of sunflower seeds, had one leg up on the top step of the dugout. He put his hand on his hips and thought about what he had to say to Merlin's comment for a couple of seconds. However, his response was not quite what the guys had become accustomed to.

"Light 'em up, guys," he said and everyone went silent. He turned his head down the dugout and flailed his arms toward the field, "I mean it. Let this cocksucker hear what you have. This is no time to be nice and quiet, it's time to break it out, Merlin, let's help Squat out. Let this asshole hear it. You all owe him one, for every single bullpen he has ever slaved through in four years, every game he's sat on the bench and cheered for you, every time he talked you guys up when you felt you were terrible. This could be his moment and it's time to jump on this guy's back to help him out."

The dugout was yelling their lungs out before Calloway was done with his sentence.

"You're going down, you fucking German!"

"We're gonna light you up, meat!"

"Just step off and throw it in the gap!"

"Big bat's coming up, you big dumb asshole!"

"This guy's fastball is higher than his I.Q.," Coop yelled, causing the bench to go into hysterics, including Coach Calloway.

Vandendrich stared over at our bench when the announcer said my name over the loud speaker. He didn't bother looking in for a sign when the umpire yelled for us to play ball, staring Nichols down during his entire windup as if to say, "You've got to be kidding me." The ball left his hand and sailed through the air like a shooting star, leaving a trail of glare in the dark, artificially lit night. I barely managed to get the bat off of my shoulder before the ball sailed past and the umpire made the motion for strike one.

Vandendrich shook his head when he got the ball back and winced his eyes toward home where the catcher was going through the motion of giving him the fastball sign. After nodding his head he went into a slow motion wind-up, trying his best to show me up. Now, I took a lot of flack for being overweight and saying stupid things, but I was still a Division I baseball player, and when that son of a bitch tried to make me look bad, my blood began to boil.

When Vandendrich got to his full leg kick, he sped up to real time motion and fired the ball high. I checked my swing, but the catcher called for an appeal to the base umpire and my heart sank when I looked down and saw Ed Masters looking back at me. My eyes pleaded with Ed, and I think he understood, even though he hated my guts.

"Did he go, Ed?" the home plate umpire yelled and pointed toward first base where Ed had his hands in his pockets to keep them warm on the unusually cold May night.

"No, Frank, he did not," Ed yelled, making a safe motion with his arms.

"You're goddamn right he didn't!" Coop yelled from the dugout where he stood on the top step.

"That's a great goddamn call, Ed," Wilson yelled.

"Fuck that," Vandendrich said, who was almost standing next to me to retrieve the ball.

"Shut your mouth," the home plate umpire said with authority.

"Whatever, I'm still going to strike this horseshit out," he laughed as the catcher handed him the ball.

"You're the horseshit," I yelled, pointing my bat toward Vandendrich's back as he walked away. Everyone on both benches went to the top step and all the fielders took two steps in. I looked at our bench where Coop was looking back and I thought, *Oh shit, did I say that out loud?*

"Oh, what the hell," Tex moaned.

"I got Vandendrich if the benches clear," Wilson Jack said, jumping up and down.

"No, I'll take his punk ass," Mitchell Lewis said, causing everyone to take their eyes off of the ball game for a split second.

Vandendrich, on the other hand, had no other physical reaction to my words besides a smirk. He turned around and started backpedaling toward the mound, saying as he went, "Here comes the best fastball in the nation, chump, let's see what you can do."

"This is just like *Major League 2*," Bill Hum said with awe in his eye.

"Exciting!" Coop yelled, unable to keep his emotions in check.

I dug my back foot hard in the box and Vandendrich toed the rubber, stretching his arms high into the air in order to get his jersey off of his arm another inch or two. He patted his glove and nodded, wasting no time going into his wind-up. He let loose a fierce grunt when he let go of the ball and the only thing faster on the field than the ball was the swing of my bat and the earth shattering sound it made when I connected.

Vandendrich almost blew out a muscle in his neck he turned so fast to track the ball, but it was clearly in the gap, a sizzling one hopper off of the right center field wall. The ball squirted toward center field as I rounded first base, my eyes blurry from adrenaline. The outfielders dashed after the ball, having a long run since they were playing in for the short, fat catcher they had never heard of. The center fielder came up with the ball and threw a perfect strike to the shortstop, but I was running faster than I ever had, and it had taken the center fielder too long to get to the ball. The shortstop rushed the throw, sailing it clear over the third basemen's head and Vandendrich's glove, who was backing up the play.

Our fans and bench were erupting with cheers and applause and the whole world seemed be spinning as Coach Nichols dragged me to my feet and smacked me on the ass before yelling, "Frank we have a pinch runner. Wilson Jack for R.J. Hansen."

"I got it Tom, thanks." The umpire took out a pencil and small notepad where he made note of the change.

"Hot damn, I'm pinch running," Wilson said while grabbing a helmet and running onto the field. He gave me a high five as we passed and a, 'Fuck you,' to Vandendrich under his breath as they nearly swiped shoulders.

Benny, who was the next up to bat, was the first to congratulate me when I reached the bench. "Now pick me up," I said with the biggest smile I'd ever had in my life. I looked up into the stands at Beth's face while the rest of his team mobbed me.

Benny grinned. "You might need sunglasses for this show, son."

Vandendrich, ever the cocky bastard, shook off every off-speed pitch he had when he saw Benny at the plate, and threw a fastball, trying to prove a point that I got lucky.

When Benny turned on the low and inside fastball it seemed to hang in the air forever. The game was going to be tied up for sure, and as the outfield went back, the only question was whether or not the ball was going to be out of the park. The question was answered when the man in right field jumped high over the wall but the ball fell just over his mitt for a home run.

After the ball dropped, the earth shook back into fast motion, and the rest of the night went like a blur, burning hard into the memories of everyone that saw and providing another front porch legend for the team to pass on.

*****

After the game was over, I had a difficult time making it through the crowd to find Beth. Every player and their parents wanted to congratulate me on my triple, but as excited as I was in the moment and as rejuvenated as I felt in my baseball career, the only thing I could think of was Beth, and the moment I had seen her face in the stands before the game.

As I worked my way through the crowd, I found her in the distance, standing on her tip-toes, trying to find me. As I weeded my way through the crowd, I felt the same emotion of joy I felt when I made contact with the ball, and my adrenaline started to pump just like I was rounding the bases. When our eyes met my heart almost exploded and my face split in two by a smile. It was a sense of happiness that even the sight of Cassie Roth blocking the path couldn't wipe away.

"Great job, Squat!" she yelled, wrapping her arms around me before I could resist. I could still see Beth over Cassie's shoulder, and the joy in her face melted a bit when she saw Cassie step forward and embrace me.

"What are you doing tonight?" Cassie asked with her hands all over me. "We have to hang out!"

"Excuse me," I said while calmly sidestepping her, and then briskly walking to where Beth was still waiting for me. Cassie watched in awe as I confidently grabbed my ex-girlfriend by the shoulders and began to kiss her. She dropped her bag and kissed me back. As we wrapped our arms around each other we could hear nothing besides the beating of our hearts, and nothing else mattered but the rekindled love expressed by our lips.

Chapter Forty-Three
Looking Ahead

"The only reason I don't like playing in the World Series is I can't watch myself play."
    -Reggie Jackson

So, that was awesome...

*****

    We took three out of four games from Indiana that weekend and followed it up the next weekend with a clean sweep of Michigan State, propelling us back up into the Big Ten standings and guaranteeing us a spot in the conference tournament.
    I discovered a new motivation for baseball after getting back together with Beth, and I thanked Benny endlessly for his help, and apologized again for our previous argument. I was determined to follow in Benny's footsteps for the last week or two of our careers at Michigan, and enjoy every second I got to be at the field, even if I wasn't in the line-up. "See," Benny told me after I talked about how much more I was enjoying baseball. "Isn't it a great feeling? Now the toughest part is never losing it, no matter what. Don't let anybody or anything ruin your joy for the game again. It's a special thing."
    There was no way we could win the regular season conference championship, but we were feeling confident at this point that we could make a good run at the tournament championship because no one in the conference was as hot as we were. Minnesota was our final Big Ten opponent before the post-season, and our last chance to give ourselves a better position in the tournament. Currently, Minnesota was neck in neck with Ohio State for first with Illinois running third and us, Penn State, Michigan State, and Northwestern rounding out the top six.
    Coach Nichols decided to start Franklin on Friday night, much to Calloway's disgust, and save Coop for Sunday because he had been complaining of arm problems. Coop said he was willing to tough it out, but the coaching staff didn't want to risk anything, so they gave him a couple more days off.
    When Friday came, Nichols gave the team a great speech about tradition, how we had made him proud, and how we were all worthy of being called Michigan men. Then he told us about our current situation, and what the

series with Minnesota meant to our team, "They knocked you guys out last year, so even though we all know that we have solidified a spot in the post-season, I want nothing more than to go out and show these guys they got lucky last year and if they meet us in the tourney, we are going to mop the floor with them. If we split we can easily get into third place, or if we take three of four or sweep we can get into second, which is pretty damn impressive considering our slow start."

Later, after the hoopla in the locker room had died down, the majority of the pitching staff was relaxing in the locker room and shooting the bull.

"So what are those jackass scouts telling you guys?" Wilson Jack asked while flipping through the channels on the TV. Every pitcher besides Franklin was sitting inside waiting for the game to start while the position players were on the field taking an infield.

"Don't be sour because they aren't talking to you, Wilson," Coop said with a smirk, prompting Wilson to give him the finger. "Calm down, Wilson, I'm just fucking with you."

"Yeah, well, you don't even know," Wilson said. "The scouts are to talking to me, they are saying stuff like, 'Hey, have you seen John Cooper?' or 'Excuse me, I'm trying to get by.'"

Coop laughed. "C'mon, you've had a pretty solid season. They aren't saying anything to you?"

"No, Cool Cliff told me I was terrible. He said that I had to mix in at least one strike per batter in order to be effective at the next level." Wilson joined in with the rest of the room and laughed at himself. "Okay, really. I want to know what they've told you. The draft is only a week after the Big Ten Tournament so they must be all over your nuts right now."

"Yeah," Coop said, "most of the teams are trying to convince me not to get an agent, saying if I do it they'll promise me more money. Otherwise I might have to hold out before I get what I want. Besides, Squat said he could get me millions. He made me sign my name to a napkin that said he'd be my agent."

The room laughed together and then Tucker asked, "What about you, Merlin? What have they told you about agents?"

"Agent?" Merlin laughed. "I'm a fifth year senior, bro. That means I'm just hoping to get drafted and sign for a six pack and gas money to get to spring training. There are only about two or three teams even looking at me. There's something about that whole jail time fiasco that made all the scouts drop me in the blink of an eye, I can't imagine why."

*****

When the game was about to start a man with a horse stitched on his baseball cap calmly walked into the stadium and looked around, trying to decide where to sit down. There wasn't a whole lot of time left until the draft, and with a couple of pretty good prospects between us and Minnesota, there were a lot of scouts in the stands. Most of them were grouped right behind home plate with their aluminum radar gun cases gleaming in the sun. There weren't many people sitting between the group of scouts and the press box, so the man decided to sit there by himself.

He sat a half dozen rows behind the scouts and started to listen to them talk to each other. It always amazed him how they ran games against each other, trying to get other organizations to think they weren't interested in certain people so they could steal them in the draft. Affiliated baseball was a dirty and political business, and he was glad he wasn't part of it.

"I'm Cool Cliff," said a curly haired man with a dark complexion and a Milwaukee Brewers hat. "Milwaukee Brewers. This is usually where I sit."

"Brent Yarborough," the man in the horse hat said. "I'm with the Chillicothe Paints and I'm sorry, I didn't realize I was taking anyone's spot." Brent looked around at the empty bleachers to either side of him. Then, when Cool Cliff kept standing in front of him and waiting for him to move, he gave in and scooted down the bleacher a few feet and Cliff sat down with a groan.

"Thanks."

"No problem."

"So the Chillicothe Paints, huh? That's in the Frontier League, right?"

"That's right."

"Let me guess," Cliff said with a grin. "You're here to look at Ben Marker."

"Well, Marker and possibly a few guys from this Minnesota squad."

"Yeah," Cliff agreed, "they have some pretty good prospects, too." Cliff was quiet for a second before adding the question, "So do you hope to get into affiliated ball someday?"

"Well, Cliff, I have to tell you the truth, I like the independent leagues much better."

"Oh, you must have gotten turned down by every major league organization then, am I right?" Cool Cliff laughed and Brent decided to give him a courtesy chuckle. "That Ben Marker," Cool Cliff said after he finished laughing, "I'm not sure if he's going to do much in professional baseball. He's really helped his team in college, but the only tool he has is his emotion, and you just can't bring that to the table every day in a professional schedule. It's too demanding, and if that kid doesn't have his passion for the game, he doesn't have anything."

"Cliff, that's exactly why I'm here," Brent said with a knowing smile. "Because I don't have to deal with the bullshit of developing players with just one tool, and don't have the passion for the game that Ben Marker has. That's why you affiliated guys screw up so much; you never check to see if the kid has guts or not, you just look at his muscles and write down a number. I like going to games and getting guys just like him, guys that help their team win and give it all they have. I'm glad you turn your nose up at guys like that, because I know the Paints will always be there to scoop them up. Don't worry though," Brent slapped him on the back, "when he hits .350 in the first month of the independent season, I'll be willing to sell his contract to you along with a big crow sandwich."

*****

After the game, Benny was approached by the scout he'd been in contact with for the last two weeks. He offered Benny a job on the spot, all the while telling Benny that he had the greatest talent for the intangibles he'd ever seen. He offered him a contract, a whopping six hundred dollars a month, a host family to live with, and sixteen dollars a day for meal money when the team went on the road. Benny accepted.

"Congratulations, Benny, you've earned it," Brent said. "I know all about your career and I know how tough it is to get respect with your size. Well, those days are over, and we're really excited about you playing for us this summer. You'll have a spot in our outfield as soon as your season is done."

Benny fought back tears as he shook the man's hand. "You don't know how much I appreciate the opportunity to play professional ball. It's a dream come true."

"The pleasure is all mine," Brent said. "I've never seen anyone play the game the way you do. And I don't think you'll last long on our team before the affiliated teams start waking up."

"Thanks again," Benny said while clearing his throat.

"You're welcome," the scout said with a smile. "Listen, I need to get on the road. I have a kid in Indiana that I need to go look at - I'll see you after the Big Ten Tournament?"

"I wouldn't miss it."

"Alright, take care, Benny."

"Wait," Benny said, stopping the man before he could walk away. "I have a favor to ask."

"What is it?"

"If it isn't too much trouble, don't tell my coaches about signing me. I'd like to tell them myself."

"Sure, no problem. Is that all?"

"Yeah that's all."

"Alright Benny, I'll see you later."

"You too," Benny said, adding after the scout had walked a ways away, "drive safely!"

*****

Coop was on the mound during the first game of the Saturday doubleheader when he first felt the twinge in his elbow. He was winning the game by the score of 5 runs to 2, but after recording the first out of the fourth he shook his arm a couple of times, trying to force the pain out.

He thought about calling Calloway out to the mound, but we needed the game, and Coop felt a sense of responsibility to push through it and do his part. He had been known for his selfishness most of his life, but not now. Now, as he stood there and looked in for the sign on that hot May afternoon, he could see the end of his college career, and he wasn't willing to pack it in just yet.

Walker called two fastballs in a row to start off the next hitter and Coop was able to put one of the two in the strike zone. The hitter didn't offer at either pitch and the count was even at one pitch and one strike when Walker called for a slider. The pain had worked its way out of his arm with the first two fastballs and Coop was starting to dismiss it as a muscle spasm or pinched nerve. But when he let loose of the slider he felt another explosion near his elbow and he couldn't help but show it in his face after he let the pitch go.

Coop was lucky he threw the pitch in the dirt because if the ball would have been hit back at him he could have been seriously injured. Walker walked out in front of the plate before he threw the ball back to the mound, sensing that something was wrong. He took a quick glance at the dugout and then fired the ball back to Coop, who tucked his mitt under his arm and rubbed the ball after getting it back from his catcher.

Nichols was on the top step of the dugout when he saw the pain in Coop's face, and he was about to go out and get him when Coach Calloway caught his sleeve. "Give him one more pitch, Tom. Maybe he just twisted his ankle or something."

Coach Nichols fidgeted nervously. "If he looks over here even once, I'm going to get him."

But Coop didn't look over. He didn't look over on purpose because he knew that Nichols would come get him if he did and he didn't want to show the coaches or the scouts in the stands that he was injured. Instead he put the ball in a fastball grip and started shaking off pitches until Walker called it. A fastball would hurt the arm the least of any pitch he had, and he was determined to give his arm one more throw before he decided that he'd blown it out.

The ball went straight into the ground when he released it and Coop instantly went into a squatting position. He threw his mitt to the side and grabbed his pitching elbow with his non-pitching hand, trying to hide his face from everyone that was looking. Nichols reached the mound as soon as he possibly could, and escorted Coop off the field.

"Limp off the field, Coop," Nichols said in his ear before putting his arm around him. "Limp off the field so the scouts think you injured your ankle." Coop looked at his coach with tears in his eyes and complied. He would thank his coach later for his quick thinking, but it wouldn't matter.

Chapter Forty-Four
Tourney Time

"Baseball is a lot like life. The line drives are caught, the squibbers go for base hits. It's an unfair game."
    -Ron Kanehl

    Archie nodded at Harold and cleared his throat, starting the countdown to live broadcast. "The first round of this year's Big Ten tournament finds the Michigan Wolverines pitted against the Penn State Nittany Lions. The Penn State team still has half of their starters from last year where the Wolverines upset the then second place Penn State. This year is a different story as Michigan walks confidently into the tournament hosted by regular season champs Ohio State, who waits for the winner of this match up. The other side of the bracket finds Minnesota waiting for the winner of Illinois and Michigan State, all teams that Michigan had their way with this season. You know, it's interesting Harold, as we open this tournament, I don't see anyone on this list that I'm afraid of. Ever since the Wolverines lost three of four games to this Nittany Lion ball club, we have been cruising. In fact, most of our conference losses came to inferior opponents at the beginning of the schedule. We are running so hot right now, if we can just get past Penn State, we could sweep this thing out from under the host Buckeyes without blinking, your thoughts?"

    "Yeah," Harold said. "The Buckeyes are still pretty angry over the games in Ann Arbor this year and I think they'll be fired up to play us at their place. I also heard through the grapevine that their coach took the team on a camping trip this week to loosen them up, which I thought was an interesting tactic."

    "An interesting tactic," Archie interrupted, "and another oh-so-useless piece of information yet again. I'm glad to see you haven't been slacking, Harold."

    "Not in my vocabulary, Archie," Harold said with a wink.

    "I tend to believe not much is, Harold, but that's beside the point. Let's get back to talking baseball folks, because this Wolverine team has made one heck of a turn around this year and boosts some of the best prospects in the nation. They enter Big Ten tournament play with a 30-24 record, which is great considering the awful spring trip they suffered through this year. They finished third in the Big Ten, and look much improved from the squad that finished sixth last year.

"Michael Merlin, the projected All-American closer for Michigan, is 2-2 this season with a 2.14 earned run average and a school record 13 saves. The strength of this year's squad may be their leadership, but I tell you what, there are several freshmen that have made huge contributions. Pete Alger, for one, has made 37 starts for the Wolverines in left field this year. Pete, a defensive specialist, has only made one error this season, and leads the team with 8 bunts for base hits and 11 infield singles. Paul Walker has been a steady contributor to the Wolverine offense all year, and by tournament time, here, it looks like he is starting to get more comfortable behind the dish. Albert McKinney is a big freshman surprise, he entered their season planning on red-shirting and now he is hitting a very respectable .289 with 14 doubles and 7 home runs. That goes without mentioning Tucker Howard, who has just recently worked his way into the staring rotation. Tucker, after starting out the year with an earned run average of just below my age in dog years, has strung together some really good outings including a clutch win in game four against Minnesota to save a series split for the Wolverines.

"Unfortunately, we have been told that projected first round draft pick John Cooper is not available to pitch in the Big Ten tournament opener. We have some conflicting reports, and we aren't quite sure what is wrong with John, but he fell ill after his start against Minnesota last weekend and apparently he still feels under the weather. Losing Cooper could be huge for this squad. Harold, your thoughts?"

"That's right," Harold said. "We're going to see Wilson Jack start in the first game here. According to my stat sheet he is 5-5 with a 4.73 ERA. The big question for Wilson is whether or not he is going to know where the ball is going. If he can throw strikes he can pitch against any team in America, if he can't, watch out in the booth. We have just as good of a chance of catching a ball as the catcher does."

"You heard it here, Wolverine fans," Archie said. "What would our broadcast be without Harold deep sixin' the Michigan nine with his historic jinx..."

*****

Archie wasn't lying, he really did jinx Wilson. At least that was what Wilson said after he heard the radio recording the day after he pitched. A day where he went three and a third, allowing seven runs on four hits and eight walks. He threw a fit when Nichols came out to the mound to take him out of the game. After he handed off the ball he ran off the fielding yelling every cuss word that came into his mind. When he reached the dugout he went straight over to the bubblegum bucket and smashed it on the dugout steps.

"Goddamnit, motherfucker, son of a whore!" Wilson yelled while taking off his cap, throwing it to the ground, and kicking it across the dugout.

"Settle down, Wilson!" Calloway yelled from the far end of the bench. "Good God, it looks like we should have given you the gum jar to throw on the mound instead of the ball, shit." Calloway grunted and shook his head, turning his attention back to the game and Bill Hum, who had come in to relieve Wilson. Wilson wanted to run down to the end of the bench and punch Calloway in the face, but instead he held it in, trying to breathe like I had taught him during the winter.

Unfortunately, it was too late to overcome the Penn State team that handled us earlier in the season, and we were facing the loser's bracket after only one game. Nichols tried to keep things positive after the game, but he couldn't help but to be frustrated by the loss. He wouldn't let himself think that if we would have only had Coop to pitch the opener against Penn State, we could have beaten Ohio State and very easily found ourselves in the finals.

Fortunately for us, Franklin sucked it up and pitched a gem of a game in the first game of the loser's bracket against Illinois. Every time Franklin got someone from Illinois to pop out, ground out, or strike out, Calloway was visibly shaken. No one ever found out why Calloway didn't care for Franklin and his way of going about things, but one thing was for sure, Franklin finally found a way to stay in the game; he didn't give up a hit until the eighth inning. After striking out the first batter of the eighth with a disgusting slider in the dirt, the second batter threw the bat at the ball and poked one over Smalls' head. The next hitter hit a ground ball through the middle. Smalls and Wes dove toward each other for the ball, but both came up short. They took Franklin out with the runners on first and second, bringing Merlin in a bit early to ensure the win.

"I'm proud of you, Don," Smalls said, slapping Franklin on the ass when the infield came together as Nichols walked up to the mound.

"That was one gutsy performance," Tex said.

"What can I say, Don?" Lou asked.

Wes nodded. "You dominated today, Don."

"Don Franklin," Walker said through his catcher's mask. "I'm speechless."

Franklin gave Smalls a funny look, and then asked through heavy breathing, "What's with everyone calling me Don?"

"What do you mean?" Smalls said with a knowing grin. "You're a fucking sophomore, no more stupid freshman nicknames, remember?"

Franklin laughed as Nichols reached the mound. "What's so funny guys?" Everyone dropped their smiles until Nichols added, "Besides how stupid Franklin made the Fighting Illini look today."

The grins came back to their faces and Nichols looked down to the bullpen, signaling for Merlin to enter the game. When he turned back and took the ball from Franklin he said, "It's been a pleasure coaching you, Franklin."

Franklin handed him the ball, but paused when it sank in what Nichols said. "What was that, Coach?"

"Are you kidding?" Nichols pointed toward the stands behind home plate where over a dozen scouts were on their cell phones. "You hit 93 today with 12 strike outs. You're a stud; I apologize for Coach Calloway and myself that we didn't see it earlier. Now go take a bow for your performance." Franklin smiled and walked back toward the dugout where his teammates were waiting to shake his hand. The crowd went wild from the point where Franklin left the game until the final out was recorded. Merlin made short work of Illinois in the eighth and ninth, and a day later, it was rematch time with the Golden Gophers of Minnesota.

Minnesota was coming off an upset loss to Michigan State where they played terribly, and they were looking pretty determined to turn it around. Chase Warner was on tab to start for our squad, but Nichols thought he would give Tucker the starting nod because he had such success against the Gophers the previous weekend. Warner was a bit upset by the news, but he had a good head on his shoulders, and looked forward to starting the next game against the loser of Illinois and Ohio State.

Before the game started Tucker had a terrible feeling in his stomach a lot like he had when he started against Notre Dame.

"Merlin," Tucker said in the dugout while the coaches were meeting at home plate. "I feel great."

"Uh-oh," Merlin said. "That means you're probably going to give up lasers all over the place." Merlin looked down the bench. "Hey, Varner, quick, tell Tucker how terrible he is."

Varner scrunched his eyebrows for a second and asked, "What?"

"You heard me, make fun of Tucker."

"Okay. Tucker, you're a pussy daddy's boy."

Tucker frowned. "I don't think this is the answer, Merlin."

Merlin persisted. "No, c'mon Varner. I'm talking about his talent, make fun of his talent."

"Okay. Tucker you're going to throw fucking beach balls up there today, I'm not even sure which side of the fence to play on."

Tucker grimaced. "Fuck this, I'm ready."

Four innings and five strikeouts later, Tucker was cruising. He sprinted back into the dugout after the bottom of the fourth, taking his seat fast and wrapping his arm so he could find Varner, who was leading off the inning.

Varner grabbed his bat out of the bat rack and started walking up the dugout steps where Tucker was waiting. "Are you planning on touching a ball today? How about you lead us off one time."

Varner smirked. "Out of the way, Daddy's Boy."

When Varner got up to the plate he didn't bother looking down at Nichols for his sign. The third baseman was playing him deep and close to the outfield grass because he hit a hard grounder at him the time before. He angled the bat as the pitcher released the ball and laid down a perfect bunt. By the time the third baseman got to it, he didn't even attempt to throw to first because Varner was already a few steps past first base.

"Uh-oh, here we come," Merlin yelled from the dugout.

Pete was up next and even though the third basemen took a few steps in, Nichols put on the drag bunt, hoping to at least get a sacrifice out of the play. Pete dug out of the box hard, his bunt traveling a little too far toward the third basemen but far enough away for his only play to be at first base. Fortunately for us, he rushed his throw toward first and sailed the ball over the first basemen's head and allowed Varner to move to third and Pete to move to second on the throwing error.

"Snowball fight!" Tucker yelled from the bench, drawing a dirty look from Calloway.

"Shut your mouth if you want to stay in the game," Calloway said, but Tucker ignored him.

Smalls was the next hitter and Minnesota's coach must have thought we weren't going to score many runs in the game, so he decided to draw the infield in. Smalls saw the infield in and took three huge hacks, trying to hit a sacrifice fly, but failing to draw contact on any of them. Smalls was the last hitter in the lineup, which meant Benny was up next, so everyone was pretty optimistic on the bench that we were at least going to get one run out of the rally. Benny swung and connected on the second pitch, hitting a hard line drive toward the second basemen who scooped it up quickly and fired home, catching Varner trying to score on a bang-bang play.

Tex was the next hitter of the game and the infielders move back to their regular positions with one out. When Tex looked down to Nichols for the sign; he expected a first and third play since they had the speedy freshman Pete at third and Benny on first, but Nichols just clapped his hands and told Tex to give it a ride.

He had gone 0 for 4 against the same Minnesota pitcher in Ann Arbor the weekend before and he had already struck out in his first at bat of the day. He took the first pitch on purpose, hoping he could get ahead in the count, and trying to get his timing on the pitcher. But the pitcher threw the ball hard and down the middle with confidence in this defense, and smiled broadly when Tex didn't swing. The next pitch was a slider out of the zone and Tex chased, trying to spray the ball into right field. He stepped out of the box after the second strike and looked toward the bench where we were all on our feet cheering. Then he looked down to Benny on first base clapping his hands, Pete on third, and Nichols in the third base coaching box telling Tex to focus. Then, while looking away from Nichols, he caught a glimpse of the third basemen, which the Wolverine offense had already picked on twice in the inning. He was playing back on the edge of the infield because he knew the big Texan had never dropped down a bunt in his life.

The next pitch was a high fastball, meant to strike Tex out, but the pitcher didn't get it high enough, and Tex was able to get the barrel on top of it and send a bunt down the third base line. Pete was startled, but he sprinted home ahead of the third baseman, who was crashing toward the ball, and scored easily. The third baseman strained hard to get to the ball, grabbing it and firing it toward first, not worrying about Pete with two outs in the inning. Tex lumbered down the line in slow motion, and even though he only had a few steps left when the third baseman grabbed the ball, it was still a close play. The

Minnesota coach sprinted onto the field to argue when the first base umpire raised his hands to call Tex safe.

"Hey, Jake Taylor," Hum said when Tex came in the dugout after the inning with a huge smile on his face. "I can't believe you just did that."

"Yeah, but I don't have the bad knees," Tex laughed, grabbing his mitt and heading back in the field.

It looked like one run was all Tucker would need, as he put away Gopher batters like nothing. He challenged them with pitch after pitch, continuing to get the best of them until the bottom of the ninth when he walked two consecutive batters with two outs and Nichols had to go to Merlin.

"I had it today, Merlin," Tucker said with a smile when he handed him the ball.

"Shit yeah, you did," Merlin said. "I'll close her up for you, bro."

The batter that Merlin had to face was all too familiar. He only stood five foot seven inches tall and weighed less than a hundred and seventy pounds, but the year before he somehow managed to push one over the center field fence and end our season. Merlin didn't want a repeat performance, and he didn't want to risk a bloop base hit. Even though he had Walker catching behind the plate and he wasn't too sure about his blocking skills, he threw two forkballs in a row. Both darted under the hitter's bat for strikes, but the second one got through Walker's legs and let the runners advance to second and third. With two strikes on the hitter and an open base, Merlin knew he couldn't lose. The next pitch was his best fastball, right at eye level, but the batter was able to hold back. The one ball two strike pitch was a slider low and away to even the count at 2-2. Merlin threw the same pitch on 2 and 2, and the hitter took it again for ball three. The Michigan fans erupted, hoping for a chance to win the game, but Merlin was confident and nodded yes when Walker called for another forkball.

Merlin knew he was in trouble as soon as the ball left his hand. It slipped through his fingers instead of popping out with its usual knuckling action and the ball spun and hung up around the hitter's bellybutton. The batter was waiting back, expecting the off speed pitch with the base open and got his best swing on the floating pitch.

As Benny ran for it he could feel fear leaking through his stomach, and his legs unwillingly slowed down, but then he had this vision of himself playing independent baseball, a legit prospect, acknowledged so by fans and players alike, even Cool Cliff. Thinking this way he ran harder and the image in his head became clearer. He was playing for the Chillicothe Paints, lighting up the Frontier League, and soon affiliated teams were begging and fighting for his contract. Now he was in the minor leagues, tearing his way to the top in an unprecedented fashion, nothing could stand in his way. He was in the big leagues, and a teardrop formed in his eyes as he stretched an arm out for the ball. He was still too far away, but the wall was approaching fast. He jumped, refusing to spot the wall, or worry about injury. Yet the wall continued to advance, and though Beth and her friends were on their feet shrieking out a warning, Benny hit it with a skull-breaking bang, and the wall embraced him headfirst. He turned from the wall with a stumble, seeing the dent he made first, then the ball in his glove. Benny lost vision out of one eye at a time as he held the ball triumphantly toward the infield umpire, his smile never fading a bit as he fell to his knees. His last sight was the stadium erupting, his family and teammates rejoicing, and the umpire calling it the final out of the game.

Chapter Forty-Five
On the Edge between This Year and Next

"You may glory in a team triumphant, but you fall in love with a team in defeat. Losing after great striving is the story of man, who was born to sorrow, whose sweetest songs tell of the saddest thought, and who, if he is a hero, does nothing in life as becomingly as leaving it."
-Roger Kahn, The Boys of Summer

We ended our season quietly with Benny in the hospital, bowing out in the next game to Ohio State, 4 to 2. The game didn't matter much to the guys on the team; our minds and hearts were with Benny. We were all in the hospital room the next day when he passed away; he never regained consciousness after his collision with the wall.

It was awhile after the season was over before Coach Nichols was able to get himself and his coaching staff back in the mindset of working again. The team's success had gotten Morgan off of his back, but that was the least of his concerns. He had never had anything happened to him in his life like what happen with Benny, and he had a difficult time recovering. Sometimes he would just sit in his office and weep for his fallen player whenever he caught a glimpse of his picture in the program or saw his name on the roster from last year.

A letter of condolences from the Chillicothe Paints lay on Nichols' desk for weeks after his death and he wasn't sure whether he should frame it or throw it away because it was too painful to read. Benny had agreed verbally to join the team after the season was over, but he had kept it a secret from everyone. Somehow it made Tom feel a little bit better, knowing that not only did Benny die doing what he loved, but he did it knowing that he had accomplished something, that someone had finally rewarded him for his effort and determination.

Nichols was sitting in his chair only a few days after returning to work, twirling a pencil in his fingers and staring at the letter from Chillicothe when he heard a knock on the door. Tom shot out of his chair and rushed to the door, swearing that he had seen Benny's face through the glass for a second, but as he approached, it faded away and when he opened the door he saw a face he never expected to see again.

"Do you have a few minutes, Coach?" a man in his late twenties asked. He wore a nice shirt and tie complimented by a blue blazer. His hair was gelled up to look like he had just gotten out of bed and the look on his face told Tom that he was nervous enough to not know whether he should smile or not.

"Of course," Nichols said, more out of shock than anything else. He offered a seat to the man and then sat down behind his desk, trying to pick his jaw off the floor. "I never expected you to speak to me again, Shane."

"Neither did I," Shane said.

"I'm sorry," Tom said, not knowing what else to say.

"Me too," Shane said, lifting a giant weight off of both their shoulders. "I was wrong, for everything I did, and I missed out on a lot because of it. I had an attitude, and I got cut for it. I was so angry with you that I didn't enjoy anything until I shoved it in your face, and even when I did, it didn't help me. I was unhappy, in every aspect of my life, and I couldn't figure out why. I finally got sick of blaming you."

"I've regretted it every day since."

"There's no reason to say that, Coach."

"Sure there is," Nichols said. "I should have known the impact it would have on you. I should have just worked with you, but I was too quick to make an example out of someone. I just wanted to be the best coach I could."

"Well look at you now, Michigan man, back where you belong."

"It's been a tough year."

"I heard."

"About Benny?"

"Yeah, I'm sorry."

"It's okay," Nichols said. "I've finally come to grips with it I think. He was such a great kid, the world is a worse place without him."

"It's why I'm here."

"What do you mean?"

"I'm not sure," Shane said while rubbing his hands together. "I guess I mean that when I saw you were the coach here I still felt a need to hate you. I saw that you were doing well and I still felt like I had to hate you for what you did, like I was being forced to. But when I saw how that kid Ben died, and I read about his life and the quotes of his teammates about his character, I was blown away about how one person could affect so many. And I guess I'm here to tell you how you affected me, how even after I hated you all these years I finally realize that I'm a better person because of what you did, and I didn't want to go another day without coming here and telling you."

"Thank you," Nichols said while rubbing his eyes, unable to express his relief. "I appreciate it." Shane nodded like he was out of words and not sure what else to do. He stood up like he was going to leave and Nichols circled his desk and hugged him. Shane smiled when Nichols finally released him and gave him a few more kind words about Benny. He reassured Tom that Benny hadn't just touched the lives of the people who knew him, but that his story had changed the lives of everyone who heard it, including himself. He admitted he probably would have kept living in a world fueled by a need to hate instead of a willingness to forgive had he not heard about Benny. Instead, he had recognized the brevity of life and took action to change from the inside out.

Then Shane shook Tom's hand and walked out the door, promising to keep in touch. Nichols waited for him to disappear around the corner of the hallway before going back into his room. Shane looked over his shoulder one last time before he went out of sight, giving Tom a nod of the head, making Tom swear he saw Benny's face one more time.

Epilogue
Life Goes On

"But at my back I always hear
Time's winged chariot hurrying near."
　　　- Andrew Marvell (1621-1678)

I finished telling the story of my senior year to my son and smiled at the memories that I had cleaned up a bit for his ears. "I know that you're a young man, but I just don't feel like I can tell you the complete extent of what I experienced in college. I guess some of it will have to be a surprise."

"I can take it dad," he said with disgust. "I *am* eighteen now."

"Yeah, I know."

"Hey, whatever happened to some of those guys?"

"Oh, I don't know. You know about Coop and how he rehabbed his arm and came back throwing harder, right? I think that idiot got drafted even higher than he would have if he didn't get hurt. It's a good thing I made him sign that napkin about becoming his agent. He tried to get out of it, but I nailed the bastard in court."

"Yeah, I think I've heard about Coop about a million times."

"Well, he would have done better in the big leagues if he wasn't such a moron."

"Dad, he made the All-Star team his second year in the league, I looked up his stats."

"Yeah, but I still think Merlin had a better career."

"Of course he did, he broke just about every relief record in the books. He's a sure first ballot Hall of Famer. Who I want to know about is Franklin and some of those other guys."

"Franklin got drafted and signed after that year, just like Nichols thought he would, but not before he went in and gave Calloway a good piece of his mind. I still don't know why they were so hard on him. Anyway, he played for awhile in the minors and now he owns a used car dealership in southeast Michigan somewhere."

"So that Q-Bert guy, he was a freshman?"

"Yeah, he toned down the act a bit after we caught him in the freshman level Psychology class, but we promised not to tell anyone. He really was pretty damn smart, because he sure fooled all of us, and then he stole the equipment room blind when he left, never heard from him again. I heard something later that he only did it because he had some huge gambling debt to payoff.

Apparently, he wasn't a very good poker player. Coop, Hum, and I kind of blamed ourselves for not telling anyone." I shrugged.

"What about Wes, Lou, Varner, and all those guys?"

"I don't know what those guys are doing. I know that our positive influence turned Varner around, though, and he actually managed to graduate. The last I knew he was going back to school to do film. Apparently, he became a huge John Wayne fan after he met my dad." I laughed at my own joke, even though it was true, and turned my attention to the three letters on the living room counter, and the reason I had gone into the story in the first place.

"Son," I said, "I know that you take my advice with a grain of salt, but I know a thing or two about playing college ball." I stopped to clear my throat and my son picked up the National Letters of Intent one by one to examine the name attached to each.

"Notre Dame," I said as he picked up the first letter, "is a great school, with a great tradition, and a great baseball team. On the other hand, it's a Catholic school and the student body is entirely male, so you might want to take that into consideration."

My son set down the first letter and picked up the second one. "I'm not sure if I can say enough about that one. You know about me, my history at Michigan, the tough times, and the nickname they gave me because I never played."

"Squat," my son said with a laugh. I laughed too. I can laugh at it now.

"Yeah. It was a long time ago, and there are parts I regret, but sometimes regret isn't a bad thing." I sighed loudly before I knew what I was doing. "But I love that place, no matter what I went through there. On the other hand, I would understand if you were too sick of hearing my stories and want to create your own somewhere else."

My son nodded and picked up the third letter, a letter which caused me great distress and I couldn't hide the sweat beading on my forehead as my one and only son scanned the letterhead. "Now, I've let this last one go on for way too long." My son looked over the top of the letter with a big grin. "Ohio State is just out of the fucking question." I grabbed the paper, ripped it in half, and my son and I shared a laugh.

"I love you, Dad."

I smiled as my boy reached down, picked up the pen, and set it down on the letter that had a huge "M" on the top.

"I love you too, Benji." I gently ruffled his hair and embraced him with a hug after he was finished signing the letter.

Something came over me when I hugged my son, my chin digging into his shoulder, and I couldn't help holding the embrace for a few seconds longer than we were accustomed to in my house. When I opened my tear-filled eyes, still clutching my son tight, I saw Beth standing behind us and smiling. At that moment all I could think about was Benny. Benjamin Douglas Marker, one of my best friends, my hero, the man who saved my chance for happiness when he saved my relationship with Beth, and taught me how foolish we were to pray for rain.

Instead I prayed to God and to Benny that night, just like I had every night since college, thanking them both for being in my life. Sometimes I wondered if they were in it together, to build my character, to lift me up when the time was right. *He's going to Michigan*, I thought with a smile, *a switch hitting outfielder with no speed, no arm, but a head like a bull. I'm not sure if I've ever seen anyone play like him... except... say, Benny? You did just talk to Beth for me, didn't you?*

The End